Analysing the Structure of Econometric Models

ADVANCED STUDIES IN THEORETICAL AND APPLIED ECONOMETRICS
VOLUME 2

THE SPECIAL SCOPE OF THE SERIES

The fortress of econometrics has often been laid siege to from one or a few sides only. According to their inspiration or inclination, authors have laid stress on model specification, parameter estimation, testing and prediction or more generally the use of models (prediction in particular being a rare bird in econometric literature). Special topics, such as errors in the variables, missing observations, multi-dimensional data, time-series analysis, dynamic specification, spatial autocorrelation, were dealt with as and when the need arose.

No econometric exercises will ever be complete. Nevertheless, in setting up such an exercise as part of an operational economic investigation, one may reasonably be expected to try and encompass in it as many aspects of econometric modelling as may present themselves. This series is devoted to the publication of work which, as far as possible, addresses all aspects of a "complete econometric modelling" approach; for instance, spatial econometrics or policy optimisation studies which account explicitly for the specification, estimation or analysis of components of those models in the widest sense, including any complementary components from the environment in which the economic model must operate.

The very objective of the series may limit its extensions; but as André Gide put it (Les faux monnayeurs), "il est bon de suivre sa pente, pourvu que ce soit en montant".

PREVIOUSLY PUBLISHED:

1 J.H.P. Paelinck (ed.) Qualitative and Quantitative Mathematical Economics, 1982. ISBN 90 247 2623 9.

All correspondence should be addressed to A.J. Hughes Hallet or to J.H.P. Paelinck at the Erasmus University, PO Box 1738, 3000 DR Rotterdam, The Netherlands.

Analysing the Structure of Econometric Models

edited by

J.P. Ancot

1984 **MARTINUS NIJHOFF PUBLISHERS**
a member of the KLUWER ACADEMIC PUBLISHERS GROUP
THE HAGUE / BOSTON / LANCASTER

Distributors

for the United States and Canada: Kluwer Boston, Inc., 190 Old Derby Street, Hingham, MA 02043, USA
for all other countries: Kluwer Academic Publishers Group, Distribution Center, P.O.Box 322, 3300 AH Dordrecht, The Netherlands

Library of Congress Cataloging in Publication Data

Main entry under tilte:

Analysing the structure of econometric models.

(Advanced studies in theoretical and applied econometrics ; v. 2)
Includes index.
1. Econometrics--Addresses, essays, lectures.
I. Ancot, J. P. (Jean-Pierre) II. Series.
HB141.A55 1984 330'.028 83-23757
ISBN 90-247-2894-0

ISBN-13: 978-94-009-6100-5 e-ISBN-13: 978-94-009-6098-5
DOI: 10.1007/978-94-009-6098-5

PREFACE

Understanding the structure of a large econometric model is rather like the art of winetasting or like the art of playing a musical instrument. The quality of a wine results from a complex combination of various elements such as its colour which should be clear and crystalline, its smell which can be decomposed into a general aroma and a variety of particular characteristics, more or less persistent depending on the type and the age of the wine, its taste, of course, which again is a complex system whose equilibrium and charm depend on the whole set of ingredients: alcohol, tannin, glycerine, sugar, acidity . . . Similarly, a clarinetist's musicianship depends on the quality of his instrument, on his embouchure, fingering, tonguing and articulation techniques, on his sense for rhythm, phasing and tone colour. However, the enchantment produced by a Romanée-Conti or by a brilliant performance of Brahm's F minor sonata for clarinet and piano arises from a process which is at the same time time much simpler and much more complex than the straightforward juxtaposition of individual causal relations.

In recent years econometricians and macro-economists have been challenged by the problem of keeping abreast with an ever increasing number of increasingly more complex large econometric models. The necessity of developing systematic analytical tools to study the often implicit and hidden structure of these models has become more evident. For this reason, the Applied Econometric Association organised an international workshop at the Erasmus University in Rotterdam, the Netherlands on December 10-12, 1982 to investigate and evaluate methods of structural analysis of econometric models. The present volume takes up this theme; however, it is not a collection of proceedings of the workshop –to call it that would do great injustice to a number of highly valuable contributions to the workshop which could not be included in this book– but a set of articles whose conception and realisation originated from the material presented at the workshop and the discussions which arose at that occasion.

The book has been rather loosely divided into two parts, distinguishing between basically qualitative methods of structural analysis and basically quantitative methods.

From the outset, D. Royer and G. Ritschard evaluate the relative merits of the qualitative analysis of causal structures. They argue that the tools which are developed to conduct such analyses, however powerful and efficient they may be, should be used with care and discretion. Structural analysis of econometric models should not rest blindly on a more or less mechanical implementation of the techniques available but it should, on the contrary, always be backed and guided by the explicit formulation of the theoretical foundations of the model.

Graph-theoretic techniques form the basis of stepwise procedures for structural analysis of M. Garbely and M. Gilli and of M. Boutillier. The authors use these techniques to structure causal relations in the models into blocks and hierarchies which can often further be simplified through the elimination of inessential circularities. They apply their methods to a number of quarterly and annual models for the United States and France.

J.P. Auray and G. Duru develop a mathematical structure which allows for an operational definition of structural analysis fitting the requirements of the social sciences. Their approach proceeds from a weakening of the axioms defining topological spaces and rests on their concept of poor structures. The operational character of the mathematical instrument is illustrated by means of an application to the French input-output table.

Some of the ideas presented in the previous chapters are demonstrated by J.P. Decaestecker and M. Mouillart who analyse the structure of the SABINE quarterly disaggregated model of consumption and savings behaviour of households.

A.A. Keller advocates the use of the so-called semi-reduced form of an econometric model –a form intermediate between the structural form of the model and its reduced or final form– to identify and to analyse the essential features of the structure of the model from the point of view of fundamental economic mechanisms, such as supply and demand interactions.

R.A. Dana and P. Malgrange deal with the analysis of complex non-linear dynamic systems. Using Kaldor's 1940 model, they show that the qualitative properties of different discrete versions of these models may reveal considerable discrepancies. They suggest that the use of ergodic theory may help solving the problems resulting from chaotically evolving variables.

The structure of rational expectations behaviour is the subject of the paper by A.S. Brandsma and A.J. Hughes Hallett. Rational expectations terms often arise in a dynamic model, the authors argue, as the result of a noncooperative game between economic agents or groups where the behaviour of one set of agents is not fully or accurately observed. They use the result of this formalisation to examine the quantitative significance of these rational expectations terms for policy analysis in the context of wage bargaining in the Dutch economy in the period 1976-80.

D. Bureau, D. Miqueu and M. Norotte develop a small-scale model to highlight the basic static and dynamic characteristics of disequilibrium models, and to establish a simple but comprehensive link between modern disequilibrium models and more traditional macro-economic models. Like several of the previous authors, they pay attention to the modelling of the dynamics, which, in particular, should be founded on behavioural assumptions consistent with the short term adjustment processes.

Monetary econometric modelling has been a very lively area in the Netherlands since the mid-seventies. In his paper M.M.G. Fase describes a quarterly monetary model of the Dutch economy. He analyses the properties of the model from the point of view of its *ex post* forecasting ability and he presents a number of impulse simulation results obtained from the model. The position of his model within the

Dutch model building tradition is discussed and its merits for policy preparation are evaluated.

C. Le Van criticises the lack of coordination between general theoretical ambitions of many models and their limited empirical relevance. The empirical realisations of models often are such that, for example, theoretical inconsistencies arise between their short term and long term properties. The argument is illustrated by means of the import function in two French models.

As this preface began, the book ends on a gastronomic note, subtitled by Th. ten Raa as *The Economy as an Onion*. Mashed onions should be condemned and the integrity of time and space in economic modelling should be restored. The fundamental theorem which makes this possible is the Schwartz kernel theorem reconciling alternative points of view concerning space-time modelling. However, I should like to take advantage of my editorial privilege to point out that I cannot agree with the author's suggestion that a good wine should be wasted for the sake of the digestion of the mashed onions!

Jean-Pierre Ancot
Rotterdam, August 1983

TABLE OF CONTENTS

PART I
QUALITATIVE ANALYSIS

CHAPTER 1

QUALITATIVE STRUCTURAL ANALYSIS: GAME OR SCIENCE ?

D. Royer and G. Ritschard
University of Geneva, Switzerland

1. INTRODUCTION

Prior to any assessment of the scope and limits of qualitative structural analysis, there is an obvious task to be done: defining what can be expected from such an analysis which can by no means constitute an end in itself.

As is well known, the significant improvements of computer techniques in the past two decades have allowed the building and use of econometric models of an ever increasing complexity. Whatever the complexity, it is nowadays always possible to solve a model to get raw forecasts or to simulate the consequences of a given set of policy measures. The problem nevertheless remains to evaluate the relevance of the solutions, which are obviously heavily dependent on the a priori theoretical assumptions embodied in each equation *and* in their global organisation.

If the theory underlying every particular equation is often easy to pinpoint (that is, if the model is not a pure computer product), that is not very often the case for the model considered as a distinct entity. For a given economist, for instance, forecasts of the real GDP will not carry the same degree of reliability, according to the overall structure of the model, Keynesian or Monetarist.

At the risk of sounding repetitive, let us emphasise again that understanding a model is not just understanding each of its equations. It also implies a strong command of its global functioning and coherence. But this very task borders rapidly on the (wrong) side of feasibility as the number of characteristics considered grows in size.

Now, this is precisely what qualitative structural analysis should be all about, which in a broad sense encompasses all techniques aiming at clarifying this intractable structure.

Owing to the vertical and horizontal complexity of the structures to be studied, it is obviously out of the question to consider a unique approach. Therefore, the very term structural analysis is bound to embody a wide range of methods, each of which being aimed at showcasing a particular aspect of the model. To consider only the best known methods, eigenvalues characterise the dynamic behaviour of the system, multipliers give information about total impacts of the exogenous variables, whereas structural shocks inform us about the sensitivity of the model to changes in the specification of particular parameters (or equations).

Several taxonomies have been suggested in the literature, see, for instance, the definition of inner and outer methods of analysis due to Deleau and Malgrange (1978). In this paper dealing with *qualitative* methods, we draw an obvious distinction between quantitative or numerical methods and qualitative methods.

The most general characterisation that can be given for the former lies in the necessary full quantification of the model to which they are applied. Beside the problems raised by the linearisation of the model, still a prerequisite for a great deal of these methods, the relevance of numerical methods lies mainly in the scope of the properties under study. One could, for instance, question the relevance of the property of asymptotic stability demanded from short term econometric models whose structure (that is the full specification of the numerical value of all parameters) is obviously valid in a sub-asymptotic time span.

Qualitative methods grew partly out of a certain scepticism with numerical results, and their initial aim was the study of more robust characteristics independent of the point validity of the empirical content of the model. Therefore it is the very nature of information taken into account, rather than the results, which generates the various aspects of qualitative structural analysis. Moreover, the operational properties required from these methods made it necessary to remain within classes of homogeneous information (presence or absence of variables, signs of the partial derivatives, and the like). As is well known, it is not easy to feed computers with heterogeneous information! As we will see, this situation has led to the development of analytical tools whose interest cannot be denied from a purely technical point of view. Unfortunately, when considering the finality of structural analysis, i.e. bringing into focus the explanatory content of a model, their validity is not all that obvious and it would at least need to be proven within some future true economic study.

Indeed, the main difficulty encountered when dealing with qualitative methods is closely related to the high degree of generality of assumptions used. And this high degree of generality is paid for by too great a number of degrees of freedom, which renders a synthetic presentation of results highly difficult, and their interpretation just as difficult.[1] Thus it is our opinion that the scope of qualitative methods cannot be assessed purely by means of the efficacy of the instruments (software). It must be essentially considered in the light of the problems encountered when deciphering computer print-outs.

This is not to deny that efficient instruments are not a necessary step toward making the methods operational. But, on the other hand, if the emphasis in the literature has been put strongly on performance of algorithms and is almost non-existent when dealing with the economic relevance of the results, one is led to wonder whether this bias is exogenous and transient or whether it is endogenous and deeply rooted within the approach itself.[2] Even when economic models are dealt with, they only come in as an illustration of the algorithm, and little attention is paid to the actual meaning of the results.[3]

In this article we intend to present some reflections on qualitative analysis which has grown out of our own experience in developing *and using* these methods, with a special emphasis on the pitfalls in interpreting the results. We believe that this could turn out to be useful to the users of such methods (after all they are in a way meant to be used), as time and again we come across enthusiastic researchers who hope to break through the profound mysteries of a model, but end up quite perplex when confronted with an impressive series of minimum covers (defined below) or qualitative solutions.

Bearing this in mind, we shall first deal with the analysis of causal structures, surveying the concepts of causal outline, matching and minimum covers. We then turn to qualitative calculus, before considering what, in our view, is the logical and most fruitful outcome of this approach: geometric structures.

2. LIMITS OF THE ANALYSIS OF CAUSAL STRUCTURES

The concept of causal structures in economic models stems from an axiomatic definition of temporal causality, asymmetric by definition to which any process of understanding is bound to be closely related. Owing to the problem of observing data, among others, any attempt to model an economic phenomenon implies a certain degree of interdependence, i.e. of reciprocal causality, characterised by circuits. Therefore, with respect to the time period of observation and of the model, axiomatic causality gives rise to a *within* period dynamics, of which only the periodical equilibria are modelled. The so-called dynamics of the model represents only the *between* period links of these equilibria.

Obviously, the concept of simultaneity underlying equilibrium models does not preclude a given form of recursivity in those models, related to slower or negligible feedbacks.

When present in a model, this partial recursivity easily gives rise to an interpretation in terms of fundamental periodic causality. Bringing out this recursivity has thus been a very natural object of the first efforts in a systematic analysis of the causal structure, which is quite simply given by the subset of endogenous variables entering each equation.

Following the pioneering work of Simon (1963) in terms of linear algebra, graph theory has provided the operational tools for solving these problems.[4] Defining a causal structure is indeed tantamount to the definition of a directed graph.

Partial recursivity, commonly known as the *causal outline* of a model, obtains straighforwardly by determining the classes of interdependent variables linked together by at least one circuit (strong components), and then by ordering these classes according to the non-circular paths leading from one to the other.

This first aspect of the analysis of causal structures is the most operational one in terms of the efficacy of the instrument.

As to the results, it is worth mentioning that the causal outline gives the separable or quasi-separable submodels directly. Let us recall that a submodel is separable if, once isolated from the whole model, it gives rise to the same conclusions (and, of course, the same solutions) as those obtained from the whole model. As to quasi-separability, it is a similar but weaker concept inasmuch as it only implies that the rest of the model be exogenous with respect to the submodel considered. Thus *quasi-separable* models correspond to the strong components, the *separable* models being the components of the first level of the hierarchical structure, i.e. those that do not depend on other endogenous variables.

Bringing out such separable submodels is then of obvious interest, be it for estimating them, solving them, or for the possibility thus offered of studying a sequence of models without disregarding any relevant information.

Even though it is rather unambiguous, this type of analysis is strictly limited by pragmatic considerations. Most macroeconometric models exhibit indeed a large strong component, with a few variables appearing before that component (the prologue) and after (the epilogue). The strong component includes most of the endogenous variables of interest, whereas the prologue usually introduces semi-endogenous variables (exports as a function of foreign demand). The epilogue is then a collection of economic indicators. This state of affairs therefore takes a lot out of what can be expected from the study of the causal outline.

We are now very naturally led to consider the second aspect of the analysis of causal structures, that is the analysis of the interdependencies that characterise strong components.

The problem here is basically to translate the interdependencies in terms of their fundamental periodic causality. In practice this is achieved by the extraction of recursive reading schemes which ideally should correspond to the theoretical content of the model. In this respect it is important to emphasise that, as opposed to the uniqueness of the causal outline, there are usually several classes of reading schemes, each of them depending on the *matching* of variables and equations chosen, which represents the direction of causality to be read from the equations.

This problem of matching should not be treated light-heartedly, as in many cases it conditions the interpretation of the whole model. Think of the well known accounting identity used as an equilibrium condition on the goods market: $Q-C-I=0$, which links production (Q), consumption (C), and investment (I). If it is to be read $Q=C+I$, it implies a Keynesian (demand-driven) interpretation of the model. If, on the other hand, it is read $C=Q-I$, it characterises a totally different situation (closely related to either the Classical or the Repressed Inflation equilibria), where supply drives demand on the goods market.

These reading schemes can only be obtained at the cost of some simplification in the model (removal of arcs or redating of variables), the significance of which must be minimised. The first difficulty encountered is the choice of the relevant criterion function.

Automatic operational procedures have been developed, which rely exclusively on purely mathematical criteria. By considering only the binary information characterising the casual structure, it has been suggested to minimise the number of variables to be treated; in other words to minimise the number of predetermined variables in order to render the strong component perfectly recursive.[5] The corresponding sets of variables are then called the minimum covers.

The efficacy of the corresponding algorithms depends both on the size of the model (number of variables) and its density (number of non-zero elements in the Jacobian matrix). Macroeconometric models usually exhibit a very sparse matrix, which makes the algorithms fairly efficient.

There is no doubt that the concept of minimum covers is an important one from a descriptive point of view. Just like in data analysis, where the projections according to the largest eigenvalues give the best image of a set of points, the recursive terms associated with minimum covers represent best the causalities at stake in an interdependent structure.

They can be of some help too for solving non-linear systems, as they minimise the number of variables on which a Gauss-Seidel type procedure must iterate. Unfortunately there is no built-in guarantee that such a procedure will converge.

From the point of view of explanation, the major goal of structural analysis, the relevance of minimum covers is much less straightforward.

Consider first the fact that most models usually exhibit a large number of such sets. The problem is then to choose a particular one, supposedly corresponding best to the alleged functioning of the model. One obvious criterion is the rejection of non convergent schemes, which implies the reintroduction of all quantitative information. On a purely qualitative basis, the set of minimum covers could be given a structure of topological space, thus allowing the aggregation of covers by means of a concept of neighbourhood and hence of proximity.

On the other hand, we must be aware that there is no reason for a theoretically appropriate reading scheme to correspond to a minimum cover. Consider thus a model with output Q, consumption C and employment N as endogenous variables. Due to problems of aggregation, each of these variables will embody elements of the demand and the supply sides. Consequently, the structure of the model will consist in the stacking of a supply scheme (N → Q → C) on a demand scheme (Q → N → C → Q).

It is easy to check that, for the following structure:

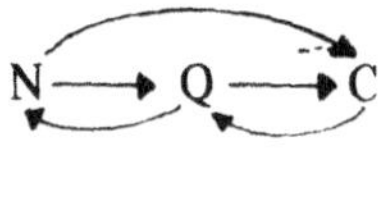

the only minimum cover is the singleton $\{Q\}$, which leads to the following recursive scheme:

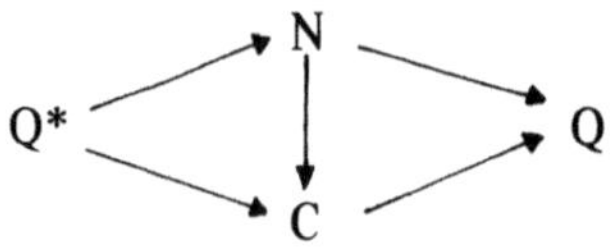

The demand side is well accounted for ($Q^* \to N \to C \to Q$) whereas the supply side is quite blurred.

The following scheme, resulting from the use of two variables (therefore it is not a minimum cover), is obviously more informative:

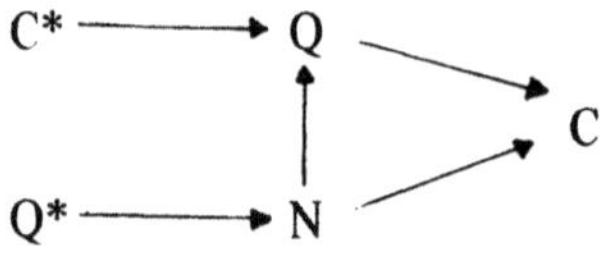

Hence, one must take great care when using the concept of minimum covers because its scope can obviously be overestimated. In particular, there is no one to one mapping between a minimum cover and the underlying dynamics of the model.

3. SCOPE AND LIMITS OF QUALITATIVE CALCULUS

The qualitative structure of a model is defined by attaching a sign (positive or negative) to the influence transmitted through the links of causality. The analysis of qualitative structure is thus based on the study of signed digraphs or equivalently on the sign content of the matrix of partial derivatives of the equations.

The concern for qualitative structures grew mainly out of problems of comparative statics, and goes back to the work of Samuelson (1947) on the foundations of economic analysis.

Put formally, the problem consists in studying the solutions x to the qualitative linear system $Ax = b$, where A is the matrix containing the signs of the partial derivatives with respect to the endogenous variables, b the sign vector of derivatives with respect to the exogenous variable whose impact is considered, and x the (unknown) vector of impact multipliers.

Qualitatively *determined* multipliers are found by scanning the set of sign vectors x that are solution to the qualitative system. They actually correspond to the components of x which remain sign constant in all solutions. Qualitatively *linked* multipliers can also be found by scanning this set of solutions, as they correspond to groups of components which have either the same sign or the opposite sign throughout all solutions.

Efficient computerised procedures are available which permit the detection of qualitatively determined and qualitatively linked multipliers in a few minutes CPU time for models up to 300 equations.

Turning now to the criticisms expressed toward qualitative calculus, let us dismiss first the case of Bassett (1969). Considering a small macroeconomic equilibrium model, this author tries to point out qualitatively defined multipliers that could not be detected by qualitative calculus. But his argument lacks the correct foundations, inasmuch as it is based on results obtained from two different sets of information. Indeed, by developing the impact multipliers analytically, Bassett uses the information corresponding to the qualitative structure of a ten equation model, which he compares to the results obtained from the qualitative structure of a three equation model. This latter model being derived from the original one by rewriting it under the form of a zero excess demand system. Now it has been established elsewhere (Ritschard, 1983) that, in such a situation, the information provided by both systems is equivalent if, and only if, the reduced system is obtained from the original one according to the procedure of qualitative aggregation. As a matter of fact, Bassett's example does not comply with this rule.

Similarly to the analysis of causal structures, the sensitive issue in qualitative calculus is not its actual implementation, but the scarcity of significant results provided by this approach. Setting aside a few small scholarly models, it so happens that qualitatively defined multipliers are almost never to be found. The most relevant results obtained concern only qualitative links among multipliers. Thus, in most cases, purely qualitative hypotheses will not ensure a positive impact of autonomous expenditures on output in a Neo-keynesian model, but will only exhibit a qualitative link between output and investment.

There are two natural ways to strengthen the hypotheses in order to get more significant results. One of them consists in shortening the intervals of variation of exogenous variables, and leads to the geometric approach treated in the next section. The other incorporates further restrictions on the partial derivatives of the model. Considering for instance the stability of the within-period dynamics, a prerequisite for any analysis of comparative statics, the sign of the Jacobian determinant can be imposed.

According to Cramer's rule $x_i \det(A) = \det(A_i)$, including this constraint in the set of hypotheses permits the definition of the sign of all multipliers x_i whose associated determinant $\det(A_i)$ is signed under pure qualitative hypotheses.

As natural as it may be, the stability constraint unfortunately appears to quickly become inoperative if the size of the model goes beyond twenty equations.

Because the techniques of qualitative calculus apply equally well when extra qualitative equations are added to the system $Ax = b$, any information capable of being put in that form should be included. Take, for instance, the model:

$$C = f(Q)$$
$$I = g(Q)$$
$$Q = C + I + G$$

which defines consumption C, investment I and output Q as a function of autonomous expenditures G. By differentiating and adding up each equation, we get

$$(1 - f' - g')dQ = dG$$

This equation can be translated into qualitative terms:

$$(+)\ dQ = (+)\ dG,$$

given the assumption of a marginal propensity to spend less than unity ($f' + g' < 1$). It can be noted that this restriction, which ensures the qualitative definition of the multiplier dQ/dG, is equivalent in this case to the imposition of a negative sign for the Jacobian determinant.

When justified, this type of restriction appears as a powerful tool for qualitative calculus. The search for ***relevant*** restrictions, which certainly cannot be automated, is nevertheless a very difficult task. Its difficulty is actually the main, if not only, barrier to a more systematic use of qualitative calculus.

4. SCOPE OF THE GEOMETRIC COMPARATIVE STATICS

It appears quite natural to move from the open intervals $(-\infty, 0)$ and $(0, +\infty)$ of qualitative calculus to compact intervals taking into account a more precise knowledge on admissible values of partial derivatives. A marginal propensity to consume is certainly positive, but in normal situations it is almost as certainly included in the interval [0.5, 0.9]. Besides, setting the upper and lower bounds equal, this approach can also account for the exact value of certain coefficients, like those of the definitional relations for instance.

For a linear system $Ax = b$, where the elements of matrix A and vector b are allowed to vary over appropriate intervals, the geometric approach consists in studying the set of feasible values for the state variables x. This feasible set is compact (Rossier, 1982) when det(A) does not change sign within its domain. In more precise terms, this set is a geometric figure of a polyhedral type, not necessarily convex, and called a polytope, whose dimension is given by the number of relations in the system $Ax = b$ which contain variable elements.

There are basically two ways to interpret the shape of these polytopes. First, the set of feasible solutions can be explored by repeated simulations. Each simulation will correspond to a specific value for the parameters resulting, for instance, from a random drawing from the intervals of variation. This approach is basically time consuming and not very tractable, but its main flaw lies in its inability to give a precise definition of the contour of a polytope, and particularly in its inability to detect non-convexities.

A more satisfying approach is the purely geometric approach of Rossier (1979, 1982) which consists in studying the polytope by means of its projections on axes and specially selected planes. This procedure will thus give a full description of the feasible set of the endogenous variables, taking simultaneously into account all the relevant assumptions on possible values for the parameters.

There may, of course, remain qualitatively undetermined multipliers in a geometric analysis: it would be an exceptional occurrence that the polytope generated by the various intervals lie in a single orthant. These indeterminacies do not, however, have the unfortunate consequences they have in the pure qualitative case. Even if the set of feasible values for a multiplier includes zero, the information obtained in this way can be processed because each point of the polytope can be associated to a given combination of the values of all variable parameters.

The contribution of the geometric analysis to the understanding of a model goes well beyond the raw display of feasible values for the multipliers. Indeed, each critical (angular) point on the boundary of the projection of a polytope in a given plane corresponds to extreme values of the variable parameters. And each edge linking these points is generated by the variation of a single parameter. The study of the critical points, and more generally of the boundary of the projection, gives information as to the sensitivity of the endogenous variables to the various variable parameters. Combinations of values leading to the most favourable points of the polytope can thus be pointed out.

The geometric approach is not restricted to the analysis of multipliers since it can be applied to any system liable to be linearised under the form $Ax = b$, where for instance the variables are expressed in absolute changes or rates of variation. Besides, an appropriate rewriting of the system extends the same treatment to exogenous variables and parameters. Thus intervals of variation can equally be considered for exogenous variables.

In this respect it appears particularly interesting to consider only the controllable exogenous elements (policy measures) as variable. When the polytope is projected in a plane corresponding to conflicting objectives, the various trade-offs resulting from non-dominated policies are explicitly displayed. Moreover, the slope of the edges generated by the variation of one policy instrument gives a measure of the relative efficacy of that instrument. In the plane employment-balance of trade in a demand model considered by Ritschard and Royer (1983), a weakly negative slope for the edges associated to public expenditures shows the conflicting nature of these objectives with respect to this policy instrument, as well as its greater ability to control employment than the balance of trade.

When non-controllable parameters can take on values over some interval, the resulting polytope should be analysed with respect to the transformation of the partial polytopes corresponding to policy measures. The resulting moving polytopes are especially useful for the understanding of switching conditions which give rise to non-convexities. Such situations come up when a structural parameter conditions the impact of one or several instruments (see Hislaire and Mirlesse, 1982).

5. CONCLUDING REMARKS

Grown out of suspicion toward quantitative results and an often deep scepticism as to the robustness of economic theory, qualitative structural analysis seems bound to return home. But the question is: in what shape?

Significant (or at least informative) results can only be obtained in non-scholarly cases by the techniques of geometric comparative statics, which requires a sound theoretical background as well as a high degree of quantification.

Should we then conclude with a negative assessment? The assessment certainly seems to be negative if one reduces qualitative structural analysis to developing yet more algorithms, whose relevance becomes less and less obvious. In this respect we still need a new Ragnar Frisch to coin the structural equivalent to 'playometrics'! On the other hand, if one considers the learning effect, or more generally, the guidelines offered by the practice of structural analysis in building a model, the conclusion can be more optimistic. Improvement, and hence a growing credibility in macroeconometric models, can only be achieved by means of sound theoretical foundations *and* a greater transparency in their operational implementation.

NOTES

1) This situation can be compared to the subject of aggregation.
2) It is in this respect instructive to realise that a great deal of the papers on qualitative methods are published in non-economically oriented journals. See, for instance, Gilli and Rossier (1981), Ritschard and Rossier (1981), and Rossier (1982, 1983).
3) Two exceptions can be found in Ritschard and Royer (1983) and Mirlesse (1983).
4) Algorithms most commonly used can be found in Rossier (1979).
5) For technical aspects see Rossier (1983).

REFERENCES

Bassett, L. (1968), 'The Solution of Qualitative Comparative Static Problems: Comment', *Quarterly Journal of Economics,* 82 (3), pp. 519-523.

Deleau, M. and P. Malgrange (1978), *L'analyse des modèles macroéconomiques quantitatifs,* Paris, Economica.

Gilli, M., G. Ritschard and D. Royer (1983), 'Pour une approche structurale en économie',

Revue économique, 34 (2), pp. 277-304.

Gilli, M. and E.Rossier (1981), 'Understanding Complex Systems', *Automatica,* 17 (4), pp. 647-652.

Hislaire, J. and D. Mirless (1982), 'Geometric Multipliers: The Case of Foreign Trade in GS-4', 3rd International Workshop of the Applied Econometric Association, Erasmus University Rotterdam.

Mirlesse, D. (1983), 'Multiplicateurs géométriques et effets de report', in: *Mélanges en hommage à E. Rossier* (G. Ritschard and D. Royer, eds.) (forthcoming).

Ritschard, G. (1980), *Contribution à l'analyse des structures qualitatives des modèles économiques,* Berne, Peter Lang.

Ritschard. G. (1983), 'Computable Qualitative Comparative Static Techniques', *Econometrica,* 51 (4), pp. 1145-1168.

Ritschard, G. and E. Rossier (1981), 'Qualitative and Geometric Models for Large Econometric Models', *Large Scale Systems,* 2 (4), pp. 269-290.

Ritschard, G. and D. Royer (1982), 'Parités flottantes en déséquilibre: le cas de la Suisse', *Prévision et Analyse Economique,* 3 (1) (forthcoming).

Ritschard, G. and D. Royer (1983), 'A Geometric Approach to Disequilibrium Exchange Rate Fluctuations: The Case of Switzerland', *European Economic Review,* 22, pp. 373-404.

Rossier, E. (1971), *Economie structurale,* Economica, Paris.

Rossier, E. (1982), 'L'inverse d'une matrice d'intervalle', *Revue Française d'Automatique d'Informatique et de Recherche Opérationelle,* 16 (2), pp. 99-124.

Rossier, E. (1983), 'Pour un schéma de lecture des modèles économiques complexes: application à MINI–DMS', *Revue Française d'Automatique d'Informatique et de Recherche Opérationelle,* 17 (1), pp. 21-41.

Royer, D. (1980), *Contribution à l'analyse qualitative des modèles de décision,* Berne, Peter Lang.

Royer, D. (1981), 'Structure causale de la forme normative d'un modèle économique. Fondements théoriques et illustration', *Publications économétriques,* 14 (1), pp. 63-92.

Samuelson, P.A. (1947), *Foundations of Economic Analysis,* Harvard University Press, Cambridge Mass.

Simon, H.A. (1963), 'Causal Ordering and Identifiability', in: A. Ando, F.M. Fisher and H.A. Simon, *Essays on the Structure of Social Science Models,* MIT Press, Cambridge Mass.

CHAPTER 2

TWO APPROACHES IN READING MODEL INTERDEPENDENCIES

M. Garbely and M. Gilli
University of Geneva, Switzerland

1. INTRODUCTION

In order to introduce the basic notions used in our analysis, let us consider the structural form of our econometric model given by the set of n structural equations $h(y,z) = 0$, where $y, (y \in R^n)$ and $z, (z \in R^m)$ are the endogenous and exogenous variables respectively. To be regular, such a model has to verify the existence of a complete matching between the set of relations and the set of endogenous variables. This means that it has to be possible to assign a different left-hand variable to each equation, which enables us to write the model as a set of n explicit functions $y_i = g_i(y;z)$. Then, if the model is written in this form, a non-zero derivative $\partial g_i/\partial y_j$ indicates the existence of a causal link going from variable y_j to variable y_i. The set of all these links defines what is called the *causal structure of the model*. The present study is based exclusively on information of this type.

It appears that the causal structure is equivalent to a graph $G = (X, A)$, where the vertices $X = Y \cup Z$ are the variables of the model and the arcs A are all the pairs $x_i \rightarrow x_j$, x_i being one of the right-hand variables in the equation explaining variable x_j.

The analysis of the causal structure will be carried out from the graph G, whose properties are equivalent to the properties of the model. As already mentioned, the arcs correspond to the direct causal links in the model. Thus, if a vertex x_j can be reached from vertex x_i by a path in graph G, there exists an indirect causal link in the model going from variable x_i to variable x_j. Two variables x_i, x_j are considered interdependent if a direct or indirect causal link exists from x_i to x_j as well as from x_j to x_i. In graph G these two variables will belong to a circuit.

A first task consists then in finding the sets of interdependent variables. To do this we consider the set $R(x_o)$ of all vertices which can be reached from x_o by a path and the set $Q(x_o)$ of all vertices from which x_o is reachable by a path. Then, the intersection $R(x_o) \cap Q(x_o)$ forms the biggest set of interdependent variables containing variable x_o. In graph G such a set is called a strong component. The strong components of a graph constitute a partition of the set of variables.

To the initial graph G it is then possible to associate a reduced graph G_r, whose vertices are the strong components of G and in which there will be an arc between two vertices of the reduced graph if there is at least one arc in G between the vertices corresponding to the two strong components. The reduced graph G_r is representative of all the causal links between the interdependent sets of variables or blocks existing in this model.

The reduced graph G_r is used to derive the recursive properties of the model, i.e. the establishment of a hierarchy among the blocks as well as the determination of separable submodels for example.

In practice one observes that the block structure of economic models is quite particular. Indeed, most of them have a very large block of interdependent equations, containing almost all the endogenous variables of the model; this leads to the following familiar pattern of the Jacobian matrix:

source set

interdependent set

sink set

Thus, the importance of techniques dealing with the analysis of the causal structure inside a block is evident.

2. ESSENTIAL ELEMENTS FOR INTERDEPENDENCY

A block or interdependent structure is characterised by the existence of a path between any pair of vertices involving many circuits. In practice even blocks of relatively modest size contain a number of elementary circuits, i.e. circuits which do not go twice over a same vertex, of the order of several hundreds of thousands. This leads to really complex situations. In consequence of this complexity a model may show some misbehaviour that requires the understanding of its global functioning. In general, however, this is not possible without using simplified or condensed forms of the system. Nevertheless, as simplified models often give rise to some inconsistency, there is a need for guides, or procedures, to a global understanding of complex interdependent systems which do not imply any loss of information.

In this context two approaches, which claim to contribute to the understanding of complex interdependent systems, will be presented. Fundamentally, we seek for some elements which are essential for the interdependency of the model. The first approach brings into focus some set of variables which are involved in all the feedbacks and which therefore may be considered as starting points for a possible sequential reading. The second approach points out those causal links which are indispensable to keep the system interdependent and which can be used for simplified representations.

2.1. Essential feedback vertex set

Briefly conceived, we propose to cut the circularity of the model at a certain number of variables and to analyse the resulting recursive structure.

The set of variables we seek for has then to be such that any circuit of the model contains at least one of these variables. The vertices representing these variables in the graph are split into two parts, one containing only outgoing arcs and the other only ingoing arcs. The new graph thus obtained does not contain any circuit and allows therefore a hierarchical ordering of the variables. Moreover, such a graph contains a unique set of arcs which are responsible for all the paths.

It is clear, however, that we are only interested in minimal sets having the property of cutting all the circuits. The problem of finding those sets is known as the minimal feedback vertex sets (Guardabassi (1971)). The minimal feedback vertex sets which are minimum are called essential sets and the variables forming the sets are called essential variables.

Formally, the problem consists in finding minimal covers of the following bipartite graph

$$G_T = (T, C, \Gamma) ,$$

where C is the set of all the elementary circuits of the strong component and T the set of arcs in the sub-graph defined by the strong component. Γ is the mapping giving the correspondence between the elements of T and C. A minimum cover is then a set $A \subset T$ such that

$$\Gamma(A) = C \quad \text{and} \quad \nexists B \subset A \quad \text{such that} \quad \Gamma(B) = C .$$

Since the number of vertices in the strong component is usually much smaller than the number of arcs, we would prefer to look for sets of vertices which cover the circuits in a graph $G_V = (V, C, \Psi)$. Moreover, we should mention that in most cases the definition of a graph G_T or G_V is practically impossible due to the fact that even in small blocks the number of circuits is extraordinarily high.

In any case, such a problem is known as NP-complete, i.e. the computing time needed to solve the problem is a non-polynomial function of the size of the strong component considered. In most cases, such problems, even if relatively modest in size, cannot be efficiently solved when presented in the above form.

We give here the layout of a procedure which allows us to obtain the above sets at reasonable cost, at least as far as economic models are concerned, since the graph associated with an economic model becomes less dense as the model becomes bigger.

As mentioned before, the computational difficulties come from the need to enumerate and store all the elements of the set C. To obtain an efficient procedure we use a method which avoids:

– the storage of the elements of C, using an iterative construction of the covers.
– the enumeration of redundant elements of C.

The second point qualifies the method as a topological one. The iterative algorithm of the construction of covers is described in Gilli and Rossier (1981). The fundamental idea of the iterative procedure is the following:

– given a set of covers E_r, corresponding to r circuits of the graph, compute the set of covers E_{r+1}, corresponding to the r preceeding circuits, to which a new circuit c_{r+1} has been added. Thus the procedure needs only an enumeration of the elementary circuits and no storage of them.
– secondly, the procedure for seeking the circuits is a particular one which excludes the enumeration of a circuit c_j verifying $c_i \subset c_j$. Such circuits are absorbed by circuit c_i. This means that all the covers for circuit c_i are also the covers for circuit c_j.

Once an essential set is found we transform the original graph into a graph without circuits. As all the circuits contain variables of the essential set, all the feedbacks can be cut by splitting the corresponding vertices. Thus, they will form two new sets, one containing only outgoing arcs and the other only ingoing arcs.

To this graph we apply the techniques for the analysis of recursive causal structures (see Gilli (1982)) summarised hereafter:

– establishment of a hierarchy among the variables by grouping them into succeeding levels, so that causal links can only go from lower numbered levels to higher numbered ones.
  The splitted vertices of the essential set, containing only outgoing arcs, form evidently the first level. Dropping these vertices gives rise to a subgraph which again contains vertices with no ingoing arcs and thus forms the second level. This procedure is carried on until all the levels have been found.
– summary of all causal links by means of a matrix B, in which the element b_{ij} qualifies the link going from variable y_j to variable y_i. If the rows and columns correspond to the variables in the order they have been identified in the succeeding levels, then matrix B is obviously triangular.

It might now be interesting to point out in the graph the arcs which are responsible for all the dependencies. Such arcs, called basic arcs, form a minimal graph. In our graph, which is without circuits, such a minimal graph is unique. The elements of matrix B will be set equal to the following symbols, according to the type of causal link existing from variable y_j to variable y_i:

$$b_{ij} = \begin{cases} \text{B} & \text{basic causal link} \\ \text{D} & \text{direct causal link} \\ \text{I} & \text{indirect causal link} \\ \cdot & \text{no causal links} \end{cases}$$

For an illustration we will use the following graph:

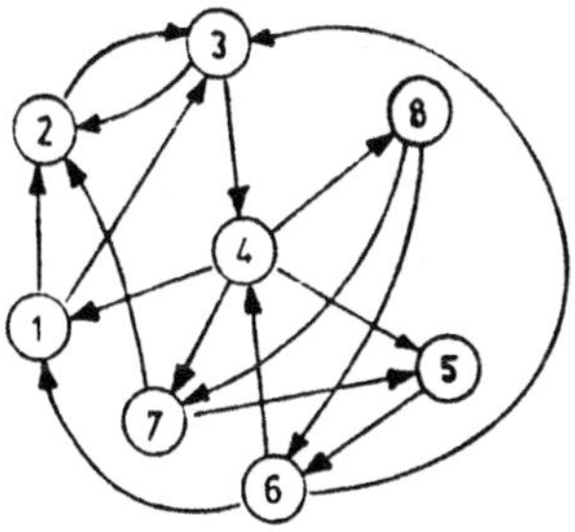

It appears that every elementary circuit of this strongly connected graph contains either vertex 3 or vertex 6. The essential set is thus given by (3,6).

Splitting vertices 3 and 6 as described above will cut off all the circuits. The vertices can then be grouped into levels and matrix B is constructed.

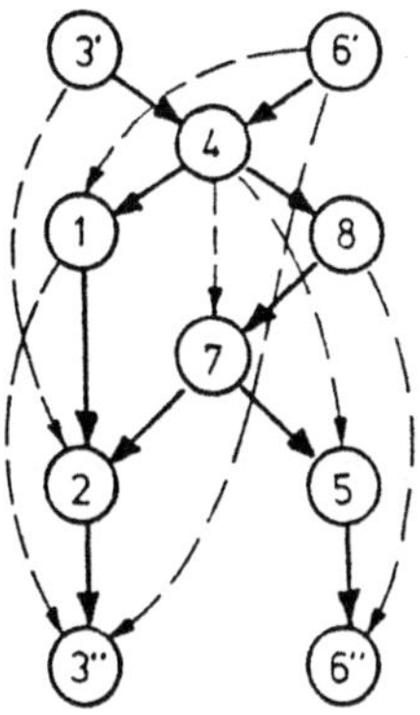

B =

		3'	6'	4	1	8	7	2	5	3''	6''
Level 1	3'	1									
	6'	·	1								
Level 2	4	B	B	1							
Level 3	1	I	D	B	1						
	8	I	I	B	·	1					
Level 4	7	I	I	D	·	B	1				
Level 5	2	D	I	I	B	I	B	1			
	5	I	I	D	·	I	B	·	1		
Level 6	3''	I	D	I	D	I	I	B	·	1	
	6''	I	I	I	·	D	I	·	B	·	1

Here the arcs drawn in fat lines represent the minimal graph. With respect to the weakening of the complexity provided by the new graph, the advantage of such a representation seems evident.

2.2. Minimal set of causal links

Finding the most simplified structure without any loss of information about mutually dependent variables gives rise to the following question: which are the causal links that are essential for the model's interdependency and, in a complementary way, which are the links that could be suppressed.

To that end, we define a *causality basis* as a minimum set of direct causal links preserving the interdependencies between the variables of the model.

Formally a causality basis is represented by a *minimal graph*, or basic graph, for the directed graph G associated with the model.

A minimal graph for graph G = (Y,A) is a partial graph $G_B = (Y,A_B)$, where A_B is a subset of A such that the reachability in G_B is the same as in G. Clearly this means that to any direct or indirect causal link from y_i to y_j in G corresponds at least one link in G_B. The subset A_B of A is minimal, i.e. the suppression of any of its arcs would modify its reachability.

As mentioned before (see section 2.1.) the minimal graph for a graph without circuits is unique and fast to compute. Moreover, in that case the arcs A_B of the minimal graph are responsible for all the dependencies in graph G.

However, in the case of a strongly connected graph, the minimal graph is in general not unique.

Our purpose being to simplify a structure as much as possible, it is clear that we are only interested in minimal graphs having a minimum number of arcs. We call them the *smallest minimal graphs*. Even then, as is shown in the following example, this problem will not have a unique solution.

For the graph:

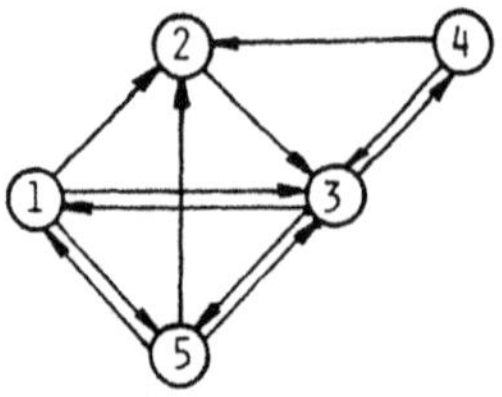

the following four partial graphs are minimal graphs but only the last two are smallest minimal graphs:

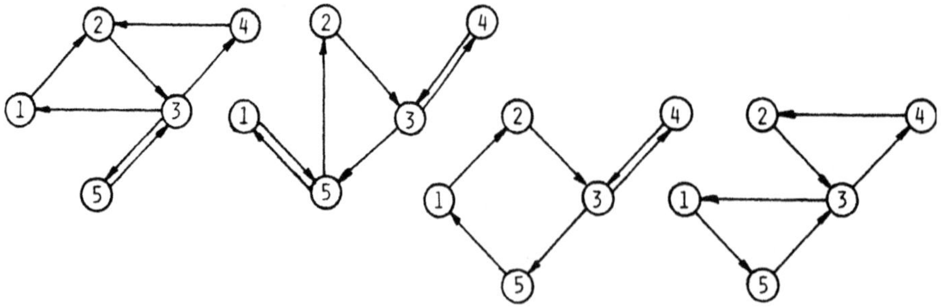

The different minimal graphs for a strongly connected graph have some interesting common elements which are called the basic arcs. A ***basic arc*** is defined as an arc belonging to each minimal graph.

The problem of finding a smallest minimal graph can be reformulated into the well-known travelling salesman problem (Held and Karp (1969)). To do so we associate with the graph G its transitive closure G_T[1]. If G is strongly connected, G_T is complete and symmetric. Every arc $y_i \rightarrow y_j$ of G_T is valued by a weight c_{ij}, where

$$c_{ij} = \begin{cases} 1 & \text{if the arc } y_i \rightarrow y_j \text{ exists in G} \\ \infty & \text{if not.} \end{cases}$$

Then the solution of the travelling salesman problem giving a path of minimal cost going over all the vertices in G_T is equivalent to a smallest minimal graph.

However, it should be recalled that the travelling salesman problem is NP-complete. Therefore, it seems natural to take advantage of the particular properties of graphs associated with economic models. In fact, those graphs happen to be very sparse and it was possible to develop an efficient procedure for finding a smallest minimal graph.

In a first stage the procedure defines some simplifications in order to reduce the size of the graph. For example, let us consider equations of the following type:

a) an equation containing only one argument variable and the variable explained by this equation steps into only one other equation.
b) an equation containing only one argument variable.

In graph G these situations yield the following configurations:

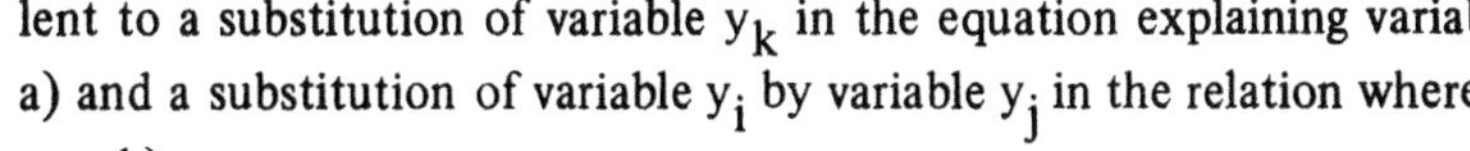

Then in case a) we can drop vertex y_k and replace both arcs $y_i \rightarrow y_k$ and $y_k \rightarrow y_j$ by one arc $y_i \rightarrow y_j$. In case b) vertex y_i is dropped and the outgoing arcs of vertex y_i are transformed into outgoing arcs of vertex y_j. In terms of the model this is equivalent to a substitution of variable y_k in the equation explaining variable y_j for case a) and a substitution of variable y_i by variable y_j in the relation where y_i occurs for case b).

Such simplifications allow us to identify basic arcs on the one hand and arcs which certainly do not belong to any minimal graph on the other hand. So, in the examples considered, the arcs $y_i \rightarrow y_k$ and $y_k \rightarrow y_j$ for case a) and the arc $y_j \rightarrow y_i$ for case b) are basic arcs. If arc $y_i \rightarrow y_j$ exists in case a), it cannot belong to any minimal graph. Other similar simplifications can be done automatically (see Garbely (1982)).

These different simplifications yield a simplified graph, the size of which is in general reduced by about 40%. Evidently a smallest minimal graph for the simplified graph allows the identification of a smallest minimal graph for the original graph.

The simplifications which yield a condensed form of the causal structure also partition the arcs of graph G into three sets:

– basic arcs
– arcs which cannot belong to any minimal graph
– arcs which may or may not belong to a minimal graph

For their interpretation it is important to note that basic arcs do not depend on the choice of a particular smallest minimal graph. Each basic arc is such that, if it is suppressed, the interdependent structure will be split into two blocks at least. A causal link of the model corresponding to a basic arc in the graph is fundamental for the model's interdependency.

On the other hand, if one removes causal links corresponding to arcs which can not belong to any minimal graph the model's interdependency will not be modified.

The method proposed for finding a smallest minimal graph is based on the principles of depth first search technique as presented by Tarjan (1972). A detailed description of the procedure as well as an operational computer algorithm is reported in Garbely (1982).

For a small illustration let us consider the following strongly connected graph:

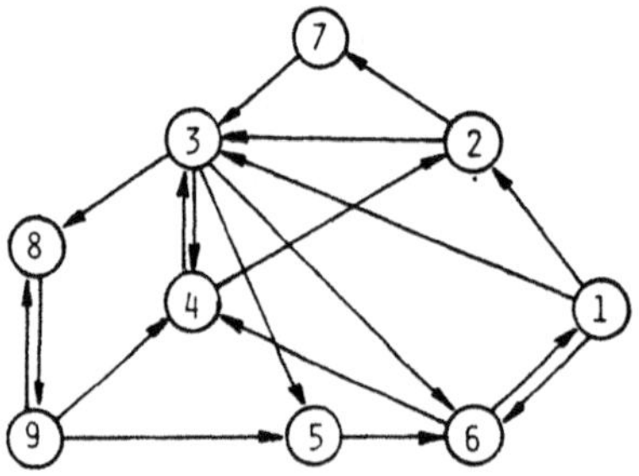

for which a smallest minimal graph is given by;

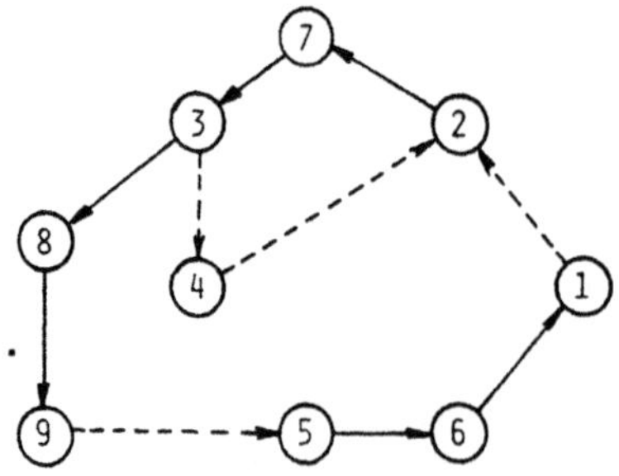

The arcs in fat lines are basic arcs. The arcs $2 \rightarrow 3$ and $9 \rightarrow 8$ cannot belong to any minimal graph.

As already mentioned, strongly connected graphs may have a large number of smallest minimal graph. (A complete symmetric graph of n vertices has $(n-1)!$ smallest minimal graphs.) Nevertheless, due to the sparsity of the structure of economic models, their smallest minimal graphs are not so numerous and not very different from each other. On average, more than 60% of the arcs of smallest minimal graphs are basic arcs.

Still, the interpretation of a causality basis corresponding to a smallest minimal graph depends on the choice of a specific minimal graph. Therefore, causality basis are specially useful for reading the model's interdependencies as a whole.

The average number of outgoing arcs per vertex of a smallest minimal graph is about 1.2, while this number lies between 2 and 4 in the original graph of interdependent economic models. Obviously, this makes the reading (and drawing) of the interdependencies much easier.

A causality basis does not bring the model's variables into a hierarchic order and so it does not refer to a particular underlying dynamic, which would imply recursivity. Since in a causality basis every variable can be considered as a starting point for the reading of the model, different underlying dynamics can be taken into account.

However, the elements of a causality basis are not only interesting as a whole. Causal relations corresponding to basic arcs are fundamental for the causal structure of a model. So, the analysis of paths and circuits formed by basic arcs can be used as a framework when comparing different causal structures.

If a model user wants to omit one or more causal links, for instance because their coefficients are not significant, he has to be aware of three cases:

- the causal links cannot belong to any minimal graph. Then they can be omitted without any influence on the causal structure of the model.
- the causal links are basic arcs. The interdependent block will certainly split into at least two blocks.
- the causal links are neither basic arcs nor arcs which cannot belong to a minimal graph. Then, if more than one link is omitted, the block structure of the model has to be reconsidered.

3. ILLUSTRATION

The two approaches for reading the interdependencies are illustrated by means of a quarterly macro-economic short-term forecasting model for the US economy[2]. The model is formed by 215 equations and contains a single big interdependent block of

128 variables; this is, as already mentioned, very common for macro-economic models.

In the following presentation only the causal structure of the interdependent block has been considered and only causal links of the current period are discussed. This analysis does not include feedbacks generated by lagged endogenous variables and therefore the conclusions concern the interdependencies within one period.

The symbols used for the variables in the block are briefly explained in the annexe.

The preliminary analysis of the recursive properties, the essential sets and the hierarchical ordering in the modified graph have been performed with the CAUSOR program described in Gilli (1982). The smallest minimal graph and the partition into basic arcs, arcs which never belong to a minimal graph, and the other arcs have been computed with a program described in Garbely (1982).

Although the interdependent block considered contains only 2.5 outgoing arcs per variable on average, its complexity is quite important. We will see how we can get some insight into the global working of such a system.

3.1. Recursive and block-recursive schemes

The cardinal number of the essential sets is 14 and the algorithm identified two sets with 12 common variables. The two sets are:

GNP,PD,PS,GNPP,DIV,RCB,SBIV,RTB,PSFW,LRAC,LRMKUP,WBP- { CON,DC / YD,PCON }

In a preliminary step the algorithm transforms the initial graph into a smaller graph by elimination of particular vertices. Some of them may be substituted in the two sets above and therefore the number of different essential sets may be much larger. We do not give here the list of all these possible substitutions, as they are of little interest as far as our analysis is concerned.

We chose the essential set containing the variables CON and DC. Applying the technique described in section 2.1 for splitting all the vertices, we obtained a recursive structure for which we computed a hierarchy among the variables. The causal scheme obtained will not be presented here, but we will refer to it later, when discussing the use of different orderings for solving the model.

We will now describe a method which leads to a more synthetic representation of the causal scheme of our block. The modifications with respect to the previous procedure are:

- instead of splitting the essential variables, we remove only the ingoing arcs which are responsible for the interdependencies.
- we do not remove the ingoing arcs which are only responsible for circuits shorter than a given threshold.

This will transform the interdependent structure into a block-recursive one, the complexity of which is less important if, in a first step, one looks only at the causality between the blocks and, in a second step, one analyses the structure of the blocks.

We see that for this method we need the *smallest minimal graph* for identifying the particular arcs responsible for the interdependencies. The main steps of this method are detailed hereafter for our example:

- choose a variable of the essential set as starting variable for the block-recursive scheme and check if this variable belongs to a long circuit and has ingoing basic arcs. If this is not the case, another variable has to be chosen. (In our case, we choose GNP as starting point and the smallest minimal graph (see figure 2, p. 29) shows that the arcs GEX → GNP and GPDI → GNP are in-going basic arcs belonging to long circuits.
- remove the ingoing basic arcs identified as belonging to long circuits. (In our case, GEX → GNP and GPDI → GNP).
- repeat these two steps for all long circuits not yet cut. (In our example, DIV and arc CF → GNP). We stop when no more essential variables exist which have ingoing basic arcs belonging to long circuits.
- compute the strong components of the modified graph (arcs have been removed). Repeat the complete procedure as long as the graph contains large strong components one wishes to decompose. (In the example, this leads to the identification of the feedbacks RPS → LRAC, RCK → LRAC and YD → DC).

Figure 1 shows the picture associated with this block-recursive structure, where only the basic arcs between the blocks are reported. The feedbacks that have been removed are drawn in dotted lines and evidently go from bottom to top. In the scheme, all the other arcs go from top to bottom and therefore unfold a possible sequence of mechanisms in the model.

The remaining blocks contain variables involved in short circuits. These blocks may be considered either as 'faster submodels' or submodels which in a first step do not depend on the main feedbacks.

One may ask whether such a scheme is of great use for understanding a model, as it depends on the choice of a particular essential set and is therefore not unique.

Two arguments will be presented in favour of such a presentation:

- almost all the schemes one can obtain with the technique explained previously have some common patterns. This is due to the fact that the unfold circuits are

Figure 1: Block-recursive decomposition

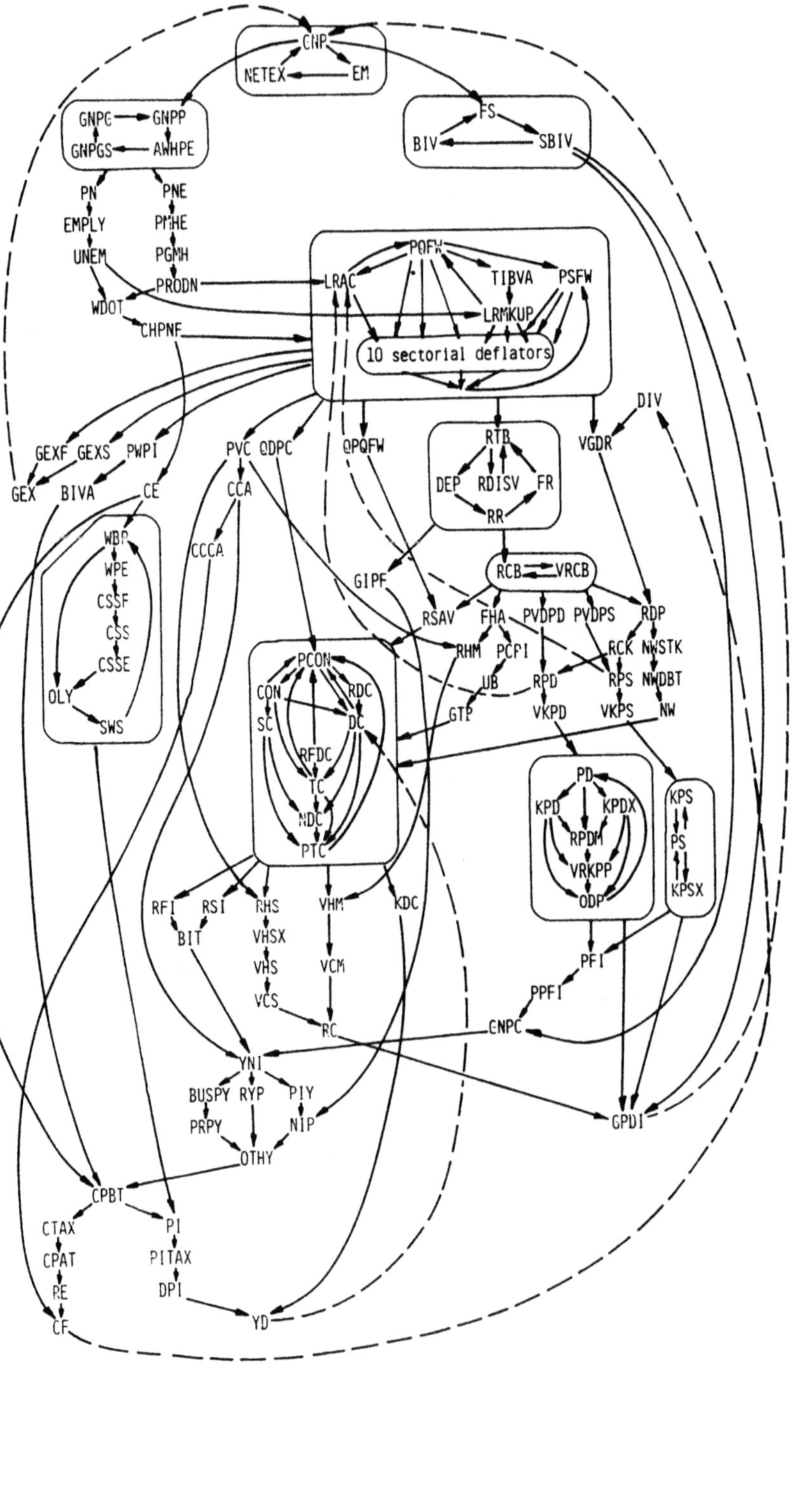

similar, regardless of the starting point that has been chosen.

– when a model has to be solved, the choice of the resolution scheme is crucial with respect to the performance of the solution algorithm.

We will briefly discuss the second of the above arguments by presenting the results of an exercise in which different resolution schemes have been used for solving the interdependent block of our model by means of an iterative Gauss-Seidel procedure.[3]

The exercise consisted in solving the interdependent block for two periods using first the block-recursive scheme given in the preceding figure. The performance for this ordering, expressed in total number of equations solved with the Gauss-Seidel procedure, has then been compared to the performance for a fully recursive scheme (where all ingoing arcs to the essential variables have been cut), as well as to the performance obtained with an ordering corresponding to the algorithm described in van der Giessen (1970). The summary of the results is the following:

Method	Iterations period 1	Iterations period 2	Equations computed	%
Modified essential sets	8	7	3209	100
Essential sets	18	18	4608	144
van der Giessen ordering	22	23	5760	180

Detail for resolution with modified essential sets (block structure)

Block	Size	Period 1 Iterations								Period 2 Iterations						
1	3	7	5	3	3	1	1	1	1	7	5	3	3	1	2	1
2	3	6	3	3	1	3	1	1	1	6	3	3	3	1	2	1
3	4	5	4	2	1	1	1	1	1	5	4	2	2	1	1	1
4	15	3	3	2	2	1	1	1	1	3	3	3	2	1	1	1
5	5	17	16	13	9	4	4	2	1	17	15	12	9	5	4	1
6	2	3	2	2	2	1	1	1	1	3	2	2	2	2	1	1
7	7	3	3	2	1	1	1	1	1	3	3	2	2	1	1	1
8	9	3	3	2	2	1	1	1	1	3	3	2	2	1	1	1
9	6	3	3	3	2	1	1	1	1	3	3	3	2	1	1	1
10	3	2	2	2	1	1	1	1	1	2	2	2	1	1	1	1

The exercise shows, at least for this example, an appreciable gain in computing costs. Nevertheless, we think that a much more important aspect consists in the fact that this way of solving allowed the identification of a subsystem of the model, whose behaviour was responsible for a bad performance of the other methods.

3.2. Basic arcs and smallest minimal graph

Applying the proposed procedure to the interdependent block containing 322 arcs we find a smallest minimal graph of 157 arcs. This corresponds to an average number of outgoing arcs per vertex of 1.2. arcs. (For economic models this number ranges from 1.1 to 1.3).

The strong component has 102 basic arcs, which means that 65% of the arcs of a smallest minimal graph are basic arcs. This again corresponds to the average of economic models.

Moreover, the different simplifications yield 10 arcs which cannot belong to any minimal graph. To an arc $y_i \rightarrow y_j$ of this type corresponds always a path $y_i \dashrightarrow y_j$ formed exclusively by basic arcs. Therefore, the enumeration of these arcs is of litle interest for our analysis.

Figure 2 shows a graphical representation of a smallest minimal graph associated with the interdependent block of the model. The arcs drawn in fat lines represent the basic arcs.

The depth first search algorithm identifies only one smallest minimal graph. In order to find all smallest minimal graphs a procedure involving combination calculus is needed. However, as we mentioned in section 2.2., in the case of economic models smallest minimal graphs are not very different from each other. Therefore the conclusions of our analysis would not be deeply modified by the choice of another smallest minimal graph.

Considering the paths formed by basic arcs only, we see that neither the prices and deflators nor the variables corresponding to the money stock and reserves have ingoing basic arcs. This does not mean, of course, that these variables are not caused by those of the block, but that the way they depend on other variables is not unique. Moreover, variables referring to consumer expenditures have no outgoing basic arcs. Thus the model takes into account different causal influences of these variables on the rest of the block.

Let us condense the variables into 10 main sectors and consider only the causal links represented by basic arcs. This yields the scheme in figure 3. It is important to note that thise scheme only gives information about causal links which *must* exist if the model has to be interdependent.

Similar schemes can be useful when comparing different causal structures as well as when choosing a specific essential set. If we condense the elements of both the sets identified in section 3.1. according to the 10 main sectors of this scheme, it appears that the common elements of the sets are involved in the four following sectors: National income and GNP, prices and deflators, interest and rental rates, and finally investment expenditure. The elements, which are different in the two essential sets, refer in both cases to consumption expenditure. This points out that the results of the analysis would not have been deeply modified if one had chosen the other set.

Figure 2: Smallest minimal graph

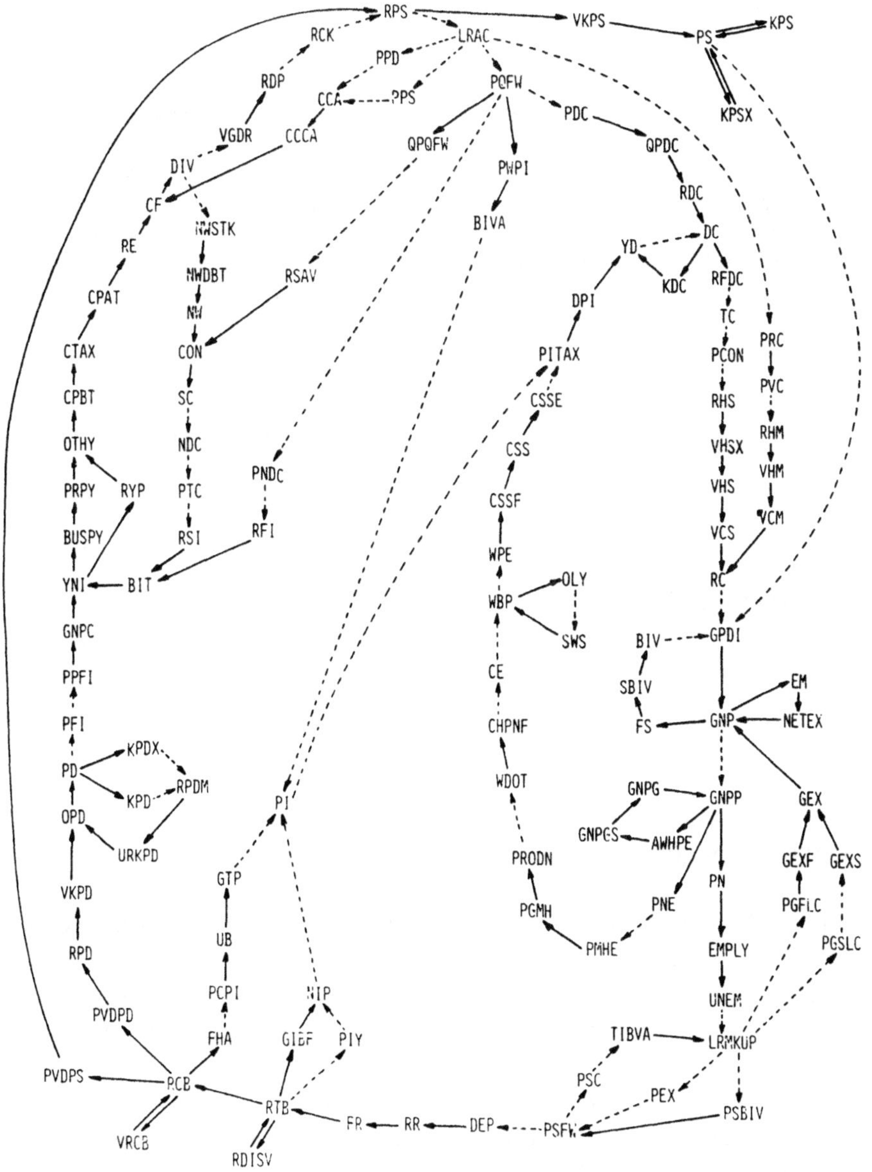

Figure 3

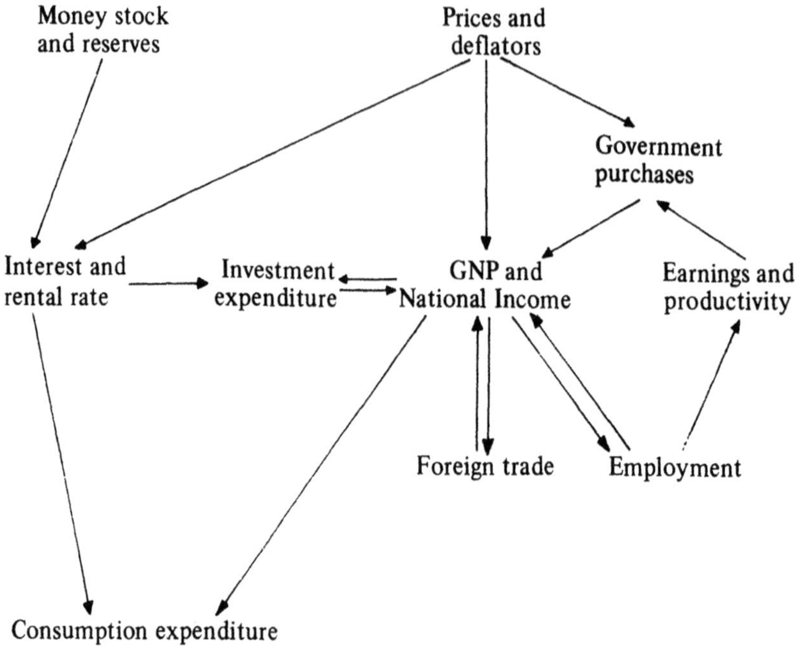

4. CONCLUDING REMARKS

The paper shows how to combine two tools for the analysis of the interdependencies in an economic model.

Each method shows interesting results on its own. Moreover, they have the great advantage of being performed by efficient procedures for which the programs have been made available.

Taken together, the two approaches allow us to tune the level of decomposition and partition of the complex linkages. The remaining blocks in these ordered structures may be considered as 'faster submodels'. The mechanisms can therefore be read in a two-stage process: the first stage considers the links between the blocks, whereas the second one details the inside of a block. This technique greatly facilitates the understanding of an interdependent model. For the solving process, the interest of such schemes has also been put forward.

APPENDIX: Endogenous variables of the interdependent block

AWHPE	WORKWEEK, PVT EMPLOYEES*	PIY	PERS INT INCOME $
BIT	IND BUS TAXES $	PMHE	MANHOURS, PVT EMPLOYEES
BIV	INVENTORY INVESTMENT	PN	EMPLOYMENT, PVT*
BIVA	INVENTORY VAL ADJ $*	PNDC	DEFL, CON EXP, NONDUR*
BUSPY	BUS & PROF INCOME $*	PNE	EMPLOYMENT, PVT ESTAB*
CCA	CAP CON ALLOW, TOT $*	PPD	DEFL, PFI, PROD DUR EQ*
CCCA	CAP CON ALLOW, CORP $*	PPFI	DEFL, PFI, TOT
CE	COMP OF EMPLOYEES $	PPS	DEFL, PFI, NONRES CONSTR*
CF	CASH FLOW $	PQFW	DEFL, FW PVT GNP (NOT)*
CON	CONSUMPTION*	PRC	DEFL, RES CONSTRUCTION*
CHPNF	COMP/MHR, PVTNFM (I)	PRODN	OUTPUT/MHR, NORM PVTFM (I)
CPAT	CORP PROFITS AFTER TAX $	PRPY	PROPRIETORS INCOME $
CPBT	CORP PROFITS BEFORE TAX $	PS	PFI, NONRES CONSTRUCTN*
CSS	CONT SOC INS $	PSBIV	DEFL, INVENTORY STOCK*
CSSE	EMPLYR CONT TO SOC INS $	PSC	DEFL, CON EXP, SERVICES*
CSSF	FED GOV REC, SOC INS TAX $	PSFW	DEFL, FW SALES (NOT)
CTAX	CORP TAX LIABILITIES $	PTC	DEFL, PERS CONS EXPEND
DC	CON EXP, DUR*	PVC	DEFL, PVT ON IN PLACE*
DEP	CHECKABLE DEPOSITS $*	PVDPD	PV DEP ALL, PROD DUR $
DIV	DIVIDENDS $*	PVDPS	PV DEP ALL, PROD STR $
DPI	DISP PERS INCOME $	PWPI	PRODUCER PRICE INDEX*
EM	IMPORTS*	QPDC	EXPECTED %CHG, PDC
EMPLY	EMPLOYMENT, CIVILIAN	QPQFW	EXPECTED %CHG, PQFW
FHA	FHA MORTGAGE RATE $*	RC	RESIDENTIAL CONSTRUCTN
FR	FREE RESERVES $	RCB	AAA CORP BOND RATE $
FS	FINAL SALES	RCK	COST OF CAPITAL
GEX	GOV PURCHASE OF G & S	RDC	RENT, CON DUR
GEXF	FED GOV PUR, TOT	RDISV	DISCOUNT RATE (EFF) $*
GEXS	S & L GOV PUR, TOT	RDP	DIV/PRICE RATIO*
GIPF	FED GOV INT PAYMENTS $*	RE	UNDISTRIBUTED PROFITS $
GNP	GROSS NATIONAL PRODUCT	RFDC	RENTAL FLOW, CONS DUR
GNPC	GROSS NATIONAL PRODUCT $	RFI	FED GOV REC, IND BUS TAX $
GNPG	GOVT GNP	RHM	RENT, MULT FAM HOUS
GNPGS	S & L GOV GNP*	RHS	RENT, SING FAM HOUS
GNPP	GROSS PRIVAT PRODUCT	PRD	RENT. PROD DUR, MARG
GPDI	GROSS PVT DOM INVESTMENT	PRDM	RENT, PROD DUR, MEAN
GTP	GOV TRAN PAYMENTS $	RPS	RENT, PROD STR
KDC	STOCK, CONS DUR	RR	REQUIRED RESERVES $
KPD	STOCK, PROD DUR, TOT	RSAV	AFT-TAX RET TO SAV
KPDX	STOCK, PROD DUR, POL CON	RSI	S & L GOV REC, IND BUS TAX $
KPS	STOCK, PROD STR, TOT	RTB	TREASURY BILL RATE $*
KPSX	STOCK, PROD STR, POL CON	RYP	RENT INCOME OF PERSONS $*
LRAC	LONG RUN AVERAGE COST	SBIV	INVENTORY STOCKS*
LRMKUP	LONG RUN MARKUP	SC	CON EXP, SERVICES*
NDC	CON EXP, NONDUR*	SWS	SUP TO WAGE & SAL $
NETEX	NET EXPORTS	TC	PERSONAL CONSUMPTION EXP
NIP	NET INTEREST PAYMENTS $	TIBVA	AV IND BUS & VA TAX RATE
NW	NET WORTH, TOT $	UB	FED GOV UNEM BENEFITS $*
NWDBT	NET WORTH, BONDS $	UNEM	UNEMPLOYMENT RATE

NWSTK	NET WORTH, EQUITIES $	URKPD	UTILIZATION RATE, KPD
OLY	OTHER LABOUR INCOME $*	VCM	VALUE CON IN PLACE, MF*
OPD	ORDERS, PROD DUR EQ*	VCS	VALUE CON IN PLACE, SF*
OTHY	OTHER INCOME $	VGDR	STD DEV, DIV GROWTH
PCON	DEFL, CONSUMPTION	VHM	VALUE MULTI FAM STARTS*
PCPI	CONSUMER PRICE INDEX*	VHS	VALUE SIN FAM STARTS
PD	PFI, PROD DUR EQUIP*	VHSX	VALUE SFS + AD + MOB H.*
PDC	DEFL, CON EXP, DUR*	VKPD	EQ (KPD/GNPP) x 100
PEX	DEFL, EXPORTS*	VKPS	EQ (KPS/GNPP) x 100
PFI	PROD FIXED INVEST, TOT	VRCB	STD DEV, RCB $
PGFLC	DEFL, FED GOV PUR, OTHER*	WBP	WAGE & SAL, OTHER (PVT) $
PGMH	MANHOURS, TOT	WDOT	% CHG, COMP/MHR PVTNF*
PGSLC	DEFL, S & L GOV PUR, OTHER*	WPE	WAGES/YR, PVT EMPLOYEES $*
PI	PERS INCOME $	YD	DPI, INC RENT ON CONS DUR $
PITAX	PERS INCOME TAXES $	YNI	NATIONAL INCOME $

NOTES

1) The transitive closure of a graph $G = (Y, A)$ is the graph $G_T = (Y, A \cup A_T)$, where A_T is the minimal number of arcs necessary to make G_T transitive. A graph is said to be transitive if the existence of a path from y_i to y_k implies the existence of an arc $y_i \rightarrow y_k$.
2) It is a model built by Joël Prakken of the Economic Department of IBM, Armonk NY.
3) We are very grateful to Harry Eisenpress of the Economic Department of IBM, Armonk NY, for his efficient support in this matter.

REFERENCES

Garbely, M. (1982), 'Bases de causalité dans les modèles économiques interdépendants', *Cahiers du département d'économétrie,* Université de Genève.

Giessen, van der, A.A. (1970), 'Solving Non-linear Systems by Computer: a New Method', *Statistica Neerlandica,* Vol. 24, No 1.

Gilli, M. and E. Rossier (1981), 'Understanding Complex Systems', *Automatica,* Vol. 17, pp. 647-652.

Gilli, M. (1982), 'TROLL PROGRAM CAUSOR, A Program fo the Analysis of Recursive and Interdependent Causal Structures', Technical Report No 37, Massachusetts Institute of Technology, Boston.

Guardabassi, G. (1971), 'A Note on Minimal Essential Sets', *IEEE Trans Circuit Theory,* CT-18, pp.557-562.

Held, M. and R. Karp (1969), 'The Travelling Salesman Problem and Minimum Spanning Trees', *Operations Research*, Vol. 18, No 6, pp. 1138-1162.

Tarjan, R. (1972), 'Depth-first Search and Linear Graph Algorithms', *SIAM, J. Comput*, Vol. 1, No 2, pp. 146-160.

CHAPTER 3

READING MACROECONOMIC MODELS AND BUILDING CAUSAL STRUCTURES

M. Boutillier
Observatoire Français des Conjonctures Economiques, Paris, France

1. INTRODUCTION

From previous studies (see e.g. Muet (1979) or Laffargue (1980)), it turns out that analysing and understanding a model means neglecting some connections, interpreting *one* equation as fixing the level of *one* economic variable, ordering the equations in order to solve them, etc. All these operations can be gathered in the concept of reading.

A model may be 'read' in various ways; its first reading is implicitly contained in its writing but another one may appear more relevant with regard to what the actual building has produced as well in qualitative as in quantitative terms. In the long run, our aim will be to develop tools to allow us to make the best reading.

Concepts of reading and causality are closely related; a causal meaning is linked to every equation and the structural form of a model makes causal structures clear, i.e. the structure of every economic mechanism and the interconnection structure of all the mechanisms.

We present the concept of causality relation developed in the first step of reading; we see that there is no one-to-one correspondence between an equation and an economic mechanism and this multivocity influences hierarchical and circular causalities which are by-products of the causality and are built in the *second* step of the reading.

This second step deals with ides from Hénin (1974), Rossier (1979) or Gilli (1979). The weakness of the second step results and the phenomenon of causal circularity justify the introduction of the concept of loop (or feedback). That concept, for which we try to find an economic interpretation, is essential in this process and the determination of the feedbacks is the *third* step of the reading.

Different approaches, like those of Keller (1970), Deleau and Malgrange (1978), Gilli and Rossier (1981) and Brillet (1981a) have distinguished between two meanings of the feedback set; the first one is such that its cardinality is minimised and the second one is such that the quantitative impact (error) due to its deletion is minimised.

We attempt to conclude by proving the relevance of the second point of view with regard to the actual reading of a model by a macro-economist.

2. FIRST READING STEP: BUILDING A CAUSALITY RELATION

In 1960, Strotz and Wold have stressed the gap between descriptive models (well known as 'black boxes') and causal models as in macroeconomics. In the latter models functional relationships between variables are not only guessed but are given a causal meaning: thus the dissymmetry between explanatory variable and explained variable introduced by econometricians and the dissymmetry between cause and effect are the same, even if this causality may appear with a probabilistic dimension.

The peculiarity of accounting identities is avoided when we realise that *one* variable involved in the equilibrium described is explained as the balance of this equilibrium; thus its level is determined by the values of the other variables. Furthermore, we may assume that a model is correctly specified when every accounting identity is assigned to the determination of one variable.

Therefore, without loss of generality, we assert that the i-th equation of the structural form depicts the determination mechanism of the i-th endogenous variable (thus the i-th variable appears in the i-th equation).

Accordingly, we introduce the causality binary relation C and the causality graph G:

$$\begin{aligned} y_i C y_j &\leftrightarrow y_i(t) \text{ is 'cause' of } y_j(t) \\ &\leftrightarrow y_i(t) \text{ appears in the j-th equation which determines } y_j(t) \\ &\leftrightarrow (y_i, y_j) \text{ is an arc of G.} \end{aligned}$$

There, we assume that this definition implies the reflexivity of C since '$y_i(t)$ appears in the equation which determines $y_i(t)$'; for short, we shall say that '$y_i(t)$ is 'cause' of $y_i(t)$'.

Given this convention, we easily deduce that the boolean matrix associated with graph G and with this binary relation C is the boolean matrix $\tilde{G}_0$ associated with matrix G_0 which describes all the simultaneous interdependencies in the model structural form:

$$y_i C y_j \leftrightarrow (y_i, y_j) \text{ arc of G} \leftrightarrow (\tilde{G}_0)_{ij} = 1 \leftrightarrow (G_0)_{ij} \neq 0$$

$$y_i \not{C} y_j \leftrightarrow (y_i, y_j) \begin{array}{c}\text{is not an}\\ \text{arc of G}\end{array} \leftrightarrow (\tilde{G}_0)_{ij} = 0 \leftrightarrow (G_0)_{ij} = 0$$

$\tilde{G}_0$, C and G are three equivalent representations of the causality in a given model.

With the help of the reflexive and transitive closure C^+ for C and G^+ for G, we compute a transitive causality relation which is a preorder and which depicts all the chains of causes and effects in the reading of the model (linked to C and G):

$$y_i \, C^+ \, y_j \;\leftrightarrow\; (y_i, y_j) \text{ arc of } G^+ \;\leftrightarrow\; \text{in G, there is a path from } y_i \text{ to } y_j$$

$$\leftrightarrow\; y_i(t) \text{ is an indirect cause of } y_j(t)$$

Let us consider the computation of C and, more precisely, the related computation of a one-to-one correspondence between the endogenous variables and the model equations. The result of the first reading step is a consequence of the state of mind of the 'reader': he asserts that the equation to which he assigns a variable is depicting the mechanism which leads to the definition of the level of this variable. Then, the result is not unique and, in the case of divergent reading, the assignment changes; a good example is the Phillips curve which defines the wage level as a function of the price level p and of the unemployment level U_n:

$$w = \mu p - \upsilon U_n + w_0$$

In a neo-keynesian framework, such as the introduction to modelling by Muet (1979), or the reading of the small theoretical model of the CEPREMAP by Laffargue (1980), this function is interpreted in the usual way, i.e. where p and U_n are the 'cause' of w; inversely, in the model FIFI –simplified by Muet– or in the neo-classical reading of the CEPREMAP model by Laffargue, it is understood as an employment supply equation and thus p and w are the 'causes' of U_n. Consequently,

Neo-keynesian reading	Neo-classical reading
p C w	p C U_n
U_n C w	w C U_n

G: 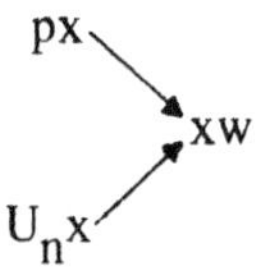

G: 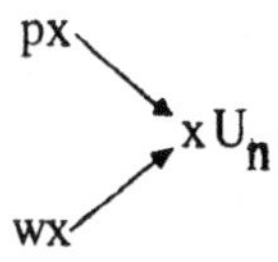

The multiplicity of the assignments and therefore the multiplicity of the causality relations implies the multiplicity of the readings; all these multiplicities are related to the interdependence property of the models.

3. SECOND STEP OF THE READING: BUILDING STRICT AND CIRCULAR CAUSALITY RELATIONS

Using the binary relation C and its reflexive and transitive closure C^+, we define an equivalence relation C_C and partially ordering relation (or partial order) C_S:

– *Circular causality* C_C:

$$y_i \, C_C \, y_j \leftrightarrow \left\{ \begin{matrix} y_i \, C^+ \, y_j \\ \\ y_j \, C^+ \, y_i \end{matrix} \right\} \leftrightarrow \text{a circuit goes through } y_i \text{ and } y_j \text{ in G.}$$

It is an equivalence relation whose equivalence classes are the strongly connected components (S.C.C.) of the graph G. The reduction of G gives the graph G* whose vertices y_i^*, y_j^* . . . are the S.C.C. of G.

– *Strict causality* C_S:

$$y_i^* \, C_S \, y_j^* \leftrightarrow (y_i^*, y_j^*) \text{ is an arc of } G^*.$$

$\leftrightarrow$ in G, there is a path from y_i belonging to the S.C.C. y_i^* to y_j belonging to the S.C.C. y_j^*

It is a strict (partial) ordering relation on the S.C.C. of G.

The second step in the reading is precisely the joint elaboration of the relation C_C which provides the blocks of endogenous variables (or the subsystems or the S.C.C.) and of the relation C_S which orders them strictly by levels. Simon (1957) has already underlined the importance of the 'causal ordering' obtained and he related it to requirements of the human mind for clustering knowledge or ideas and for organising them in hierarchies or trees; here, we aggregate the 'strongly connected' variables in blocks and we organise these blocks linearly in such a manner that their relationships become evident.

As in the following arbitrary example, we obtain remarkable visual representations, by means of graph G* or the associated boolean matrix (which becomes block-triangular given appropriate row and column permutations). The matrix representation also illustrates the link between the result of this step in the model reading and the recursivity; it justifies the use Strotz and Wold (1960) had made of the word 'vectorial causality' for what we call strict causality because the vector of variables which are in the same block at a given level is 'cause' of another vector of variables in a block at a lower level.

$$\begin{bmatrix} B_1 & & & & & \\ 0 & B_2 & & & & \\ 1 & 1 & B_3 & & & \\ 1 & 0 & 1 & B_4 & & \\ 0 & 0 & 0 & 1 & B_5 & \\ 0 & 1 & 1 & 0 & 1 & B_6 \end{bmatrix}$$

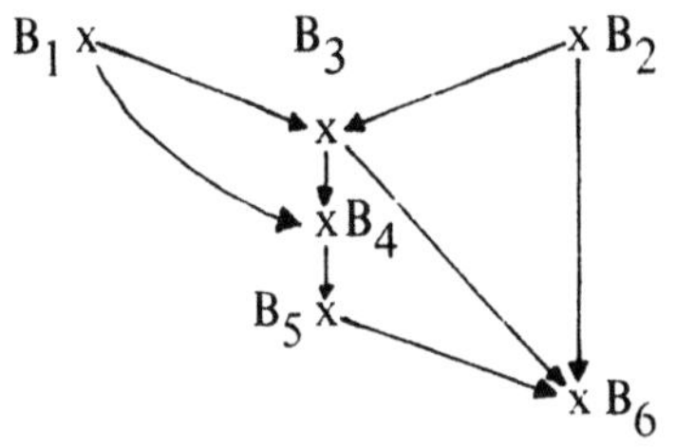

Before examining the results of the reading steps in some empirical models, let us note that this second reading step does not depend on the result of the first reading step and hence is an invariant of the model (see Boutillier (1982)). In other words, relations C_C and C_S are unique for a given model, and are not related to the chosen variables-equations assignment and to the binary relation C.

By means of a search algorithm for the S.C.C., written in PASCAL code (which automatically also performs the second reading step), we analyse both readings of the small theoretical model of the CEPREMAP by Laffargue (1980), the quarterly Wharton model (equations listed by Gilli (1979)), the quarterly model of Fair (1976), the yearly MINI-DMS (in the 'new basis' version of Brillet (1981b), the quarterly model FRB-MIT-PENN (its equations are in Ando, Modigliani and Rasche (1972)), and the quarterly model METRIC (in its first version –see Metric (1977)).

The results which have often been obtained elsewhere are confirmed: totally recursive prologue and epilogue (two sequences of one-vertex S.C.C.) surround a large block (a large S.C.C.) where we find the bulk of the variables (66 to 93%). In other words, the boolean matrix of almost every macroeconomic model is as follows (from Népomiastchy, Ravelli and Rechenmann (1978)):

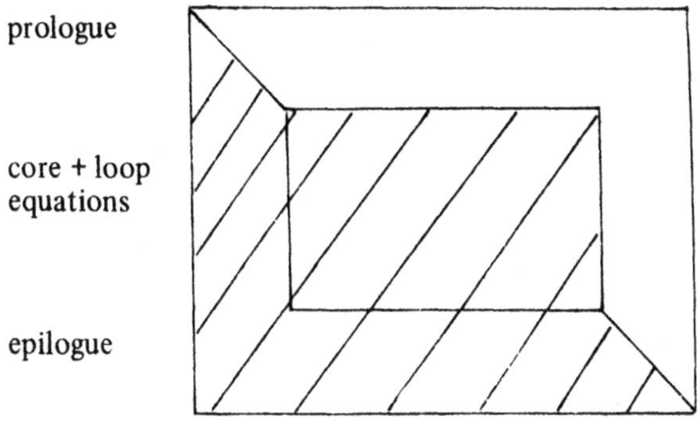

The results of the analysis are presented in table 1; it can be checked that the large central block contains almost every economically important variable in each

Table 1. Results of the second reading step

	Number of endogenous variables	Number of causal relations	Computing time (1/100 s.CPU)	Number of blocks	Scale of the large block
CEPREMAP small model keynesian reading	15	25	0.5	2	14
CEPREMAP small model classical reading	15	25	0.5	2	14
WHARTON	77	187	3.0	27	51
FAIR	83	219	3.2	9	75
MINI–DMS	166	662	7.4	52	115
FRB–MIT–PENN	168	360	6.3	42	127
METRIC	426	1025	16.2	114	313

model.

Nevertheless, if these results are robust (because not at variance with the first step results), they are insufficient; they do not give real insight in the macroeconomic structure apart from illustrating the importance of the interdependence in the macroeconomic models. This step must therefore be extended by the decomposition of the large block and the computation of a finer hierarchy between the significant variables.

4. THIRD STEP OF THE READING: BUILDING AN APPROXIMATE HIERARCHICAL CAUSALITY RELATION

The circular causality C_C which we have introduced above appears as a contradictory concept since the causality implies an asymmetry and the circularity a symmetry. On the other hand, the economic reality is made up of sequences of decisions and actions so that from the point of view of model specification models should have a structural form based on a diagonal or triangular matrix G_0 (i.e. without simultaneous interdependence).

According to Bentzel and Hansen (1954) and Strotz and Wold (1960), the difference between the microeconomic sequences and the macroeconomic interdependencies is explained by the –constrained– choice of the time basis in macroeconomic modelling. The basis, quarterly or yearly, is longer than that of the economic events; this is the foundation of the simultaneous interdependencies and justifies the causal circularity.

By his 'correspondence principle', Fisher (1970) proves the following proposition: an interdependent model is an approximation or a description of an equilibrium state of a sequential model if the interdependent model is stable; therefore, the interdependent model is the limit of the converging process of the sequential one and hence the result of an equilibrium process established during the unit time interval (quarter or year).

Thus, behind the causality relation C contained in the macroeconomic model and its asymmetry between cause and effect, we perceive a temporal asymmetry which is embodied in the underlying sequential model; thereby, the circular causality C_C becomes intellectually admissible.

For instance, if we consider the causal circle of Strotz and Wold:

$$\begin{cases} p(t) = a_1 + b_1\, q(t) \\ q(t) = a_2 + b_2\, p(t) \end{cases}$$

We assume that q(t) is cause of p(t) and that p(t) is cause of q(t). This assumption seems to be contradictory unless we understand it as an equilibrium where some mutual relations have to be satisfied; more precisely, the equilibrium is reached during the unit time and the 'true' equations are:

$$\begin{cases} p(t) = a_1 + b_1\, q(t - \Delta\theta_1) \\ q(t) = a_2 + b_2\, p(t - \Delta\theta_2) \end{cases}$$

Again we find Fisher's framework where the model is simultaneous because the time basis is larger than $\Delta\theta_1$ and $\Delta\theta_2$ and there the sequential processes are converging towards equilibrium values described by the causal circle.

Now, let us consider the bicausality of Strotz and Wold:

$$\begin{cases} q(t) = c_1 + d_1\, p(t) & \text{(demand)} \\ q(t) = c_2 + d_2\, p(t) & \text{(supply)} \end{cases}$$

Both equations assume that p(t) is cause of q(t). But this surprising redundancy hides the following model:

$$\begin{cases} q_d(t) = c_1 + d_1\, p(t) & \text{(demand)} \\ q_s(t) = c_2 + d_2\, p(t) & \text{(supply)} \\ q_d(t) = q_s(t) & \text{(equilibrium)} \end{cases}$$

Once again, the equilibrium is obtained by a sequential adjustment process on p:

$$p(t) = p\left\{t, q_d(t-\Delta\theta), q_s(t-\Delta\theta), p(t-\Delta\theta)\right\}$$

Consequently, in both cases, circularity expresses a sequential adjustment process (this is a well known idea in economics; see the auctioneer model). The equations are depicting either the joint determination of supply and demand or the equilibrium state reached iteratively on a market.

Both cases are so closely related that they are associated with the same graph G:

Starting with this simple case (two variables and only one circuit), it is possible to extend all our conclusions to more complex cases (many variables and a large graph with many circuits of any length); in that case, the model combines numerous distinct but simultaneous equilibria with probably varying time bases.

Analysing these simultaneous processes is precisely the aim of the third step of the reading; its object is the search for the sequential equilibrium processes which underlie the simultaneous interdependencies and hence the search for the relevant economic circuits of the model; this is often described as the search for the loop variables (or feedback variables) of the model.

In their method for analysing models called 'method of solution structures' (méthode des structures de résolution), Deleau and Malgrange (1978) emphasise the loop variables. The main feature of these variables is to destroy the model interdependence if they are kept constant; in other words, to make them exogenous gives a recursive submodel in which the causality relation C is hierarchical (the associated graph G has only one vertex S.C.C.). Deleau and Malgrange's method was developed in order to examine the loops (or feedbacks), i.e. the influence of the re-introduction of the loop variables on the recursive submodel.

Whereas Delau and Malgrange modify the model by solving it partially, Keller (1970) keeps it unchanged and determines the loop variables from the iterative solution of the model. At the k-th iteration, the starting values of the loop variables y_k allow the recursive computation of the other variables, and hence of the final values of the loop variables y_{k+1}; the solution –which is an equilibrium value if we imagine that the mathematical process illustrates an underlying sequential mechanism which is converging during the unit time interval– is obtained at the l-th iteration when the starting values y_l are equal to the final values y_{l+1}.

Keller suggests to choose the loop variables so that their deletion gives 'the largest possible subgraph which is compatible with an ordering relation', i.e. the greatest hierarchical subgraph. In other words, he searches for the smallest number of variables whose deletion gives a recursive submodel on a hierarchical subgraph. We now call feedback vertex set, a loop variable set, minimal feedback vertex set, a feedback vertex set such that no subset is a feedback vertex set, minimum feedback vertex set, a minimal feedback vertex set whose cardinality is minimal (for a given model) and model index, the minimal cardinality for this model.

Though MODULECO uses Newton-like algorithms for solving models and not Gauss-Seidel algorithms, as Keller suggests, this program also searches for a minimum feedback vertex set (see Népomiastchy, Ravelli and Rechenmann (1978)).
In this manner, we define a first approximation of the loops (or feedbacks); we call it 'mathematical' and we must remember that it minimises the loop number.

Nevertheless, Brillet (1981a) points out that the Gauss-Seidel algorithm –which is interpreted economically as an equilibrating process during the unit time interval– does not always converge with a minimum feedback vertex set, and one is often forced to enlarge the feedback vertex set to obtain convergence. Thus, the solution algorithm which is closest to the economic interpretation of interdependence is not always compatible with the minimality of the loop number.

When reading for instance Muet (1979) or Laffargue (1980), it appears more relevant to see the loops as marginal corrections of the recursive submodel; in the general equilibrium described by the model, this 'economic'[1] approach distinguishes between a strong element represented by the recursive submodel and a weak element represented by the loops. Thus we try to obtain a recursive submodel by minimising the *impact* and *not the number* of the loop variables. Thereby, when the 'mathematical' approach only requires qualitative data, the 'economic' approach has to take into account the numerical (or quantitative) dimension of the model; in this last case, we must minimise the *error* following from dropping the loops (or feedbacks).

Thus, we obtain two approaches which are not always well distinguished and which generate an approximate hierarchy, finer than the one obtained in the second step of the reading. We think that the 'economic' approach gives a relevant hierarchical approximation inasfar as the reading is made by an economist and we suggest to keep it for the third reading step. Contrary to the second step which is an invariant under the first step result, this third step depends on the assignment of variables to equations as made in the first step; in particular, it is easy to prove that, for the 'mathematical' approach, the index is a function of the variables-equations assignment (see Boutillier (1982)).

To illustrate this idea, we have run the m.m.g. procedure of Gilli and Rossier (1981) on the keynesian reading graph of the small CEPREMAP model (see Laffargue (1980)). Figure 1 shows the graph and figure 2 shows the minimum feedback vertex sets.

Figure 1. Graph of the small CEPREMAP model keynesian reading by Laffargue.

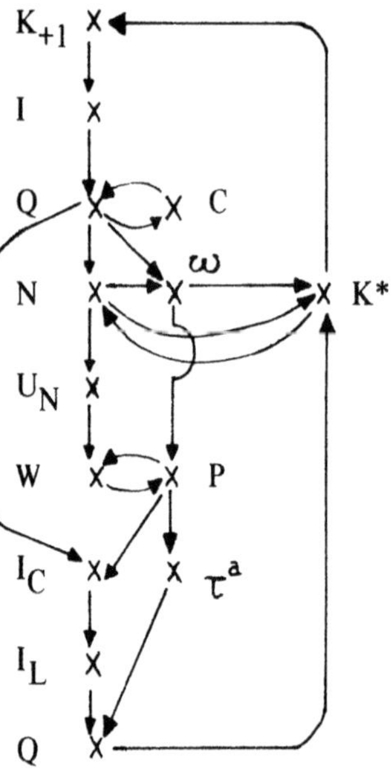

Figure 2. Minimum Feedback vertex sets of the small CEPREMAP model keynesian reading by Laffargue.

{K*, Q, p}

{K*, Q, w}

{K*, C, p}

{K*, C, w}

{N, Q, p}

{N, Q, w}

We observe that the capital cost q, which is the loop variable of the model according to Laffargue's keynesian reading does not appear in a minimum feedback vertex set (of cardinality 3). However, the results can be explained by the topological properties of the graph:

- the pairs (C,Q), (w,p) and (K*,N) form circuits of length two, and therefore, at least, one element of these pairs belongs to a minimum set;
- in the pairs (C,Q) and (K*,N), C and N are 'badly' connected in the graph (only few circuits go through them) and thereby to put them in a feedback set can increase the cardinality of the set.

All these properties are purely combinatorial, generally without any economic interpretation and thus we are not surprised to obtain minimum feedback vertex sets where we do not find the variable q as economic intuition would suggest.

Our distinction between 'mathematical' and 'economic' approaches –which is not a logical contradiction because they may coincide– is justified by this experiment as it was already by the remarks in Brillet (1981a).

Meanwhile, some permanent properties in the structure of the models involve the frequent presence of some variables; first of all, national income (or national product) which features at the centre of the real model appears in numerous circuits of length two and belongs to numerous minimum sets. On the other hand, the wage-price dynamics exist in every model and, because of the numerous circuits they generate, we find wage or, more often, price variables in the minimum sets. Therefore some topological properties of the causality graph are partially explained by the equation specification of the modeller.

The remarks on the frequent presence of some variables in the minimum feedback vertex sets are confirmed by the results of our PASCAL procedure which computes *a minimum* feedback vertex set (see Boutillier (1982)). It allows us to write the boolean matrix of a large class of models in the following shape (from Népomiastchy, Ravelli and Rechenmann (1978)):

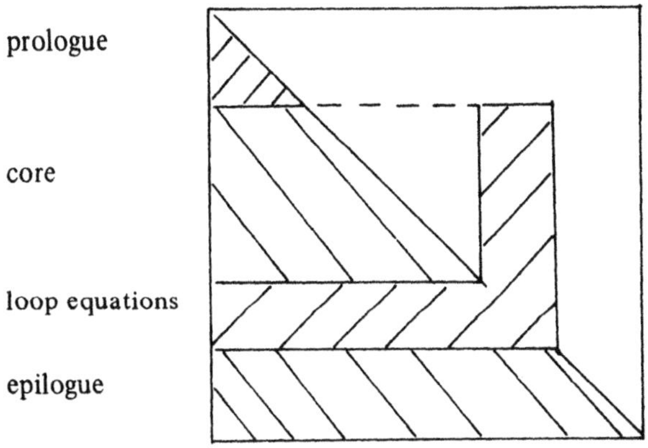

The results (for the same models as in table 1) are presented in table 2. As it was predictable, we effectively record the presence of national income (or product) variables and of price variables in every model; furthermore, for the financially integrated models (Fair, FRB-MIT-PENN and METRIC), some financial or monetary variables appear.

Table 2. Results of the third reading step

	CEPREMAP small model k reading	CEPREMAP small model c reading	Wharton	Fair	MINI-DMS	FRB-MIT PENN	METRIC
number of endogenous variables	15	15	77	83	166	168	426
number of causal relations	25	25	187	219	662	360	1025
computing time (s. CPU)	0.23	0.23	1.14	1.94	5.1	21	55
Index	3	3	7	6	7	10	22
							EXIFOB
Result	Q^1	Q^1	NI^1	X^1	aut2	$XOBE^1$	ROM^1
(minimum							MCH
feedback	P^2	τ^a	U_n	$RBILL^3$	aut1	YP^1	CHO
vertex							EFS
set)	K*	ω	Y^1	LF^3	pul^2	lnLMHT	$TXTC^3$
							XI^1
1 Production or income variable			p^2	PX^2	$pu2^2$	DCL^3	CM
							LDO
			p_c^2	IBITH	pc^2	RTB^3	RBE
							DEV^1
2 Price variable			X_m	YNLH	$df1^1$	$PXBNF^2$	IMI
							$PCME^2$
			N_m		$df2^1$	EC	$XBSW^1$
							$PXBI^2$
3 Monetary or financial variable						YPCC	$PREI^2$
							$PREA^2$
						YS^1	PCM^2
							$XBEW^1$
						$POBE^2$	XC^1
							XS^1
							XB^1

5. CONCLUSION

The purpose of this article is to summarise the analytical operations to be made by an economist when reading macroeconomic models; this process can be divided into three steps.

According to the explanatory nature of a model, we build in a first step a causality relation between the endogenous variables; because of the non-uniqueness of this relation, a further investigation must help to determine the appropriate one, maybe with respect to the third step results.

The second step provides a strict causal hierarchy between the endogenous variables but the corresponding explanatory content of the model structure is often weak.

The third step goes deeper by computing an approximate but finer causal hierarchy between the endogenous variables. Here, it is important to avoid any confusion between the mathematical treatment of the model with respect to its solution or its construction and the economic reading of the model; the latter is indifferent to the number of loops dropped to obtain an approximate hierarchy, as long as the numerical dimension of the model is exploited for minimising the quantitative impact of the loops within the interdependent system. The economic logic of the reading requires that we search for the minimum weight feedback vertex sets and this is possible when every relation is weighted with regard to the model dynamics.

NOTES

This work is derived from my thesis; I would therefore like to take the opportunity to thank the examiners, Mm. Fourgeaud, Vallee and Malgrange for their help and comments. But all remaining errors are strictly mine.

1) The words 'mathematical' and 'economic' are convenient characterisations of both approaches and do not imply any range of value.

REFERENCES

Ando, A., F. Modigliani and R. Rasche (1972), 'Equations and definitions of variables for the FRB-MIT-PENN econometric model' in: B.G. Hickmann (ed.), *Econometric models of cyclical behaviour*, NBER studies in income and wealth No 36, Columbia University Press.

Bentzel, R. and B. Hansen (1954), 'Recursiveness and interdependency in economic models',

Review of Economic Studies, Vol. XXII.

Boutillier, M. (1982), 'Lecture des modèles macroéconomiques; recherche des bouclages', Thèse de 3ème cycle, Université de Paris I (mimeographed).

Brillet, J.L. (1981a), 'La convergence des modèles: développement d'un exemple simple' *Note INSEE-Service des Programmes*, No 320/202, INSEE, Paris.

Brillet, J.L. (1981b), 'MINI-DMS, modèle macroéconomique de simulation', *Archives et documents* No 35, INSEE, Paris.

Deleau, M. and P. Malgrange (1978), *L'analyse des modèles macroéconomiques quantitatifs'*, Economica, Paris.

Fair, R.C. (1976), *A model of macroeconomic activity*, Vol. II: The empirical model, Ballinger, Cambridge, Mass.

Fisher, F.M. (1970), 'A correspondence principle for simultaneous equation models', *Econometrica*, Vol. 38, No 1.

Gilli, M. (1979), 'Etude et analyse des structures causales dans les modèles économiques', Lang (thèse de doctorat ès Sciences Economiques), Genève.

Gilli, M. and E. Rossier (1981), 'Understanding complex systems', *Automatica*, Vol. 17, No 4.

Hénin, P.Y. (1974), 'Sur la définition des structures causales en Econométrie', *Cahiers du Séminaire d'Econométrie*, CNRS No 15.

Keller, A. (1970), 'Etude structurelle de quelques modèles mathématiques de prévision économique à court terme', Mémoire de D.E.S. de Sciences Economiques, F.D.S.E. de l'Université de Paris.

Laffargue, J.P. (1980), 'Les modèles dynamiques de polititque économique: dialogue entre le théoricien et l'économètre', *Annales de l'INSEE*, No 40.

METRIC (1977), *Annales de l'INSEE*, No 26-27.

Muet, P.A. (1979), 'La modélisation macroéconomique: une étude de la structure et de la dynamique des modèles macroéconomiques', *Statistiques et études financières*, série orange, (special issue).

Népomiastchy, P., A. Ravelli and F. Rechenmann (1978), 'An automatic method to get an econometric model in a quasi-triangular form', *Rapport de recherche I.R.I.A.*, No 313.

Rossier, E. (1979), *Economie structurale*, Economica, Paris.

Simon, H.A. (1957), 'Causal ordering and identifiability', in: *Models of Man, Social and Rational*, (part 1. ch. 1), J. Wiley and Sons.

Strotz, R.H. and H.O.A. Wold (1960), 'Recursive versus non-recursive systems: an attempt at synthesis', *Econometrica*, Vol. 28, No 2.

CHAPTER 4

STRUCTURAL ANALYSIS, HIERARCHICAL FUNCTIONS AND WEAK STRUCTURES

J.P. Auray and G. Duru
University of Lyon I, France

Structural analysis is one of the modern techniques which are used in Social Sciences, and especially in Economics.

H. Laborit gives an interesting description of the subject matter of structural analysis: 'j'essaie simplement de comprendre comment 'ça' s'organise, depuis la molécule, jusqu'à l'espèce humaine sur la planète, c'est-à-dire comment chaque niveau informe au niveau sous-jacent et comment le niveau sous-jacent l'informe en retour. Or, il existe entre les niveaux d'organisation différents, des liaisons intimes, et aucun d'eux ne peut fonctionner dans l'ignorance de ce qui se passe, soit au-dessus, soit au-dessous de lui.' *

The study of structures is relevant to a variety of areas in Economics; it complements and highlights the traditional quantitative approach by means of a qualitative approach.

It is used by intersectoral analysis where one of the fundamental aspects, revealed by C. Ponsard, concerns the study of structures induced by interindustrial dominance and impact relations, resulting in a topological model of interregional economic equilibrium (Ponsard, 1969).

In the general equilibrium theory the importance of the concept of structure has been stressed by M. Guitton in 'Entropie et Gaspillage' Guitton (1975)), where the author links the concept of economic system to the idea of organisation, going beyond, but at the same time enriching, the concept of equilibrium.

In econometrics, E. Rossier (1979) in 'Economie Structurale' stresses the need to study the structures of macroeconomic models in order to supersede the theory

* I simply try to understand how 'it' is organised, from the molecule to the human species on the planet, i.e. how each level feeds information into the subsequent level and how the subsequent level returns information. Also, there exist intimate links between different levels of organisation and none of these can operate ignoring what happens, either at higher, or lower levels.'

implicit in the relations proposed and in the list of variables and equations defining these models.

*
* *

Models for structural analysis can be developed by means of mathematical structures and, in particular, by means of topological structures. But, it becomes rapidly evident that, due to its constraining axiomatics, topology is poorly equipped to describe phenomena encountered in the area of applied sciences. For instance, F. Lorrain observes that 'topological structures are probably useless to describe social networks because of the finite and discrete character of social structures' (Lorrain, 1975). Thus it seems necessary to develop a structure based on weaker axiomatics than the topological structure. Such a weakening process has been proposed by M. Fréchet (1928), later taken up again by Ky Fan, E. Cech, R. Féron and M. Brissaud and it has led to the concept of pre-topological structure, and subsequently, as a result of a further weakening of the axiomatics, to the concept of poor structures.

Definition 1: a poor structure on a set E is the pair $\sigma = (f, f^*)$ where f and f^* are two mappings of P(E) in itself such that $f^* = cfc$ where c is the mapping P(E) in itself which relates every subset A of E to its complement in E, noted cA.

Consider the following properties:

(P_1): $f(E) = E$ (or equivalently, (P'_1): $f^*(\emptyset) = \emptyset$)

(P_2): $\forall A \subset E, f(A) \subset A$(or equivalently, (P'_2): $\forall A \subset E, f^*(A) \supset A$)

(P_3): $\forall A \subset E, \forall B \subset E, A \subset B \Rightarrow f(A) \subset f(B)$
(or equivalently, (P'_3): $\forall A \subset E, \forall B \subset E, A \subset B \Rightarrow f^*(A) \subset f^*(B)$)

(P_4): f is stable for the finite intersection
(or, equivalently, (P'_4): f^* is stable for the finite union)

(P_5): f is stable for the union
(or, equivalently, (P'_5): f^* is stable for the intersection)

σ is a pre-topological structure if f statisfies (P_1) and (P_2); it is a structure of type **V** if f satisfies (P_3), a structure of type $\mathbf{V_D}$ if it satisfies (P_4) and a structure of type V_{DS} if it satisfies (P_5).

Hence, a poor or pre-topological structure is obtained through considerably weakening the axiomatics of topological structures. As a result, a large number of phenomena in the social and human sciences could be modelled by means of these structures, whereas they could not be modelled by means of topological structures.

In order to illustrate this we shall try to develop a structure for a binary relation on E.

Suppose **R** is a binary relation on E. For all $x \in E$, we write

$$\mathbf{R}(x) = \{y \in E; xRy\}$$

In analogy with the development of the natural topology of $\mathbb{R}$ on the basis of the order relation $\leqslant$, we define the structure $\sigma = (f, f^*)$ for **R** by:

$$\forall A \subset E, f(A) = \{x \in E; \mathbf{R}(x) \subset A\}$$

which is equivalent to:

$$\forall A \subset E, f^*(A) = \{x \in E; \mathbf{R}(x) \cap A \neq \emptyset\}$$

Such a structure, also called structure of the descendants for the relation **R**, is a poor structure of type $\mathbf{V}_{DS}$. It only becomes a pre-topological structure (of type $\mathbf{V}_{DS}$) if **R** is reflexive, and if **R** is reflexive, the structure σ is a topological structure provided **R** is also transitive. This example shows clearly why topological tools could not be used successfully to model relations and graphs: only quasi-orders could be considered.

The problems of connectedness are fundamental problems in the area of graph theory and, more generally, of structural analysis: the concept of connectedness being also of a topological nature, one could be tempted to characterise connectedness in graphs in a topological sense. Such an attempt has been made by M. Messeri (1973); unfortunately, because he only had topological tools at his disposal, he was forced to systematically consider the transitive closures of the graphs and as far as non-transitive relations were concerned, he could not do better than making guesses. Pre-topology allows us to handle the problem in its generality and a large number of pre-topological characterisations of connectedness in the area of graph theory are presented in Auray (1982). One of the major results is the following:

If E possesses a poor structure $\sigma = (f, f^*)$, a subset $A \subset E$ is said to be open (respectively weakly open, closed, weakly closed) for σ if and only if $f(A) = A$ (respectively, $f(A) \supset A$, $f^*(A) = A$, $f^*(A) \subset A$). When σ is a pre-topological structure, the concepts of open subset and weakly open subset, closed subset and weakly closed subset coincide: one then obtains:

Given that the binary relation **R** with graph G is defined on E, a path from $x \in E$ to $y \in E$ is any finite sequence $x_o = x, x_1, \ldots, x_n, x_{n+1} = y$ of points of E such that for all $i \in \{o, \ldots, n\}$ one has $x_i \mathbf{R} x_{i+1}$; a chain with endpoints x and y is any finite sequence $x_o = x, x_1, \ldots, x_n, x_{n+1} = y$ of points of E such that for all $i \in \{o, \ldots, n\}$

one has $x_i R x_{i+1}$ or $x_{i+1} R x_i$. If for all $(x, y) \in E x E$ there exists a path from x to y, E is said to be strongly connected (for relation **R**). If for all $(x,y) \in E x E$ there exists a path from x to y or from y to x, E is said to be unilaterally connected (for relation **R**). Finally, if for all $(x, y) \in E x E$ there exists a chain with endpoints x and y, E is said to be connected for relation **R**.

If E possesses the pre-topological structure σ of the descendants associated with a reflexive **R**, the above concepts of connectedness can be characterised as follows:

Proposition 1:

(i) E is strongly connected for **R** if and only if the only open subsets for the pre-topological structure σ are $\emptyset$ and E.

(ii) E is unilaterally connected for **R** if and only if the family of open subsets for the pre-topological structure σ is completely ordered for the inclusion.

(iii) E is connected for **R** if and only if E is connected for the pre-topological structure σ, pre-topological connectedness being defined in the same way as topological connectedness.

For the proofs of this proposition the reader is referred to Auray, Brissaud and Duru (1978), where it is formulated within the more general framework of the theory of preferential spaces.

This proposition gives an idea of the power of pre-topological tools to the extent that the use of the richer topological structures is only efficient if one works with quasi-orders.

*

* *

We will now show that the use of poor structures allows us to construct the structural analysis of a graph and in particular to generalise the classical concept of structuring function. More precisely, we will show that the concepts used in the hierarchical analysis of graphs are in fact pre-topological concepts.

We will use the following notations:

(i) if **R** is a relation on E

$$\mathbf{R}^1 = \mathbf{R}$$

$$\forall k \in \mathbf{N}^* \qquad \mathbf{R}^{k+1} = \mathbf{R}^k . \mathbf{R}$$

where $\circ$ represents the composition of the relations

(ii) if f is a mapping of **P**(E) in itself:

$$f^0 = i_{\mathbf{P}(E)} \text{ (identical mapping of } \mathbf{P}(E) \text{ in itself)}$$

$$\forall k \in \mathbf{N}^* \qquad f^{k+1} = f \circ f^k$$

where • represents the composition of the mapping of **P**(E) in itself.

Let $\sigma = (f, f^*)$ be the structure of the descendants associated with **R**; for $k \in \mathbf{N}^*$, we use the notation $\sigma^k = (f^k, (f^k)^*)$. Then one obtains:

(i) $\forall k \in \mathbf{N}^* \quad (f^k)^* = (f^*)^k$

(ii) $\forall k \in \mathbf{N}^*$ σ^k is the weak structure of the descendants associated with $\mathbf{R}^k$.

The structural analysis of the set E on which **R** has been defined uses the following property concerning weakly closed subsets:

Proposition 2:

Let $\sigma = (f, f^*)$ be the poor structure of the descendants associated with **R**. For all $x \in E$, there exists a small weakly closed subset containing x, and noted F_x; then one obtains:

$$\forall x \in E, \quad F_x = \bigcup_{k \in \mathbf{N}} f^{*k}(\{x\})$$

Proof:

We first show that the family of weakly closed subsets is stable for the intersection: Let F_i, $i \in I$ be a family of weakly closed subsets and let $F = \bigcap_{i \in I} F_i$. Then F is a weakly closed subset. Indeed, one has:

$$f^*(F) = f^*(\bigcap_{i \in I} F_i) = \bigcap_{i \in I} f^*(F_i) \subset \bigcap_{i \in I} F_i = F$$

For $x \in E$, the family of weakly closed subsets containing x is not empty, since it contains E. Let then F_x be the intersection of all the weakly closed subsets containing x: it is the smallest weakly closed subset containing x.

Let now $A = \bigcup_{k \in \mathbf{N}} f^{*k}(\{x\})$, then $A = F_x$. Indeed, A is a weakly closed subset, containing x: $x \in A$ since $f^{*\circ}(\{x\}) \subset A$;

$$f^*(A) = f^*(\bigcup_{k \in \mathbf{N}} f^{*k}(\{x\})) = \bigcup_{k \in \mathbf{N}} f^*(f^{*k}(\{x\})) = \bigcup_{k \in \mathbf{N}^*} f^{*k}(\{x\}) \subset A$$

which proves that A is a weakly closed subset.

Within all weakly closed subsets, certain subsets will play a crucial role; these are the minimal closed subsets:

Definition 2:

A minimal weakly closed subset is any non-empty weakly closed subset F of E for a poor structure σ, such that if F' is a non-empty weakly closed subset, F' contained in F implies $F = F'$.

The question now arises whether the minimal weakly closed subsets are of the form F_x: the answer is evidently yes because a weakly closed subset is not empty, and if F is a weakly closed subset, one has $F = F_x$ for all x in F. Moreover, it is worth noting that, for an arbitrary poor structure, $\emptyset$ is generally not closed: on the contrary, if the structure is a pre-topological one, $\emptyset$ is closed.

If E is finite (as it is generally the case in the treatment of applications) the existence of minimal weakly closed subsets is guaranteed. For example, let $E=\{x,y,z,t,u,v\}$ and assume the following relation:

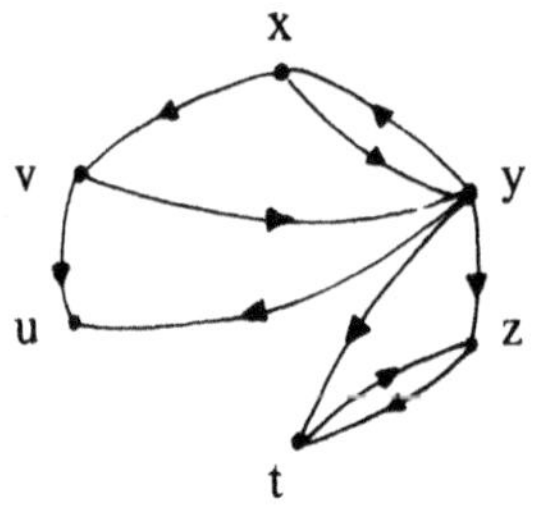

one has: $F_x = \{x, y, v\} = F_y = F_v$

$F_u = \{x, y, v, u\}$

$F_z = \{x, y, z, t, v\} = F_t$

There is a minimal weakly closed subset which is $\{x, y, v\}$. But, in general, the existence of minimal weakly subsets is not guaranteed. For example, let $E = \mathbf{N}$ and let $\mathbf{R}$ be the relation defined by $x\mathbf{R}y$ if and only if $y = x+1$; then for all $x \in \mathbf{N}$ one has $F_x = \{x, x+1, \ldots\}$. There is no minimal weakly closed subset. Neverthelss, one finds in Auray (1982) a condition for the existence of minimal weakly closed subsets based on a compactness property.

Finally, it should be noted that if F is a minimal weakly closed subset, F is not empty and $F_x = F$ for all $x \in F$.

From now on, we shall use the notation $c(k, x)$ for the set of $y \in E$, the origin of a path of length k and endpoint x, for all non-zero integer k and for all x in E. If $\sigma = (f, f^*)$ is the poor structure of the descendants associated with $\mathbf{R}$, it is easy to check that one has $f^{*k}(\{x\}) = c(k, x)$ for all x and all positive integer k.

The usefulness of the minimal weakly closed subsets in the area of structural analysis then results from the following proposition:

Proposition 3:

If x and y are two points of E, such that $F_x \subsetneq F_y$, there exists a path from x to y and there does not exist a path from y to x.

Proof:

Given that $F_x \subset F_y$, one has $x \in F_y$ and $x \neq y$ since $F_x \neq F_y$. Hence there exists a non-zero integer p, such that $x \in f^{*p}(\{y\}) = c(p, y)$ which proves the existence of a path of length p, from x to y.

If there existed a path from y to x, of length q, for example ($q \neq 0$) one would have $y \in c(q, x) = f^{*p}(\{x\})$ and hence $y \in F_x$ so that $F_y \subset F_x$ which is impossible.

The relation **R** being defined on E, one defines the relation **R*** on E as follows: for all $x \in E$ and $y \in E$, $x\mathbf{R}^*y$ if and only if there exists a path with origin x and endpoint y and a path with origin y and endpoint x. We shall use the notation $E_0 = \{x \in E; \mathbf{R}^*(x) = \emptyset\}$ and $F = E - E_0$. Then **R*** is an equivalence relation on F. By definition an element of $F/\mathbf{R}^*$ is called a strong component for the relation **R**. So, for the example used above, one has:

$$E_0 = \{u\} \quad \text{hence} \quad F = \{x, y, z, t, v\}$$

$$\text{and} \quad F/\mathbf{R}^* = \{\{x, y, v\}, \{z, t\}\}$$

One obtains the following result establishing the link between minimal closed subsets and strong components:

For all $x \in E$ we use the notation $G(x) = \{y \in F_x; F_y \subset F_x \text{ and } F_y \neq F_x\}$ and we define

$$H_x = \bigcup_{y \in G(x)} F_x$$

Proposition 4:

Let A be a part of E. The following propositions are equivalent:

(i) A is a strong component for **R**

(ii) there exists an $x \in E$ such that $A = F_x - H_x$

The proof of that proposition rests on the following lemma:

Lemma 1:

For all x and all y in E, one has $F_x = F_y$ if and only if $\mathbf{R}^*(x) = \mathbf{R}^*(y)$.

Proof of Lemma 1:

We shall assume that $F_x = F_y$ and show that $\mathbf{R}^*(x) = \mathbf{R}^*(y)$. Let $z \in \mathbf{R}^*(x)$, then there exists a path of origin x and endpoint x. Hence, there exist two integers $i \in \mathbf{N}^*$ and $j \in \mathbf{N}^*$ such that $x \in C(i, z)$ and $z \in C(j, x)$. Since $F_x = F_y$, one has $x \in F_y$ and $y \in F_x$, so that $x \in \bigcup_{k \in \mathbf{N}} f^{*k}(\{y\})$ and $y \in \bigcup_{k \in \mathbf{N}} f^{*k}(\{x\})$: hence there exists $k \in \mathbf{N}$ and $l \in \mathbf{N}$ such that $x \in f^{*k}(\{y\})$ and $y \in f^{*l}(\{x\})$. If one of the two integers k or l is equal to zero, then $x = y$ and one obtains trivially $\mathbf{R}^*(x) = \mathbf{R}^*(y)$. If none of the two integers k or l is zero, one has $x \in C(k, y)$ and $y \in C(l, x)$. Consequently, one has $x \in C(i, z)$ and $y \in C(l, x)$ so that $z \in C(j, x)$ and $x \in C(k, y)$ and again $z \in C(j+k, y)$; it follows that $z \in \mathbf{R}^*(y)$. Assuming $F_x = F_y$ it can be proved in the same way that $\mathbf{R}^*(y) \subset \mathbf{R}^*(x)$.

If $\mathbf{R}^*(x) = \mathbf{R}^*(y)$ then $y \in \aleph^*(x)$, so that there exists $k \in \mathbf{N}^*$ and $l \in \mathbf{N}^*$ such that $x \in C(k, y)$ and $y \in ¼ (l, x)$ or $x \in f^{*k}(\{y\})$ and $y \in f^{*l}(\{x\})$. Then one has $x \in F_y$ and $y \in F_x$, hence $F_y = F_x$.

Proof of Proposition 4:

(i) implies (ii): If A is a strong component for **R**, A is not empty; thus let $x \in A \subset E_1$, to show that $A = F_x - H_x$. If $y \in A$, then $\mathbf{R}^*(y) = \mathbf{R}^*(x)$ and hence $F_y = F_x$, using the above lemma. But in that case $y \in F$ and $y \notin H_x$ so that $y \in F_x - H_x$. Conversely, if $y \in F_x - H_x$, $F_y = F_x$ so that $\mathbf{R}^*(y) = \mathbf{R}^*(x)$ or $y \in A = \mathbf{R}^*(x)$.

(ii) implies (i): Let $x \in E_1$ and $A = F_x - H_x$. It is clear that $x \in A$, since otherwise one would have $x \in H_x$ or $F_x \subsetneq F_x$.

Let us show that $A = \mathbf{R}^*(x)$: if $y \in A$, then $y \in F$ and $F_y = F_x$, so that $\mathbf{R}^*(y) = \mathbf{R}^*(x)$ so that $y \in \mathbf{R}^*(x)$; if $y \in \mathbf{R}^*(x)$ then $\mathbf{R}^*(y) = \mathbf{R}^*(x)$ so that $F_y = F_x$ and thus $y \in F_x - H_x$.

Remarks:

(i) One has $H_x = G(x)$. Indeed, if $y \in H_x$ there exists $z \in G(x)$ such that $y \in F_z \subsetneq Fx$, so that $F_y \subsetneq F_x$ and thus $y \in G(x)$. If $y \in G(x)$ then $F_y \subset H_x$ and $y \in F_y$ implies $y \in H_x$.

(ii) The proposition shows that every minimal weakly closed subset contained in E_1 is a strong component for **R**. Indeed, if F_x is a minimal weakly closed subset contained in E_1, then $H_x = \emptyset$ so that $F_x = F_x - H_x$ which is a strong component for **R**.

(iii) The proof of (i) implies (ii) shows in fact that if A is a strong component for **R**, then $A = F_x - H_x$ for all $x \in A$, and if x and y are two elements of A, $H_x = H_y$.

In Auray (1982) a structural analysis has been developed based on the search for the minimal weakly closed subsets and then on that of the weakly closed subsets containing the former, in other words, the nested families of weakly closed subsets.

The use of the strong components for **R** simplifies the analysis and shows that it is an extension of the method based on hierarchical functions developed in Richetin (1975) in as far as it provides it with a topological foundation.

On F/**R*** one will build a relation $\hat{\mathbf{R}}$ called reduced relation under circuit, in the following way: if A and B are two distinct strong components for **R**, there exist x and y in F such that $A = F_x - H_x$ and $B = F_y - H_y$; we have $A\,\hat{\mathbf{R}}\,B$ if and only if $F_x \subset F_y$ (this definition is known to be independent of the choice of x and y; see remark (iii) above) and there exists no $z \in F$ such that $F_x \subsetneq F_z \subsetneq F_y$.

The relation built in this way on F/**R*** defines structural analysis.

Remark:

The analysis built in this way excludes the points of E–F: these points can in fact be reintroduced as follows: let $E' = F/\mathbf{R}^* \cup (E-F)$ and $\hat{\mathbf{R}}'$ such that $\hat{\mathbf{R}}' = \hat{\mathbf{R}}$ on F/**R***, $\hat{\mathbf{R}}' = \mathbf{R}$ on E–F and, if $A \in F/\mathbf{R}^*$ and $x \in E-F$; $x\hat{\mathbf{R}}'A$ if and only if there exists $x' \in A$ with $x\mathbf{R}x'$ and $A\hat{\mathbf{R}}'x$ if and only if there exists $x' \in A$ with $x'\mathbf{R}x$.

In fact, as soon as **R** is reflexive, the problem disappears since one then has $E - F = \emptyset$.

Example:

Let $E = \{x, y, z, t, u, v, w, s\}$ be a set of 8 elements and define the following relation on E:

One then obtains $F_x = \{x, y, z, s\} = F_y = F_z$, $F_s = \{s\}$,

$F_t = F_u = \{x, y, z, t, u, s\}$, $F_v = E$ and $F_w = \{w\}$.

One finds that $F = E - \{s, w\}$. The representation of the different subsets F_x, F_y, etc. is as follows:

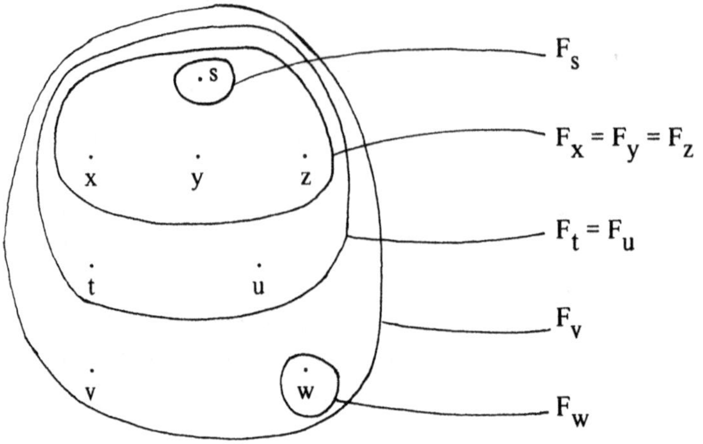

The structuring is then:

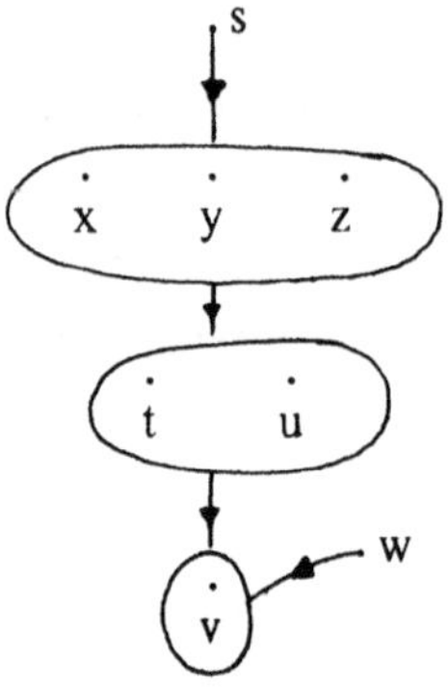

In analogy with the analysis in terms of hierarchical functions, one can define the rank of a strong component for **R**.

Let H be a set, **S** a relation on H and $\tau = (f, f^*)$ the structure of the descendants corresponding to **S**. We use the notation $\overline{\mathbf{N}} = \mathbf{N} \cup +\{\infty\}$ with the relation $\leqslant$ deduced from that of **N**, and completed by $n \leqslant +\infty$ for all $n \in \mathbf{N}$.

We build a mapping γ of H in $\overline{\mathbf{N}}$ as follows:

$$\forall x \in H, \gamma(x) = \text{Inf}\left\{k \in \mathbf{N}; f^{*k+1}(\{x\}) - f^{*k}(\{x\}) = \phi\right\}$$

Definition 3:

Let E be a set, **R** a relation on E, If A is a strong component for **R**, we call rank of A the element $b(A) \in \overline{\mathbf{N}}$ computed on $F/\mathbf{R}^*$ with the relation representing the reduced graph without closed arc progression deduced from **R**.

Remark:

If one wishes to include the points of E_0 it is sufficient to apply the above definition to the relation $\hat{\mathbf{R}}'$ defined on E′ (see previous remark).

So, for the preceding example, one would have $\gamma(\{s\}) = 0, \gamma(\{x, y, z\}) = 1$, $\gamma(\{t, u\}) = 2, \gamma(\{v\}) = 3$ and $\gamma(\{w\}) = 0$.

* * *

To conclude, we propose to use the technique developed to conduct the analysis of the graph of interindustrial impacts in an input-output table.

Let us briefly recall the principle: the input-output table consists of a square tableau with n rows and n colums where n represents the number of sectors in the economy. The element x_{ij} in this tableau represents the value of the flow from industry i to industry j. If x_i is the value of the total production of industry i, then $d_{ij} = x_{ij}/x_i$ is the percentage of the production of industry i flowing into industry j.

One can show (see Auray, Duru and Mougeot (1982)) that d_{ij} is an indicator of the direct impact of industry j on industry i (impact in the sense of dominant demand)

Starting from the matrix D of the coefficients d_{ij} and given a choice for the threshold s, one builds a relation of the impacts at level s, $\mathbf{R}_s$ starting for every pair (i, j) of industries: $i\mathbf{R}_s j$ if and only if $d_{ij} \geqslant s$ or $i = j$. The proposed structural analysis allows us then to easily highlight the network of mutual impacts.

We have proceeded in this way to analyse the French input-output table with 44 industries (1970), based on the classification defined in table 1. The resulting structural analysis using a threshold s = 0.05 is presented in figure 1.

Table 1. Industrial classification in the French input-output table

Sector Number	Sector Definition
1	Agriculture, forestry and fishing
2	Coalmining, lignite, aggregates and brickettes
3	Coke ovens
4	Crude petroleum, industrial gas and petroleum products
5	Electricity, gas, hot water and steam
6	Ores, refined materials and fissile materials
7	Ferrous and non ferrous metal ores
8	Minerals and non-metallic minerals based products
9	Chemical products
10	Metallic products except machinery and vehicles
11	Agricultural and industrial machinery
12	Office and data processing machinery and precision, optical and similar instruments
13	Electrical engineering
14	Motor vehicles
15	Other transport equipment
16	Meat and meat products
17	Dairy products
18	Other food products
19	Drink products
20	Tobacco products
21	Textile products and clothing
22	Leather, fur and shoes
23	Timber and wooden furniture
24	Paper, paper products, printing and publishing
25	Rubber and plastic products
26	Other manufacturing products
27	Building and civil engineering work
28	Recycling and repairs
29	Commercial services
30	Horeca (catering and hotels) services
31	Internal transportation services
32	Sea and air transportation services
33	Transport related services
34	Communications services
35	Banking and insurance
36	Services to enterprises
37	Housing and rent
38	Commercial educational and research services
39	Commercial health services
40	Recreational, cultural and other personal services
41	General public services
42	Non-commercial educational and research services
43	Non-commercial health services
44	Domestic and other non-commercial services

Figure 1. Structural analysis of the French input-output table with 44 sectors

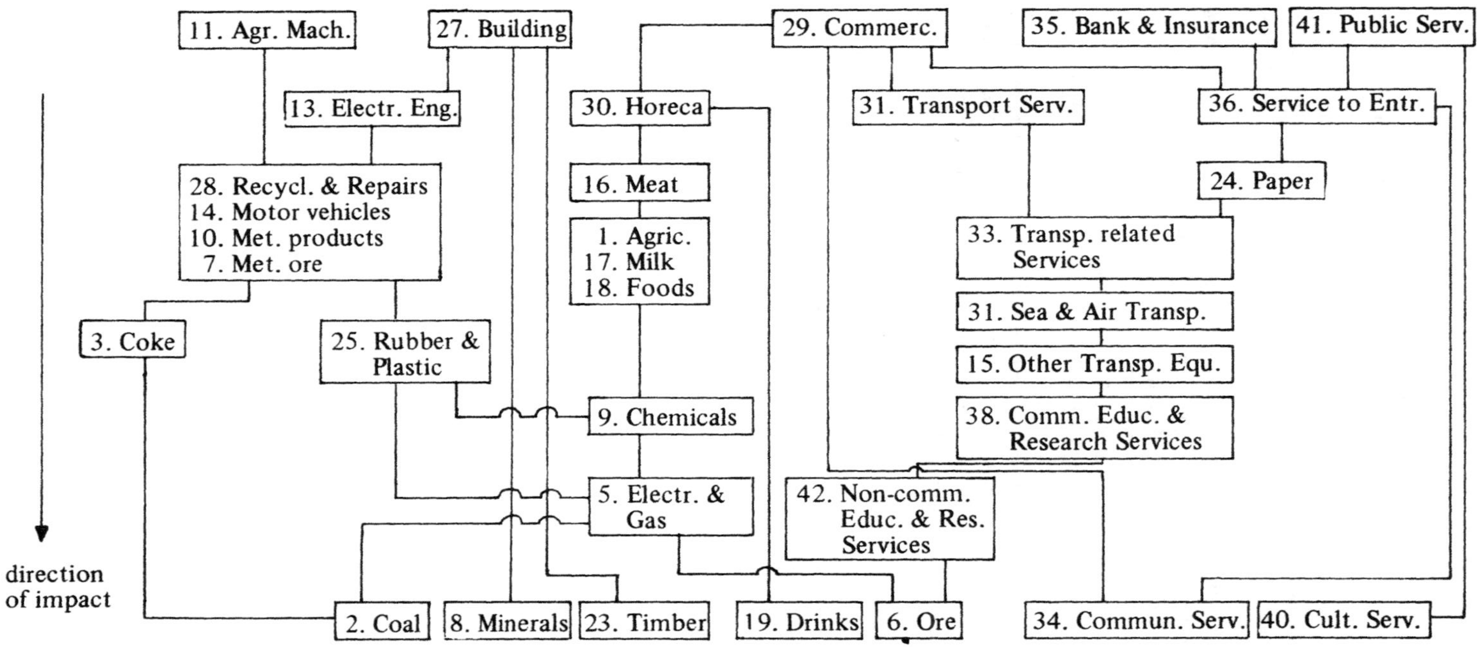

Isolated Sectors: 4. Petroleum; 12. Office Mach.; 20. Tobacco; 21. Textile; 22. Leather; 26. Other Manuf.; 37. Housing & Rent; 39 and 43. Health Serv.; 44. Domestic Serv.

REFERENCES

Auray, J.P. (1982), *Contribution à l'étude des structures pauvres,* Thèse d'Etat ès Sciences, University of Lyon I (mimeographed).

Auray, J.P., M. Brissaud and G. Duru (1978), 'Connexité des espaces préférenciés', *Cahiers du Centre d'Etudes et de Recherche Opérationnelle,* Vol. 20, No 3-4, pp. 315-324.

Auray, J.P., G. Duru and M. Mougeot (1982), *Les Structures Productives Européennes,* Editions du CNRS.

Duru, G. (1980), *Contributions à l'étude des Systèmes Complexes en Sciences Humaines,* Thèse d'Etat ès Sciences, University of Lyon I (mimeographed).

Fréchet, M. (1928), *Espaces Abstraits,* Hermann, Paris.

Guitton, H. (1975), *Entropie et Gaspillage,* Cujas.

Lorrain, F. (1975), *Réseaux sociaux et classifications sociales,* Hermann, Paris.

Messeri, M. (1973), *Applications de la Topologie à la Théorie des Graphes,* Ph.D. Thesis, University of Paris VI (mimeographed).

Ponsard, C. (1969), *Un modèle topologique d'équilibre économique inter-régional,* Dunod, Paris.

Richetin, M. (1975), *Analyse structurale des systèmes complexes en vue d'une commande hiérarchisée,* Thèse d'Etat ès Sciences, University of Toulouse (mimeographed).

Rossier, E. (1979), *Economie Structurale,* Economica, Paris.

CHAPTER 5

RATIONING AND AGGREGATION IN A MULTI-LEVEL MODEL OF HOUSEHOLD BEHAVIOUR: THE S.A.B.I.N.E. MODEL

J.P. Decaestecker and M. Mouillart
University of Paris X, France

1. INTRODUCTION

All of the existing French macroeconomic models are neo-keynesian in approach and so attach particular importance to consumer demand. Paradoxically, the modeling of consumer behaviour is based on general principles that can only yield relatively poor specifications in the light of recent developments in economic theory.

Within these models, the typical household makes a small number of decisions which can be inscribed within the format of the accounting equality between resources and expenditures:

HOUSEHOLDS' ACCOUNT

Expenditures	Resources
Consumption	(Exogenous) Income
Housing expenditures (Gross fixed investment)	Long term debts
Stocks and bonds	Short term debts
Liquid assets	

With a few exceptions (Tessier (1981) and Mouillart (1983)), the models use the following sequence to describe the household decision making process:

Stage 1: Real decisions

1. Determination of the household consumption level based on knowledge of consumer income and expectations.

2. Determination of the level of gross fixed investment based mainly on the cost of credit.

Stage 2: Financial decisions

1. Determination of the level of long term debts based on the level of gross fixed investment.
2. Determination of the level of short term debts based on consumption level.
3. Depending on the approach used, based either on wealth (COPAIN or PITI) or on a more keynesian outlook (METRIC), endogenisation of liquid assets and calculation of the balance in stocks and bonds, or endogenisation of stock and bond holdings and calculation of the balance in liquid assets.

The financial integration of the models is mainly based, firstly, on a consideration of the financial variables taken from the explanatory variables in the equations that account for real decisions, and, secondly, on the role of whichever variable (stocks and bonds, or liquid assets) is used to balance the model's real equations.

Although such models are effective tools for global macroeconomic analysis, they seem to be less effective in evaluating the consequences of economic monetary policy or in evaluating institutional changes that affect the conditions in which households make decisions. On the one hand, their descriptions of behaviour seem to be too aggregated, and on the other hand, their macro-accounting framework, although it preserves the equality of resources and expenditures, only provides model builders with statistical information that is often inadequate for a study of possible product substitution or for a study of constraints on households and postponement of non-satisfied demand.

An attempt to overcome these shortcomings has been made in the building of the SABINE model, which uses a disaggregated representation of household behaviour, in monetary and financial terms as well as in real terms, in a rationed economy with constraints that represent specific institutional characteristics, namely those existing in France since the mid-sixties. Independently of the model's statistical or descriptive qualities, great care has been taken to integrate only those behaviours or specifications which conform to a theoretical structure that was determined a priori, a structure that accounts for the constraints and the sequential pattern that condition consumer actions.

This chapter is therefore organised as follows: Section 2 contains a study of the consequences of aggregation in household behaviour modelling and of the solution adopted for these problems. Section 3 presents the main characteristics of the

SABINE model especially from the point of view of the disaggregation of goods and markets. Section 4 deals with the problems of the transition from theoretical microeconomic behaviour to macroeconomic (or mesoeconomic) specifications, showing that accounting for the effects of rationing or decision sequencing does not alter standard aggregation results.

2. AGGREGATION, RATIONING, AND MODELLING OF CONSUMER BEHAVIOUR

2.1 Most macroeconomic models assume that agents' behaviour, as well as goods, have been aggregated over those time periods that are implicitly allowed for by the limits of model size and of available statistical information.

This implicit aggregation permits the building of models in terms of relationships between variables rather than between agents. This fact, along with the lack of explicit representation of the flow of information between agents, leads to the acceptance of a direct transposition of specifications derived from microeconomic behaviour to aggregated specifications.

But such aggregation, especially when carried out on the extreme scale of models, has its own limitations if the model is to represent a rationed economy; many characteristics of such an economy will not be included in the description and this will result in an incorrect analysis of its functioning [1].

First of all, aggregation induces compensation between agents. When a constraint is introduced into an estimated model, it is assumed to affect all agents equally and in the same proportion. This excludes the all or nothing alternative that has been observed at the microeconomic level [2]. Moreover, since all agents of one side of a market are in the same position, it is possible to reason in terms of a typical agent and thereby to develop specifications representative of the behaviour of a category of agents. In order to reintroduce the effect of discrimination in rationing schemes, which seems to play a major role in the housing loan sector, the goods space may be disaggregated. Although there is not enough statistical information to distinguish between different categories of households, the same is not true of the different elements of the household financial liabilities space. If some hypotheses can be dropped, which will be discussed further below, it is indeed possible to establish a (quasi) strict relationship between certain categories of goods and certain groups of agents [3].

Secondly, aggregation introduces extraneous elements [4] which blur the distinctions between different types of rationing. Each rationing scheme introduced into a macroeconomic model must be elaborated in two stages: determination of disequilibrium between the quantity signalled and the quantity exchanged, and the distribution of this disequilibrium among the actors on either side of the market, this second stage being carried out implicitly in the literature by proportional rationing [5]. The first stage, which reveals a difference between aggregate supply and demand, very rarely corresponds to concrete decision making patterns; such a situation never occurs on the durable goods or housing markets, and will only very rarely occur (except during periods of government credit restrictions) on the housing loan market. However, this first stage presupposes the existence of a centralised system of information on quantities, an assumption which in theory is no more satisfactory than if the existence of such information on prices is presupposed.

Finally, a carelessly constructed goods aggregate greatly restricts the effectiveness of the concept of spillover of disequilibrium; practically all that remains is an intertemporal spillover. While an analysis of household behaviour stresses the importance of intertemporal rationing spillover [6], estimated macroeconomic models with rationing generate specifications which incorporate only intertemporal delays.

2.2 The building of a model of household behaviour in the presence of rationing must preserve disaggregation in the goods space, and possibly in the agent space as well [7].

The household can be viewed as a decision making unit that functions within a structure defined by a group of variables:

- Information variables: External environment or household behaviour shapes the values of information variables which reflect the constraints that the household faces.
- Control variables: The household assigns values, determined by its own decisions, to control variables. This allows objective variables to take on values that are satisfactory to the household (as high as possible and above certain limits) given available information.

An ordered set of relationships between these variables describes the internal organisation of household behaviour.

For each time period, such a structure enables the model to generate decisions which take constraints into account. It is also possible to evaluate the effects of rationing perceived by consumers; the representation will be all the more accurate if consumers have a wide range of possible choices. Even at a mesoeconomic level, such a procedure will improve knowledge of interactions between rationing and decision making.

However, at the same time, it seems unsatisfactory to retain a procedure for solving disequilibria, that is, an exchange process which would attach too much importance to a concept of regime defined by gaps between quantities exchanged and quantities signalled on the market.

It is apparently preferable to use an approach which, even though it presents quantification problems, has the advantage of producing a faithful representation of consumer and other agent decision making processes. For example, it is possible to use a structure characterised by one category of agents' domination over other agents participating in a given market. From the point of view of the representation we have adopted, such a system would imply that for each kind of decision an agent makes, there is a strong link between the agent's control variables and certain information variables whose values are mainly controlled by the dominant agent [8].

From a macroeconomic point of view, it is of course possible to adopt the idea that when only one side of a market is able to realise its plans it is because it has been able to impose appropriate constraints on the other side. However, this will not always be the case because of the spillover that usually occurs between different markets and agents. In terms of rationing schemes, finally, the formulation proposed by Broer and Siebrand (1979) makes this confrontation or sharing out of frustration explicit. Agents' relative weights in negotiations can be translated by the weights resulting from supply and demand in the determination of actually exchanged quantities as carried out in econometric estimation procedures.

2.3 Abandoning an aggregated approach and hence a procedure that ensures the centralisation of all price and quantities signals, preserves two kinds of information:

- Macroeconomic information: Information on aggregate economic variables (price indexes, the unemployment rate) and predictions of their evolution are available to agents.
- Microeconomic information: Each household checks different satisfaction levels or constraints by testing the reaction to its offers on different markets, and each household will have a different perception of the state of tension in the economy (credit structures, rationing schemes, etc.).

Such information is more or less complete depending on the type of variable or agent under consideration; the unemployment rate is known quite accurately to all households, but, on the other hand, housing prices or the rates of return on financial assets can only be determined approximately.

An approach that distinguishes [9] between a perceived constraint and an effective constraint is therefore appropriate. (Is the consumer really informed of the global constraint level when he is rationed individually?) Thus, Sneessens (1979) carefully distinguishes between the ways agents form expectations of rationing, depending on whether they are on the labour market or the goods market, and on whether the agent is a supplier (producer) or a consumer. Where consumers are concerned, the use of more qualitative information such as opinion polls permits the construction of indicators of expectations relative to different macroeconomic variables that may be considered known to households [10]. Such information can thus permit specification of how consumers perceive constraints and the macroeconomic environment. A macroeconomic constraint will therefore be in the realm of perceived constraints, and a micro (or meso) constraint will be an effective one. Moreover, avoiding the use of extrapolative mechanisms for expectations makes it easier to predict probable changes in economic structure, since the indicators can be used as predictors.

This distinction between two kinds of constraints is essential. In the relatively short term, it may be assumed that decisions made by a consumer will not be changed by a change in perceived constraints. On the other hand, if there is effective rationing on a market, an agent is forced to act differently from what he had palnned; although he can modify his decisions for later periods on the basis of new information, he cannot go back to a market that he has already visited to cancel the offers he has made.

Although the order in which a household considers different perceived constraints when making its decisions may be of little importance, the order in which the household carries out its decisions is much more significant. The sequence of consumer actions must therefore be made explicit. Sneessens (1979) has attempted to integrate this concept of sequential market visits by assuming that the typical agent will first visit a factor market and then the consumer market, an odering which corresponds to a minimal specification of ordered behaviour, given the degree of aggregation of his model. Similarly, Mouillart (1983) describes an analogous kind of behaviour in order to describe the behaviour of rationed households on the loan market with respect to different types of individual financial liabilities which can be distinguished in terms of repayment conditions and conditions governing consumer access to the markets.

In a disaggregate analysis of household behaviour with different kinds of consumer goods and housing and a broad range of financial assets, it is no longer possible to ignore the characteristics of different goods (their durability, the possibilities for stocking them, substitution possibilities, etc.) when defining spillover functions. For example, while demand for certain durable goods (cars, housing) may be postponed through the use of financial assets, food purchases or health expenditures cannot be delayed without endangering the (physiological) existence of the household. Similarly, while a demand for credit may be postponed at almost no cost[11] (unless we take into account the losses caused to the household when forced to postpone plans that were to be realised with credit: inflation, disappearance of desired goods from the market, etc.), the same is not true of all types of credit that a household may have access to. Due to certain regulations, the non-satisfaction of a credit demand may cause the household to lose the right to obtain a loan (for instance, home-saving loan) if the household's composition or income changes in the interim period.

2.4 Finally, an approach which disaggregates the goods space makes it possible to replace a rationing process based on voluntary exchange (a first stage in the determination of the macroeconomic quantity exchanged) with a compromise specification accounting better for the institutional or organisational characteristics of the markets in question.

However, given the data currently available[12], it would seem difficult to specify the characteristics of different agents with any degree of precision and therefore to solve this aspect of the aggregation problem in a satisfactory manner. It has been pointed out and stressed above that when there is credit rationing, for example, a secondary distribution of excess demand takes place, based, no longer on price determinants, but on the particularities of different consumers (sex, age, income level, etc.). Thus implicit proportional rationing schemes can no longer be considered acceptable.

The solution proposed in the SABINE model (Fanton and Mouillart (1983)) is to incorporate indicators for distribution and for the structure of disaggregated income [13]. With such a solution, the specific characteristics of households can be indirectly taken into account, and their consequences in terms of behaviour may be evaluated.

3. THE SABINE MODEL: A SYNTHESIS

3.1 SABINE is a quarterly multimarket model of household behaviour in the presence of rationing which includes more than 230 equations, 190 being behavioural relationships [14].

With this model, it is possible to describe the effects of household decisions fairly accurately when there are partial constraints on one or more of the five markets in the model:

1. The consumer goods market (10 behavioural equations corresponding to as many types of goods) [15]
2. Widely available savings instruments: savings accounts (7 behavioural equations)

3. Savings instruments with a limited number of users: stocks and bonds (8 behavioural equations)
4. The housing loan market (80 behavioural equations)
5. The real estate market (75 behavioural equations)

The following is a description of the model's basic structure (see table 1).

Household disposable income (wages and transfer income, not including taxes or other deductions) can be determined from the labour market situation and the general lines of government redistribution policy. This income is first of all used for non-durable consumption, repayment of capital on previously contracted loans, and payment of insurance premiums. In this context, these expenses may be considered mandatory and/or contractual. Also, they are largely the result of past household choices. Thus, they can be viewed as a kind of global levy on household income.

If there is any residual income after these expenditures, the household has a choice between financial savings or purchasing real estate. The strategy adopted will depend mainly on the level of financial wealth, resulting from past savings. The resources available will enable the household to finance all or part of its own real estate purchases without having to face the loan market constraint system [16]. Three categories of households can be defined according to the income level: first, households with large incomes which are able to finance housing purchases themselves; secondly, households with middle level incomes which have enough resources to make down payments and thereby obtain loans; and lastly, households with low incomes which do not possess enough financial wealth to become house owners.

The last category of households, with little wealth, is excluded from the real estate market (and therefore from the loan market). They may use their residual income to buy widely available savings instruments, or simply keep it in a liquid form.

In contrast, the first two categories of households will be more or less subject to constraints (due to monetary policy, for example). If credit is rationed, thereby making it difficult to obtain loans, they may cancel or postpone real estate purchases and choose financial savings instead. If credit is widely available at low rates, they will more readily take out loans to finance real estate purchases.

3.2 SABINE is thus a model with an ordered decision making structure. The consumer makes decisions within a constraint system which imposes an ordered sequence of actions.

In the first stage, the household carries out its most basic expenditures: non-durable consumption (under a physiological survival constraint), loan reimbursement (under a regulations constraint), and insurance premiums (under a contractual con-

Table 1. General structure of the SABINE model

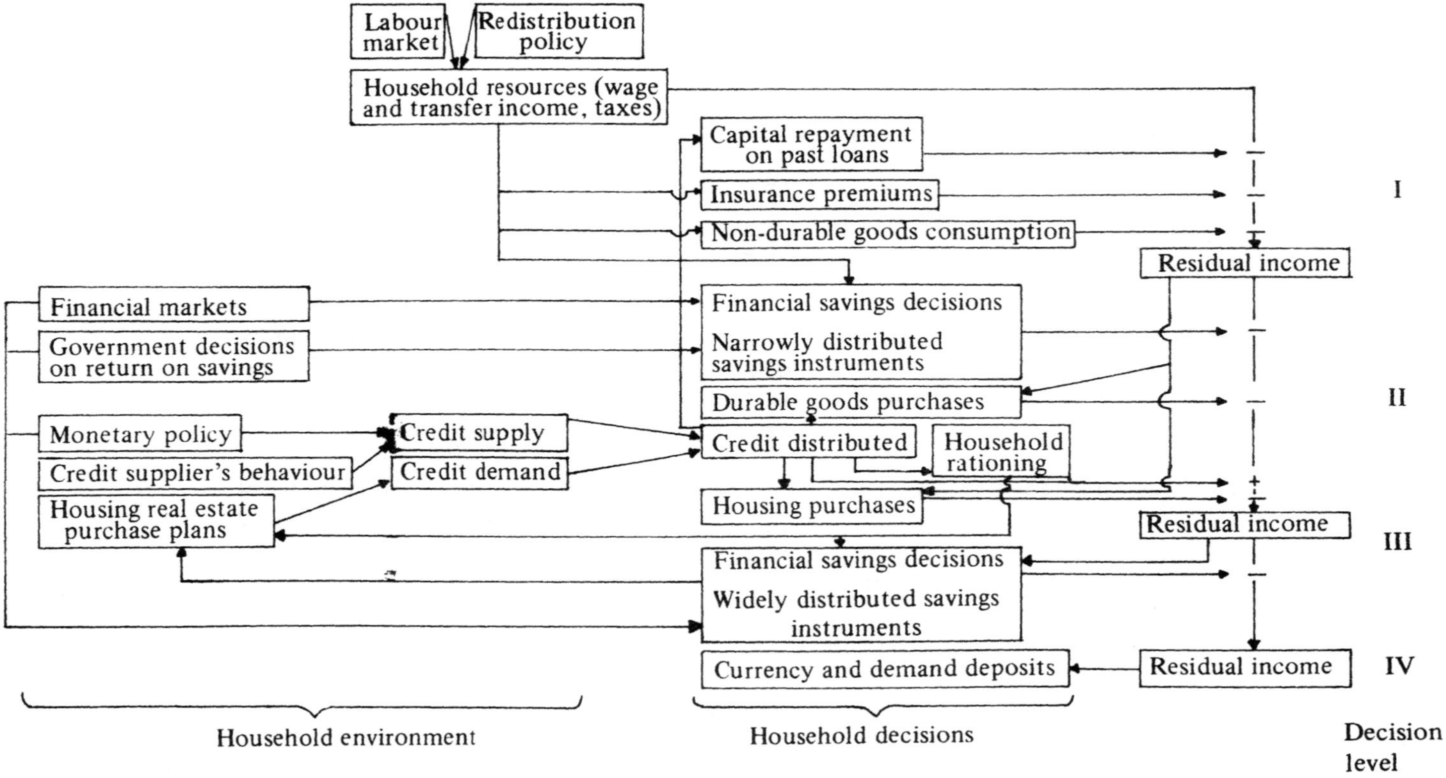

Table 2. Households' Account (each item expressed as a percentage of income); Quarterly averages: 1975–1981

Decision level	Expenditures		Resources	
I	Capital repayments	2.24	100.00	Household income
	Insurance premiums	1.14		
	Non-durable goods consumption	76.73		
	Residual income: balance from level I	19.89	19.89	Residual income: balance from level I
II	Narrowly distributed financial savings	3.28		
	Durable goods purchases	7.33	6.70	Level of household debt
	Housing purchases	7.60		
	Residual income: balance from level II	8.38	8.38	Residual income: balance from level II
III	Widely distributed financial savings	5.39		
	Residual income: balance from level III	2.99	2.99	Residual income: balance from level III
IV	Currency and demand deposits	2.99		

Source: SABINE data base

straint).

In the second stage, the household divides its residual income between real estate and financial savings. Wealth constraints and restricted access to different types of credit (depending on institutional loan market organisation) will govern household choices. When the loan market is rationed, the household, if it is under a constraint, may have to postpone or cancel its real estate purchases and turn towards financial savings. This is the third stage of decision making. The process may be schematically presented as follows:

planned real estate purchases → loans → real estate purchases → financial savings

If the household obtains the desired loans, it will execute its decisions without inter- or intratemporal delays.

This decision making sequence results from the presence of effective or perceived constraints, from the existence of intratemporal delays when certain decisions can not be acted upon, and finally from the impossibility of cancelling decisions that have already been carried out.

Because SABINE is based on a twofold disaggregation, that is, in the goods space and in the consumer space, such an ordering of decisions is possible.

The goods space is disaggregated in such a way as to describe positions on either side of five markets, each with its own special characteristics, as well as rationing spillover between markets. Moreover, a disaggregation that accurately represents the framework of institutions and regulations makes it possible to define groups of goods that are homogeneous in terms of conditions for consumer access to their markets.

In the agent space, although it is difficult to carry out a very fine disaggregation given currently available data, income structure indicators have been introduced in order to disaggregate behaviour by income level. This makes it possible to allow for the exclusion of some households from certain markets because of their income level and to allow for the consequences of discrimination between households (see table 3).

3.3 Finally, the econometric estimation of the SABINE model was based on the period from the first quarter of 1969 to the fourth quarter of 1981. The results of the estimates, equation by equation, are of good and even excellent quality: the proportion of variance that is accounted for varies from 72% to 99%.

A good evaluation of the model's performance may be gained from its ex post simulations, where each section of the model is used in interaction with the others. A study of the model's precision in determining some key variables yields the results of table 4.

Table 3. Disaggregation of household behaviour and income

Effects of growth in → on ↓	Low incomes	Middle level incomes	High incomes	Transfer incomes
Non-durable goods consumption	+	–	0	+
Narrowly distributed financial savings	–	–	+	0
Durable goods purchases	0	0	0	0
Housing purchases	+	+	0	0
Level of household debt	–	+	0	0
Widely distributed financial savings	+	+	0	0

+ positive effect; – negative effect; 0 effect nil or statistically insignificant.

Table 4. Some performance indicators for SABINE

Average percentage discrepancy between observed and simulated series	Static simulation	Dynamic simulation
Total consumption (rate of growth)	0.64	insignificant
Level of consumer debt (rate of growth)	– 5.95	– 1.90
Savings rate	0.42	1.25
Number of housing starts	–0.03	2.46

SABINE's stability and consistence with observed reality are thus sufficient to warrant a closer examination of the sequencing principles that have been applied and a further discussion of the theoretical basis of consumer behaviour.

4. THE TRANSITION FROM MICROECONOMIC BEHAVIOUR THEORY TO AGGREGATED ECONOMETRIC REPRESENTATIONS

4.1 Sometimes, it is sufficient to obtain an estimated model that 'reproduces' observed series, in a quantitatively satisfactory manner, and which can then be interpreted according to various economic theories. However, the econometrician may want, in addition, to obtain estimated specifications that can be derived directly from theoretical specifications or that fall within a given theoretical framework. Such a link with the theory will generally offer two advantages:

- One type of behaviour or a set of behavioural categories, which can guarantee a certain homogeneity in the agents' rationality underlying the model, can be taken as a point of reference.
- Constraints imposed by the theory can be used to simplify estimation problems, or to 'deduce' indicators from the estimated parameters.

We shall try to develop such a link with the theory for the SABINE model.

4.1 The problems that must be solved in order to obtain a model of an economic agent's behaviour depend on the properties that are desired for the model. At a microeconomic level, an equivalence between the given theoretical rationality and the rationality deduced from the model is required. At a macroeconomic level, whether the model is based on panel data or on pre-aggregated data from national account data, it is necessary to assume either the existence of a 'representative'[17] consumer in order to achieve the required degree of aggregation, or the existence of price and/or quantity transformations which consumer choices are based on[18]. Such transformations imply certain forms of separability in the utility functions, for example, vis-a-vis aggregates constructed on the basis of these transformations. These transformations allow for changes in the utility functions making aggregation of agents possible.

If aggregation schemes based on time (from the quarter to the year) are ruled out, the changes mentioned above may be determined by finding the applications associated with the arrows in the following graph; these are generally not injective.

$$
\begin{array}{ll}
\text{micro level} & \left\{\begin{array}{ccccc}
u_0 \in R^m & \leftarrow\text{-----} & y_0 \in R^{nxm} & \leftarrow\text{-----} & x_0 \in R^{nxm} \\
\downarrow & & \downarrow & & \downarrow \\
u_1 \in R^m & \leftarrow\text{-----} & y_1 \in R^{pxm} & \leftarrow\text{-----} & x_1 \in R^{pxm}
\end{array}\right. \\
 & \begin{array}{ccccc}
\downarrow & \qquad & \downarrow & \qquad & \downarrow
\end{array} \\
\text{macro level} & \begin{array}{ccccc}
u_2 \in R & \leftarrow\text{-----} & y_2 \in R^p & \leftarrow\text{-----} & x_2 \in R^p
\end{array}
\end{array}
$$

$p < m$; n: number of elementary goods; p: number of groups of goods;
m: number of agents

In this graph (derived from those used in Malinvaud (1956)) 'x' represents variables that are exogenous for the consumer (for example, prices and past structure of wealth), 'y' represents endogenous variables (quantities consumed, etc.) and 'u' represents the value of a criterion that is optimised through the choice of 'y', dependent on the value of 'x' and subject to certain constraints (utility, etc.).

As we have indicated above, the state of available information is a constraint (section 2.1) but it also allows us (sections 2.4 and 3.1) to restrict ourselves to the first levels (0 and 1) of the graph, without having to go into the problem of the existence of any kind of collective utility function ($u_1 \rightarrow u_2$). We may assume that, at least for a model with SABINE's institutional characteristics, the main transformations from level 0 to level 2 have been carried out if there is a consistent set of transformations from level 0 to level 1.

4.3 In fact, the two approaches mentioned in the previous section designed to obtain a macroeconomic representation, are not completely independent. Theil's approach combines certain aspects of the two; he discusses the definition of price and/or quantity aggregates which would allow the construction of well-behaved demand functions, both in terms of aggregation or microeconomic behaviour on the one hand, and in terms of treatment of statistical residuals from aggregation biases (level 1 → level 2) on the other [19]. The Rotterdam model was based on this idea.

Imposed constraints on the construction of an aggregation that is consistent with a certain framework have an effect on microeconomic behaviour and particularly on the structure of agent preferences. To put it generally, it is necessary to impose some separability between goods, hence allowing for 'blockwise' defined utility functions (Green (1964), Theorem 3, for example); the aggregates mentioned above are constructed on the basis of price and quantity information on goods within a block. This separability hypothesis can be tested by examining the sensitivities of relative elasticities of goods in one block to the quantities of goods in another block (Green (1964), Theorem 1 or Barnett (1981), section 5.6).

It should be noted that theoretical presentations or various comments on the estimation of the consumer behaviour implied by such a scheme (from Theil (1971) to Barnett (1981)), assume that this agent simultaneously decides how much of his resources to allocate to each block and on the distribution of his allocation among the various goods within a given block, even if, at the optimum, the marginal utilities derived from the aggregates corresponding to each block differ from one block to another. However, while in the absence of rationing this multi-level decision making process can be depicted as instantaneous and time-invariant relationship between levels, the same representation no longer holds in the presence of rationing, a situation where there are spillovers from one level to another. Since these spillovers are generally only in one direction, they appear to be in a certain order that cannot be reversed, at least not empirically and not within the institutional framework of SABINE.

A hypothesis of lexicographic temporal preference among blocks (which has no effect on aggregation, at least if there is no rationing on a block) can be superimposed on the weak separability hypothesis (called 'functional separability' by Leontieff) which is necessary in order to aggregate goods (level 0 → level 1). This implies that the allocation of resources among blocks is ***sequential***, but does not alter results at all in terms of the level of demand, at least in the absence of rationing [20].

One of the major consequences of this approach (system-wide or Rotterdam model) on prediction or ex post analysis of behaviour is that, if the separability hypothesis for goods, which requires a block by block breakdown of preferences, is tested, and if the approach is found to be acceptable, it means that agents actually behave as though they allocated their resources on the basis of price and quantity aggregates constructed with specifications that conform to this approach. The quantity indexes associated with such aggregates are generally of the Divisia type (Diewert (1976)), and the evolution of these indexes has, with few exceptions, a very poor correlation with indexes that are constructed simply be summing the quantities of goods within a block. The conclusion to be drawn from this fact is clear as far as prediction or core model building is concerned: a core model should only use the composite commodities corresponding to each block or each level, if there is ranking.

4.4 Before returning to a discussion of connections between ranking and rationing, two observations should be made at the microeconomic level. Concerning the specific consumer behaviour, the standard analysis of the optimisation programme without resource constraints is changed, on the one hand, by the existence of rationing, which can modify the demand function and therefore bring in discontinuities at the aggregated level, and on the other hand, by considering optimisations carried out over several time periods.

4.4.1 One way to resolve the first question is to view the aggregated demand functin as an average of demand functions for both rationed and non-rationed individuals, each group being weighted according to its proportion in the total population. The disadvantage of this solution is that it either does not integrate certain conditions necessary for correct aggregation or that is presupposes that these conditions are satisfied by the demand functions of each group of individuals. Moreover, this type of specification inevitably leads to incorrect estimation when we are dealing with lagged variables for a given group (for example, unsatisfied past demand) and when significant numbers of individuals have shifted from one group to another within the time period in question (for example, when we are dealing with 'waiting line' rationing schemes, which do not imply a correlation between an individual's rank in the line at different points in time).

In the SABINE model, the attempt to achieve a fine disaggregation which can associate one category of individuals with a particular market segment (in the case of housing and housing finance) and the hypothesis that rationing affects the whole population on a given market, minimise this risk[21].

Another procedure is to assign a shadow price [22] to a rationed good. This price is a continuous function of the degree of rationing, and demand functions for other goods can be redefined within a rationed context on the basis of this price, their form being the same as in a non-rationed context. In a non-rationed context, the shadow price is equal to the price observed. The advantage of this procedure is that rationing is no longer presented as an outside constraint to the demand functions. Even though the exact formulation of a shadow price as a function of the constraint clearly depends on the demand system and, more generally, on the preference system, these results can at least lead us to include a rationing indicator in demand functions for goods that are substitutes for or complements to rationed goods and that belong to the same level [23] in our representation.

4.4.2 In order to write down a decision programme covering several time periods, we must assume (i) that agents anticipate changes in the price and quantity system or (ii) that agents' preference systems or institutional constraints affect the quantity of resources that will actually be available to carry out their current decisions.

The first option always seems difficult to implement given the diversity of possible models for household expectations (see the current debate over the use of rational expectations models). A promising approach, both because of its empirical effectiveness and because of the analysis of the process of household expectation formation that it permits, would be to construct indicators for household opinion on prices or unemployment on the basis of opinion polls (see section 2.2). Because this work is not yet completed, we have taken the second (ii) option for the present version of our research.

This second approach has two aspects: one concerning resources, and the other concerning resource allocation. In so far as the only way in which an agent can transfer future *resources* to the present time period is by the use of credit, the problem of expectations referred to above becomes one of determining what loans are available to a given category of agents. The quantity of credit available is not completely freely chosen by households in that credit institutions measure household ability to repay (and therefore to borrow, if we assume that households always choose the length of time for a loan which will maximise the amount of the loan, on the basis of institution policy) by household income and by certain other indicators of *current* household resources. One of the simplest hypotheses regarding the role of time in *resource allocation* is to postulate that if an agent has a utility function covering several time periods, this function has a weak separability between current and future expenses. Given this assumption along with the preceding one, the representative agent may be viewed, within each time period, as solving his decision programme relative only to that period.

4.5 In an attempt to insert rationing into a sequential decision making scheme, two points must be considered. First, the rationing procedure itself is such that only one side of the market is constrained, and a disequilibrium is distributed over the two sides of the market. In SABINE the rationing procedure is represented as 'exogenous' to the decision scheme. The two are connected, however, on the basis of the quantities demanded that are generated by the scheme and on the basis of the constrained quantities that the rationing procedure determines and then retransmits to the decision scheme [24]. Secondly, different types of spillovers must be measured. Spillovers within a given time period are of two kinds: intra-level and inter-level. Intra-level spillovers are determined by possible substitution within the block associated with the level. Inter-level spillovers imply that resource allocations made prior to the level on which a spillover occurs will be increased by that fraction of the spillover that was not absorbed by substitution effects on the level above. Another kind of spillover is the one occuring between time periods [25]. Such spillover will modify demand for the good which is now rationed in the following time period.

4.5.1 To express this point formally, let us consider the levels j and j+1 associated with the composite goods x_j and x_{j+1} respectively, with representative prices p_j and p_{j+1}, and quantities q_j and q_{j+1}. We will assume that these aggregates have been constructed on the basis of elementary quantities and prices by the use of certain functions χ and Π with:

$$q_j = \chi(q_{j1}, \ldots, q_{j\ell}) = \chi(q_{j.}),$$

where the q_{ji} are the quantities of elementary goods, their prices being p_{ji};

$$p_j = \Pi(p_{j1}, \ldots, p_{j\ell}) = \Pi(p_{j.});\ q_{j.}, p_{j.} \in R^1,$$

such that: $m_j = q_j p_j = q_{j.} \cdot p_{j.}$. In the same way: $m_{j+1} = q_{j+1} p_{j+1} = q_{j+1.} \cdot p_{j+1.}$ where m_j denotes the amount of resources devoted to the expenditures of level j, before the perception of any constraint on levels above j.

Let $\hat{q}_{ji}$ be the quantity signalled on the market, $\bar{q}_{ji}$ the available (constrained) quantity and $\tilde{q}_{ji}$ the actually exchanged quantity, with[26]:

$$\hat{q}_{ji} < \bar{q}_{ji} \Rightarrow \tilde{q}_{ji} = \hat{q}_{ji}$$

$$\hat{q}_{ji} \geqslant \bar{q}_{ji} \Rightarrow \tilde{q}_{ji} = \bar{q}_{ji}$$

Without constraints on the markets at level j and prior levels: $q_{j.} \cdot p_{j.} = m_j$.

If $\tilde{q}_{ji} = \bar{q}_{ji} < \hat{q}_{ji}$, then we must divided unused resources between levels j and j+1; generally[27]:

$$S: \begin{cases} \tilde{m}_j = \tilde{q}_{j.} \cdot p_{j.} + a p_{ji}(\hat{q}_{ji} - \bar{q}_{ji}) \\ \tilde{m}_j < m_j \\ \text{and} \\ \hat{m}_{j+1} = m_{j+1} + (1-a) p_{ji}(\hat{q}_{ji} - \bar{q}_{ji}) \\ \hat{m}_{j+1} > m_{j+1} \end{cases}$$

The intra-level distribution will be a function of the rates of substitution between x_{ji} and x_{jh}, of the differences $\bar{q}_{jh} - \hat{q}_{jh}$, and of the size of the intertemporal spillover. Indeed, because of the imperfections of used goods makets, if an individual wants to transfer a fraction f in t+1 of his non-satisfied demand and if, moreover, the level of his resources available in t+1 is uncertain, he will prefer, in period t, to transfer a fraction (an increasing function of f) of his resources that are not allocated due to rationing to relatively liquid financial assets, allocating the balance to goods.

Scheme S is hence affected by the quantity of spillovers between time periods[28]. When $f \to 1$, the agent keeps as much as possible of his resources in a potentially liquid form and all *intra* level substitution between p_{ji} and goods and physical assets disappears. When $f \to 0$, q_{ji}^{t+1} is not explicitly dependent on rationing, and initial substitution within the level is possible.

4.5.2 Considering the above indications it seems clear that consistency between rationing in a ranked model and a weak separability hypothesis[29] for consumer preferences, which permits a sequential decision making scheme, essentially depends on how the different levels or composite goods are defined, and therefore on elasticities relative to goods involved in rationing or spillovers. Hence, it is important, when defining level j, to classify goods according to their elasticities vis-a-vis spillovers on the next level up (j−1); and also to the elasticities of goods on the next level down (j+1) vis-a-vis spillovers from level j. This guideline, which must be added to guidelines for a consistent formulation in terms of sequential decision making (see Green (1964), Theorems 1 and 4 and Note 20) may seem difficult to apply. In fact, however, few of the categories of goods that households face seem to be rationed (and to induce spillover effects) to any significant degree; moreover, rationing spillovers go in only one direction. Hence the number of levels containing rationed goods, which theoretically must be constructed in order to determine spillovers emitted $(m_j - \tilde{m}_j)$ or received $(\hat{m}_{j+1} - m_{j+1})$ by a given level and to determine the corresponding elasticities, is acceptably low if the degree of disaggregation for this type of goods is not too fine.

4.5.3 Unlike a complete demand model, even as detailed a model as those studied by Barnett, for example, SABINE takes borrowed household resources, particularly housing loans, to be endogenous. From the point of view of the link between rationing and ranking, certain difficulties seem to appear, since there is a specific demand for loans, sometimes constrained, and then, loans appear as a resource on the right-hand side of the budget constraint for housing purchases. The distinction between housing purchasing plans and actual purchases (see section 3.2) and the treatment of credit as a good with its own specific preference schedule, are sufficient to overcome these difficulties.

Indeed, the various constraints and institutional policies regarding housing loans mentioned in sections 2 and 3 would lead us to expect a rather high degree of complementarity between types of housing and types of loans. Moreover, the way a household chooses to take out a loan is analogous to choices made for other goods. 'Utility' can be implicitly evaluated either on the basis of the utility of housing or on the basis of the utilities of the other goods which cannot be purchased because of loan costs (repayment plus interest) which will reduce net disposable income at level I (see table 2). This type of representation thus generates substitution (and not complementarity) relationships between certain kinds of goods and borrowed resources.

5. CONCLUSION

In this paper, we have tried to show, with a minimum of technical detail, that it is possible to build a model of disaggregated household behaviour in the presence of rationing, and that such a model could fit in with a given institutional framework and be compatible with a theoretical representation which allows a certain form of aggregation.

The exact specifications used in the SABINE model are quite different from those of the Rotterdam model type. The presence of certain variables is justified because they are linked to the way households process information and thereby to the transformations that their way of evaluating the economic environment bring about on gross meso- or macroeconomic variables or on indicators linked to rationing (see section 4.4). And if the distribution of variables or goods among different levels is done while taking the remarks made in section 4.5 into account, the specifications are not explicitly made in terms of composite goods and the associated price and quantity aggregates.

The core model of SABINE seems to us to constitute a framework that can permit the construction of a model which explicitly incorporates specifications that are consistent with the principles and the framework discussed in sections 2 and 3. We have seen in section 4 that such specifications are in keeping with the aggregation or disaggregation principles that form the basis of the work of researchers such as Theil or Barnett. Such a core model will allow us to address questions on optimal policy for households, work which is now in progress.

NOTES

We are indebted to Miss L. ap Roberts for an accurate translation of the original text.

1) Examples are discussed by Drazen (1980) with reference to unemployment and money and by Mouillart (1983) with reference to household debts.
2) An agent either is or is not rationed on a given market. Thus, a restriction on housing credit will not bring about an increase in household cash flow (proportional, non-discriminatory distribution), but will cause a reduction in housing sales and construction (cancelling of plans by rationed households).
3) For example, in the case of households, a classification by income bracket coincides with a classification of different financial liabilities, and also, to a great extent, with a system of classification of housing purchased by households based on institutional and regulatory criteria (Mouillart (1983)).
4) Extraneous is an appropriate term to the extent that differences between supply and demand that are resolved by rationing measures cannot be deduced from the exchange process governing individual transactions.
5) Exceptions are Bourguignon, Michel, and Miqueu (1980) and Artus, Laroque,

and Michel (1982) who describe schemes specifying the distribution of disequilibria respectively among sectors and among components of demand.

6) A constraint on certain types of consumption will also lead to changes in total consumption structure and level (Decaestecker and Mouillart (1983)). Constraints on consumption or household debt will affect short term consumer real estate financial operations (Fanton and Mouillart (1983)).
7) The points discussed in this and the following section have been developed more thoroughly by Decaestecker and Mouillart (1982).
8) For example, household credit demand (a control variable) depends on the level of the borrower's interest rate (an information variable for the consumer, but a control variable for the supplying institution) which is partly determined by the conditions in which the supplier dominates.
9) See Benassy (1977).
10) See Decaestecker and Mouillart (1983).
11) For an analysis of the relationships between spillovers and changes in household financial holdings, see Parly and Blondel (1980). See also Deaton and Muellbauer (1980), section 13.4 about the consequences of constraints on sales (of durable goods) and borrowing.
12) There are few sources of data on income and wealth distribution, and even fewer if one needs short period data (quarterly), or if one is restricted to conventional accounting sources.
13) Moreover, such information on income is all the more useful because SABINE's data bank and the institutional characteristics of the markets under consideration make it possible to link household income level with access to (or blocking from) different parts of the real estate market or the housing loan market.
14) In order to further the construction of the SABINE model, which is currently used by the Ministry of City Planning and Housing to formulate its budgets and by the Commisariat Général du Plan to develop the Ninth Plan, a threefold project for methodological improvement was conceived: first of all, a set of highly disaggregated household behaviour functions; secondly, specifications as to the conditions under which rationing can affect household decisions and econometric rationing estimates; and thirdly, the constitution of a data base with more than one thousand quarterly series observed from 1964 to 1981 which allow for precise measurement of disaggregated behaviour functions.
15) Cars, housing services, food, health, domestic appliances, industrial products, transport and telecommunications, clothing, entertainment, other services.
16) As an example of the rationing households face, on average over the period, 20% of the demand for housing loans (in conjunction with home saving) and 8% of the demand for contractual loans went unsatisfied. This is indeed a question of *signalled* market demand. When a market is rationed, SABINE reconstitutes supply and demand separately and not only quantities actually exchanged.
17) 'Representative' at least in the statistical sense as in the contemporary work on integral or mean demand function (for example, Hildenbrand (1974) or Freixas and Mass Collell (1982)).

18) Most of the work that has been done on aggregation since Green (1964) and to a lesser extent Malinvaud (1956).
19) We should note that Theil for the most part studies finite groups of consumers while researchers such as Hildenbrand work within a measure space of agents.
20) The rather awkward term 'lexicographic termporal preference' simply means that within the time period (a quarter, for example) under consideration, decisions regarding different levels are assumed to be made at different points in time within the period and that the decision dates themselves are governed by a lexicographic preference system, independent of the preference structure governing decisions on the goods and services themselves (see table 1).
21) Also, Deaton and Muellbauer (1980) (pp. 364-65) suggest that the bias introduced into aggregates by the fact that households can belong to both 'sides' of the market is probably more marked in durable goods than in non-durable goods markets.
22) For a detailed study of this approach and an application to the linear expenditure system, see Robert and Neary (1980). For an application to a demand system where there may be a constraint in the supply on the labour market see Barnett (1981), section 2.4.
23) It is clear that most of the difficulties linked to a consideration of rationing are due to the extremely aggregated level at which we must work as a result of data availability restrictions. When panel data are available, it is possible to trace population sub-groups quite precisely and to give an exact description of the role of constraints or of their disappearance on agent decisions. Thus, Hausman and Wise (1980), in a similar problem of decision making on housing markets, are able to analyse the effect of the lifting of constraints (fictive price < observed price) in the framework of a housing aid programme where there are three different types of behaviour.
24) For details on the procedures incorporated into SABINE see Decaestecker and Mouillart (1982) or Mouillart (1983). In the present version there are 'compromise function' procedures, and 'minimum supply and demand' procedures, both applied on level 2 of table 1.
25) Demand on different segments of the housing or loan market is calculated for each period on the basis of available information, taking each level in order. Intertemporal spillovers are not carried out *directly* from a given level in 't' to the same level in 't+1', but are done via the available resources. This procedure allows us to preserve the condition on elasticities between goods in blocks which correspond to different time periods (see section 4.2).
26) In fact, if we actually took indivisibilities on the housing market, for example, into account, we would have: $\check{q}_{ji} < \bar{q}_{ji}$.
27) Of course: $a < \dfrac{\sum_{h \neq j} p_{jh}(\bar{q}_{jh} - \hat{q}_{jh})}{p_{ji}(\hat{q}_{ji} - \bar{q}_{ji})}$

Otherwise, other spillovers would have to exist from level j to level j+1. Bowden (1978) (section 6.3, p. 221 ff) gives some indications for an approximation expression for goods which are submitted to spillovers on level j.

28) We must note that since SABINE allows us to reconstitute supply and demand signalled on different markets $\check{q} = \hat{q}$, it is possible, by performing a simulation on the model both without rationing and with rationing, to measure the 'a' coefficients and to decide if their evolution depends on the degree or on the nature of the rationing. In practice, in the model's present version, a scheme like S is used only on levels II and III. Given the types of goods or assets on these levels, a high value for 'f' implies a low value for 'a'.

29) This hypothesis implies that the marginal rate of substitution between two goods belonging to the same group is independent of consumption of goods in other groups. It would be possible to adopt another representation of sequential decision making, one which, unlike ours, does not use multi-stage budgeting. This would lead to hypotheses other than weak separability (see Deaton and Muellbauer (1980), p. 133 ff). However, we have used the hypothesis which seems most suited for time sequences associated with rationing spillovers.

REFERENCES

Artus, P., G. Laroque and G. Michel (1982), 'Estimation d'un modèle macroéconométrique trimestriel avec rationnements', Séminaire R. Roy, Paris (mimeo).

Barnett, W.A. (1981), *Consumer demand and labour supply*, North Holland, Amsterdam.

Benassy, J.P. (1977), 'Effective demand, quantity signals and decision theory', *CEPREMAP*, Paris (mimeo).

Bourguignon, F., G. Michel and D. Miqueu (1980), 'Short run rigidities and long run adjustments in a computable general model of income distribution and development', *Laboratoire d'Economie Politique – Ecole Normale Supérieure*, Document No 30 bis, Paris.

Bowden, R.J. (1978), *The Econometrics of Disequilibrium*, North Holland, Amsterdam.

Broer, D.P. and J.C. Siebrand (1979), 'A simultaneous disequilibrium analysis of product market and labour market', *Erasmus University – Institute for Economic Research*, Discussion paper series 7813–G.

Deaton, A. and J. Muellbauer (1980), *Economics and consumer behaviour*, Cambridge University Press, Cambridge.

Decaestecker, J.P. and M. Mouillart (1982), 'Les comportements des ménages en présence de rationnements: quelques orientations pour la modélisation', *IX. Colloque International d'Econométrie Appliquée et VI. Colloque International sur la Modélisation Econométrique Socialiste*, Budapest

Decaestecker, J.P. and M. Mouillart (1983), 'Comportements de consommation des ménages en présence de rationnement', *Rapport D.G.R.S.T., Paris.*

Diewert, W.E. (1976), 'Exact and superlative index numbers', *Journal of Econometrics*, Vol. 4, pp. 115-146.

Drazen, A. (1980), 'Recent developments in macroeconomic disequilibrium theory', *Econometrica*, Vol. 48, pp. 283-307.

Fanton, M. and M. Mouillart (1983), 'Marchés immobiliers et dépenses logement des ménages', A.F.S.E. Colloquium, Paris, June 1983.

Fanton, M. and M. Mouillart (1983), 'SABINE: un modèle de comportement des ménages',

Cahiers Economiques de Nancy (forthcoming).
Freixas, X. and A Mass Colell (1982), 'Courbes d'Engel et demande agrégée satisfaisant l'axiome faible des préférences révélées', (mimeo), Seminar of R. Roy, Paris.
Green, H.A.J. (1964), *Aggregation in economic analysis*, Princeton University Press.
Hausman J. and D. Wise (1980), 'Discontinuous budget constraints and estimation: the demand for housing', *Review of Economic Studies*, Econometric Issue, pp. 75-96.
Hildenbrand, W. (1974), *Core and equilibria of a large economy*, Princeton University Press.
Malinvaud, E. (1956), 'L'agrégation dans les modèles économiques', *Cahiers du Séminaire d'Econométrie* – C.N.R.S., Paris.
Mouillart, M. (1983), 'Endettement des ménages et rationnement du crédit', Université de Paris X Nanterre (mimeo).
Neary, J.P. and K.W.S. Roberts (1980), 'The theory of household behaviour under rationing', *European Economic Review*, pp. 25-42.
Parly, J.M. and D. Blondel (1980), 'De la pertinence de la notion de 'report de déséquilibre' pour l'intégration des variables monétaires et financières' in: P.Y. Hénin (ed.), *Etudes sur l'économie en déséquilibre*, Economica, Paris.
Sneessens, H. (1979), 'On the econometrics of quantity rationing models', *Princeton University Research Memorandum*, No 250.
Tessier, R. (1981), 'Principes de modélisation du comportement financier des ménages', *B.R.M. Ministère de l'Economie et des Finances* (mimeo), Paris.
Theil, H. (1980), *The system-wide approach to microeconomics*, University of Chicago Press, Chicago.

PART II
QUANTITATIVE ANALYSIS

CHAPTER 6

SEMI-REDUCED FORMS OF ECONOMETRIC MODELS

A.A. Keller
University of Paris II and Groupe d'Analyse Macroéconomique Appliquée – CNRS, France

1. SEMI-REDUCED FORMS

The semi-reduced form of a model can be achieved at an intermediate step of its resolution, the structural form of the model being the direct implicit expression of the behaviour and mechanisms of the markets while the reduced and final forms of that model are the translation of its explicit representation as a function of factors determined outside the model or outside the current period. This calculation process which is stopped at some intermediate step of the resolution corresponds to an equivalent operation in the associated graph in which some auxiliary points (variables) or vertices of circuits are deleted.

The reduction process can be justified by the need to clarify the model presentation without disturbing its construction unlike certain aggregation empirical procedures which, on the contrary, are proceeding by eliminating auxiliary variables (those which make the reading of the results easier) or sectoral variables with a weak explanatory content (detailed income distribution and inter-industrial relations) or those with a weak functional contribution (as regards dynamics and economic explanation). With this approach we can carry on the analysis at such levels of complexity where it is totally under our control by means, for example, of a reduction into sub-equilibria or real general equilibria (supply–demand) or into some real monetary equilibria (IS–LM).

The interest of this semi-reduced form goes beyond the ease of reading and of theoretical control, and stems in particular from the fact that the parameterised supply and demand curves can be obtained from it. The structural values of these equations, while changing, immediately determine the position of a new ex post equilibrium (or solution) and facilitate the understanding of the analysis considerably [1]. This analysis includes setting up resolution structures in terms of feedback effects variables and of consistency variables with respect to the static simulation studies as well as revealing the model's properties via the derivation of final equations. From a more general point of view, we consider that it is possible to be interested in and even to concentrate on the inter-action of certain variables in particular.

The examples we describe hereafter are mainly simple ones (linear cases), but their complexity is gradually increased by taking into account other equilibria (financial) and extending the survey to the dynamics (lagged variables). The linear case (or linearised case) makes it possible, in particular, to implement successive deletion procedures of variables: partitioning scheme of the Gauss method, (pivot operation).

2. INCOMPLETE RESOLUTION TECHNIQUES

The technical control and exact evaluation of the results derived from a detailed model require that its fundamental properties be brought out and preferably on the basis of an associated small-scale model that we try and build as strictly similar to the full size model as can be.

We are particularly interested in the procedures of automatic building of small-scale models based on a succession of equilibria (subequilibria) by successive deletion of variables such as the search for resolution structures or of semi-reduced forms for which we are presenting, on the other hand, a translation in terms of the associated graph [2].

The use of solving structures [3] leads to modifying the model by partially solving it through fixing the initial values of feedback variables chosen from among the endogenous variables; the construction of semi-reduced forms produces the same kind of process without involving the search for feedback variables.

(i) Solving structures

Let the IS-LM model be [4]:

Equations

$$
\begin{aligned}
&\text{E1.} \quad Y = C + I + \bar{G} + \bar{X} - M \\
&\text{E2.} \quad C = b_1(Y-T) + b_0 \\
&\text{E3.} \quad I = b_3 r + b_2 Y \\
&\text{E4.} \quad T = b_5 Y + b_4 \\
&\text{E5.} \quad M = b_7 Y + b_6 \\
&\text{E6.} \quad r = b_9 Y + b_8 \bar{M}_0
\end{aligned} \qquad \text{(I)}
$$

Variables (nominal values)

endogenous	exogenous –barred–
Y : Money income	$\bar{G}$: Government expenditure
C : Consumption	$\bar{X}$: Exports
I : Investment	$\bar{M}_0$: Supply of money
T : Nominal tax receipts	
M : Imports	
r : Interest rate	

The E6 equation represents the first simplification step as the reduced expression of the equilibrium in the money market (2.3) between supply (2.2) and money demand (2.1) described by (II)

$$L^{(1)} = \frac{1}{b_8} r - \frac{b_9}{b_8} Y \quad (2.1)$$

$$L^{(2)} = \bar{M}_0 \quad (2.2) \qquad \text{(II)}$$

$$L^{(1)} = L^{(2)} \quad (2.3)$$

interest rate r works as a feedback variable, and L (demand of money) as a consistency variable. The procedure can also be applied to system (I) in which two partitionings can be obtained according to the choice of the feedback and consistency variables.

<u>decomposition A</u>

feedback : $Y \equiv Y^*$

consistency : C

$$\begin{aligned}
&\text{E1.} \quad C^{(1)} = Y - I - \bar{G} - \bar{X} + M \\
&\text{E2.} \quad C^{(2)} = b_1(Y^* - T) + b_0 \\
&\text{E3.} \quad I = b_3 r + b_2 Y^* \\
&\text{E4.} \quad T = b_5 Y^* + b_4 \\
&\text{E5.} \quad M = b_7 Y^* + b_6 \\
&\text{E6.} \quad r = b_9 Y^* + b_8 \bar{M}_0
\end{aligned} \qquad \text{(IA)}$$

<u>decomposition B</u>

feedback : $Y \equiv Y^*$

consistency : r

$$\begin{aligned}
&\text{E1.} \quad I = Y^* - C - \bar{G} - \bar{X} + M \\
&\text{E2.} \quad C = b_1(Y^* - T) + b_0 \\
&\text{E3.} \quad r^{(1)} = \frac{1}{b_3} I - \frac{b_2}{b_3} Y^* \\
&\text{E4.} \quad T = b_5 Y^* + b_4 \\
&\text{E5.} \quad M = b_7 Y^* + b_6 \\
&\text{E6.} \quad r^{(2)} = b_9 Y^* + b_8 \bar{M}_0
\end{aligned} \qquad \text{(IB)}$$

(a) The decomposition A produces the supply-demand scheme of which the complete literal expression is:

$$C^{(1)} = b_1(1-b_5)Y^* + b_0 - b_1 b_4 \quad (2.4)$$

$$C^{(2)} = (1-b_2+b_7-b_3b_9)Y^* - (\bar{G}+\bar{X}) - b_3 b_8 \bar{M}_0 + b_6 \quad (2.5)$$

(IIA)

From the results of his computation for the French economy (see Lafay (1972)) w show that the model has one solution since:

from (2.4)	from (2.5)
$b_1(1-b_5) = 0.652 > 0$	$1 - b_2 + b_7 - b_3 b_9 = 1.312 > 0$
and	; and
$b_0 - b_1 b_4 = 11.157 > 0$	$-(\bar{G}+\bar{X}) - b_3 b_8 \bar{M}_0 + b_6 = -262.0955 < 0$ in 1968

(b) The decomposition B ensures that the equilibrium condition is satisfied between the interest rate r and the money income Y on the product market ($I \equiv S$) and the supply of money, without any liquid assets trap and without 'money illusion', with the following full literal expression:

$$r^{(1)} = \frac{1}{b_3}(1-b_1-b_2+b_7+b_1b_5)Y^* - \frac{1}{b_3}(\bar{G}+\bar{X}) - \frac{1}{b_3}(b_0-b_6-b_1b_4) \quad (2.6)$$

(IIB)

$$r^{(2)} = b_9 Y^* + b_8 \bar{M}_0 \quad (2.7)$$

The numerical value of the structural parameters determines the sign of these two equations (curve slopes of opposite signs) and allows testing their correct reading:

from (2.6)	from (2.7)
$\frac{1}{b_3}(1-b_1-b_2+b_7+b_1b_5) = -0.2030 < 0$	$b_9 = 0.1940 > 0$
and	; and
$-\frac{1}{b_3}(\bar{G}+\bar{X}) - \frac{1}{b_3}(b_0-b_6-b_1b_4) = 119.7452 > 0$ for 1968	$b_8\bar{M}_0 = 98.3477 > 0$ for 1968

The two different expressions for C (consistency variable of IIA) are numerically equal at the equilibrium position, considering the values of the exogenous variables[5].

(ii) Semi-reduced forms

The model I can be described by a (boolean)[6] incident matrix and its associated graph in order to simplify the study of the interdependencies between the endogenous variables of the model:

M =

	E1	E2	E3	E4	E5	E6
	Y	C	I	T	M	r
Y	0	1	1	1	1	1
C	1	0	0	0	0	0
I	1	0	0	0	0	0
T	0	1	0	0	0	0
r	0	0	1	0	0	0

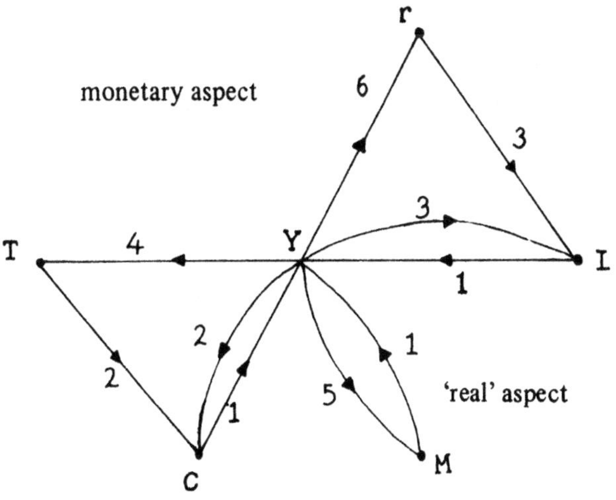

Figure 1. (Arcs numbering corresponds to that of the equations)

The associated graph shows the causal relations without any interference from the form of the equations nor from the relative importance so far. There are readings in the equations system that correspond to the properties of and operations on the graphs. (Keller and Valensi (1973) and Keller (1976)):

(a) Each strongly connected component of the graph is the illustration of a submodel. The example shown above has only one submodel since every vertex can be reached from any point. Corresponding to a decomposition of the graph into strongly connected components, there is an equivalent decomposition of the system of equations since every equation belongs to one and only one component.

(b) The graph does not contain any loop (property of the digraphs), since no simultaneous self-explanation process can be assumed in an explanatory model in which an indexed variable can only be found in one single element of an explanatory relation of the econometric or accounting type.

(c) The circuits are performing a special part, quite easy to describe. To the circuit (Y, T, C, Y) defined by the vertices, is associated a system of three equations, derived from (I) and explaining the variables associated to the vertices:

$$\begin{aligned} &\text{E1.} \quad Y = C + I + \overline{G} + \overline{X} - M \\ &\text{E2.} \quad C = b_1(Y-T) + b_0 \\ &\text{E4.} \quad T = b_5Y + b_4 \end{aligned} \qquad \text{(III)}$$

If this system is solvable, then it is possible to calculate the values of Y, C, T depending on the other variables considered as parameters. For this system to be solvable, there is a necessary and sufficient condition which is that the equations should be independent, hence that their Wronskian, being computed in relation to the variables we would like to be deleted, be different from zero. In this example, we postulate that:

$$\begin{aligned} &E1 \equiv Y - C - I - \overline{G} - \overline{X} + M = 0 \\ &E2 \equiv C - b_1Y + b_1T - b_0 = 0 \\ &E4 \equiv T - b_5Y - b_4 = 0 \end{aligned} \qquad \text{(III)}$$

We have to test the system to make sure the determinant $Det(W_1)$ is different from zero:

$$Det(W_1) = \left(\frac{\partial E_i}{\partial Y}\,;\ \frac{\partial E_i}{\partial C}\,;\ \frac{\partial E_i}{\partial T}\right)_{i=1,2,4} = \begin{bmatrix} 1 & -1 & 0 \\ -b_1 & 1 & b_1 \\ -b_5 & 0 & 1 \end{bmatrix} \qquad (2.8)$$

$$\text{thus} \quad Det(W_1) = 1 - b_1(1-b_5) \neq 0 \quad \text{hence} \quad b_1 \neq \frac{1}{1-b_5} \qquad (2.9)$$

If $Det(W_1)$ was equal to zero, it would imply that one equation at least could be described by a linear combination of equations of the model. The estimates given by Lafay (1972) imply that $Det(W_1) = 0.347$ can be assumed. The derived solutions will be such that:

$$Y = f_1(I, M, r, \lambda)$$
$$C = f_2(I, M, r, \lambda) \qquad \text{(IV)}$$
$$T = f_3(I, M, r, \lambda)$$

The variables of the circuit are specified by the remaining variables I, r and by λ which is an auxiliary variable characterising the integer valued circuit 1, 2, . . . m where m is the number of distinct solutions to the system. Thus, after having deleted C and T, Y appears to be a first degree solution to the equation:

$$(1 - b_1 + b_1b_5)Y + [b_1b_4 - b_0 - I - (\bar{G}+\bar{X}) + M] = 0 \qquad (2.10)$$

This solution corresponds to the numerical value 1 for λ. In the same way, we could be interested in the circuit (Y, r, I, Y) corresponding to the equation system (V) hereafter:

$$\text{E1.}\quad Y = C + I + \bar{G} + \bar{X} - M$$
$$\text{E3.}\quad I = b_3r + b_2Y \qquad \text{(V)}$$
$$\text{E6.}\quad r = b_9Y + b_8\bar{M}_0$$

The Wronskian $\text{Det}(W_2)$ calculated in relation to the variables to be deleted must be nonzero: let

$$\text{Det}(W_2) = b_9 - b_2 \neq 0 \quad \text{or} \quad b_9 \neq b_2 \qquad (2.11)$$

The Lafay implementation gives $\text{Det}(W_2) = 1.855$.

(d) Auxiliary relations can be deleted with a view to reduce the graph to a simpler expression, in particular in the case of graphs reduced to a quotient set while keeping the longer causality paths (Keller and Valensi (1973)).

The deletion of some arcs assumed to be auxiliary ones may also correspond to discretely selected substitutions of variables. Thus system (III) can be reduced to (IV) by deleting the explicit effect of T, for example let:

$$Y = C + I + \bar{G} + \bar{X} - M \qquad \text{(VI)}$$
$$C = (b_1 - b_1b_5)Y + b_0 - b_1b_4$$

Let us keep in mind as an inference that the deletion of some definite circuits can be made by means of the classical process of the electric networks where every circuit is replaced by a star as a substitute whose vertex figures the auxiliary variable λ and whose edges are associated to the variables of the circuit. The two above mentioned systems (IIA) and (IIB) in particular can be derived from the previous diagnosis procedures and lead to two kinds of economic explanations, the one representing the real equilibrium supply–demand (IIA) and the other (IIB) the IS–LM real-monetary equilibrium on the two markets. In fact, since all the endogenous variables are elements of the same and single strongly connected component, the variables Y and C on the one hand, and Y and r on the other are elements of the same circuit and all the other variables can disappear by successive deleting operations.

3. CONSTRUCTION OF SEMI-REDUCED FORMS

(i) Variables deleting method

The Gaussian solving method by successive variables deletion offers the advantage of being easily translated into an automatic procedure from a matrix form which is parameterised or numerically specified of the equations system of the model [7]. A recursive formula is used to express the semi-reduced form coefficients of a step p as a function of the semi-reduced form coefficients of the preceding step p–1. Let the system $A \cdot Y = 0$ contain four equations described below by a single matrix A. $A^{(1)}$ represents A in its initial state:

$$A = \begin{bmatrix} a_{11}^{(1)} & a_{12}^{(1)} & a_{13}^{(1)} & a_{14}^{(1)} \\ a_{21}^{(1)} & a_{22}^{(1)} & a_{23}^{(1)} & a_{24}^{(1)} \\ a_{31}^{(1)} & a_{32}^{(1)} & a_{33}^{(1)} & a_{34}^{(1)} \\ a_{41}^{(1)} & a_{42}^{(1)} & a_{43}^{(1)} & a_{44}^{(1)} \end{bmatrix} \quad ; \quad Y = \begin{bmatrix} Y_1 \\ Y_2 \\ Y_3 \\ Y_4 \end{bmatrix}$$

Deletion of the variable Y_1 is obtained by means of linear combinations of the rows of A. The division of the coefficients of the first row by a_{11} gives the new row.

$$A_1^{(1)} = \left[\begin{array}{cccc} 1 & a_{12}^{(2)} & a_{13}^{(2)} & a_{14}^{(2)} \\ \hline a_{21}^{(1)} & a_{22}^{(1)} & a_{23}^{(1)} & a_{24}^{(1)} \\ a_{31}^{(1)} & a_{32}^{(1)} & a_{33}^{(1)} & a_{34}^{(1)} \\ a_{41}^{(1)} & a_{42}^{(1)} & a_{43}^{(1)} & a_{44}^{(1)} \end{array}\right] \quad \text{where } a_{1j}^{(2)} = \frac{a_{1j}^{(1)}}{a_{11}^{(1)}} \text{ for } j>1 \tag{3.1}$$

Thereafter, we just have to subtract from $A_1^{(1)}$ the product of its first row by a_{21}, of its third row by a_{31}, and so on. The result is as follows:

$$A^{(2)} = \begin{bmatrix} - & - & - & - \\ - & a_{22}^{(2)} & a_{23}^{(2)} & a_{24}^{(2)} \\ - & a_{32}^{(2)} & a_{33}^{(2)} & a_{34}^{(2)} \\ - & a_{42}^{(2)} & a_{43}^{(2)} & a_{44}^{(2)} \end{bmatrix}$$

therefore

$$a_{ij}^{(2)} = a_{ij}^{(2)} - \frac{a_{i1}^{(1)} \cdot a_{1j}^{(1)}}{a_{11}^{(1)}} \; ; \; (i, j \geqslant 2) \tag{3.2}$$

The same procedure is used to calculate $A^{(3)}$, every coefficient of the semi-reduced for $A^{(p)}$ at step p $(p \leqslant 4)$ is expressed in function of the coefficients of the previous step according to the recurrent formula (3.2):

$$a_{jp}^{(p)} = a_{ij}^{(p-1)} - \frac{a_{i\,p-1}^{(p-1)} \cdot a_{p-1\,j}^{(p-1)}}{a_{p-1\,p-1}^{(p-1)}} \; ; \; (i, j \geqslant p) \tag{3.3}$$ [8]

$$A^{(3)} = \begin{bmatrix} - & - & - & - \\ - & - & - & - \\ - & - & a_{33}^{(3)} & a_{34}^{(3)} \\ - & - & a_{43}^{(3)} & a_{44}^{(3)} \end{bmatrix}$$

On the other hand, we ensure that each coefficient of the reduced form thus derived is expressed in function of the initial structural coefficients, say for $a_{43}^{(3)}$:

$$a_{43}^{(3)} = a_{43}^{(1)} - \frac{a_{41}^{(1)} \cdot a_{13}^{(1)}}{a_{11}^{(1)}} - \frac{\left[a_{42}^{(1)} - \frac{a_{41}^{(1)}\, a_{12}^{(1)}}{a_{11}^{(1)}}\right]\left[a_{23}^{(1)} - \frac{a_{21}^{(1)} \cdot a_{13}^{(1)}}{a_{11}^{(1)}}\right]}{\left[a_{22}^{(1)} - \frac{a_{21}^{(1)} \cdot a_{12}^{(1)}}{a_{22}^{(1)}}\right]} \qquad (3.4)$$

We note that this procedure can be stopped at any moment of the complete numerical solution process as soon as the real value of each unknown variable is obtained. In the example given above the procedure has been stopped at stage 3.

(ii) Programming the computations

The implementation of this deleting procedure of variables involves, however, a presentation of the equations such that the associated variables we want to delete are placed at the beginning of the index list as in the following example where the structural matrices are partitioned as follows:

$$\begin{array}{c} \\ 1\\4\\5\\ \\2\\3 \end{array}
\overset{\begin{array}{ccccc}1&4&5&2&3\end{array}}{\begin{bmatrix} B_{11} & B_{12} \\ B_{21} & B_{22} \end{bmatrix}}
\cdot
\begin{bmatrix} Y_1 \\ Y_2 \end{bmatrix}
\begin{array}{c} 1\\4\\5\\ \\2\\3 \end{array}
+
\overset{\begin{array}{cccccc}6&7&8&9&10&11\end{array}}{\begin{bmatrix} C_1 \\ C_2 \end{bmatrix}}
\begin{bmatrix} Z \end{bmatrix}
\begin{array}{c} 6\\7\\8\\9\\ \\10\\11\\ \\11 \end{array}
=
\begin{bmatrix} 0 \\ 0 \end{bmatrix}$$

These partitioned matrices are derived from B and C of the initial model $BY + CZ = 0$ where Z collects the set of exogenous predetermined variables as well as the lagged endogenous variables: we operate the permutation of the rows and columns whose numbering corresponds to that of the variables to be deleted such as (1, 4, 5). The numbering of all the variables makes it possible to calculate the semi-reduced form for the whole model, predetermined variables included. All we have to do is to construct a new matrix D by a concatenation procedure of B and C, i.e. $D = (B \mid C)$ as we will do in the applications below.

D =

	1 4 5	2 3	6 7 8 9 10 11
1 4 5	B_{11}	B_{12}	C_1
2 3	B_{21}	B_{22}	C_2

The present version of the programme [9] is therefore limited to simple operations: rewriting of a matrix by rows and columns permutation once the user has specified which variables were to be deleted; implementation of a simple algorithm for the deletion of the variables. The results are described in terms of the initial matrix, the interchanged matrix and the solution matrix which leads to the selected semi-reduced form.

4. THE USEFULNESS OF SEMI-REDUCED FORMS IN APPLICATIONS

We investigate the usefulness of the semi-reduced form by means of simple examples[10] of econometric models illustrated by Lafay (1972). The author considers four descriptions of the French economy during the years 1950–1968: two static indecomposable models, the simple keynesian model and the IS–LM model of Hicks as well as two recursive models, the oscillation model of Samuelson and the oscillation model with the integration of monetary aspects by Lovell and Prescott.

(i) Economic interpretation: global equilibrium and equilibrium value

The keynesian model is described by the following equations and variables:

Equations

E1. $Y = C + \bar{I} + \bar{G} + \bar{X} - M$

E2. $C = b_1(Y-T) + b_0$ (VII)

E3. $T = b_3Y + b_2$

E4. $M = b_5Y + b_4$

Variables*: endogenous (index):		exogenous –barred–	(index)
Y : income	... (Y1)	$\bar{I} + \bar{G} + \bar{X}$: autonomous expenses (investment, public expenses and exports)	... (Y5)
C : consumption	... (Y2)		
T : taxes	... (Y3)		
M : imports	... (Y4)	1 : constant	... (Y6)

* at constant price

The matrix D of DY = 0 where the endogenous and predetermined variables are collected in Y is:

Initial structural matrix

D_0:

	Y1	Y2	Y3	Y4	Y5	Y6
Y1	1.	– 1.	0.	1.	– 1.	0.
Y2	– 0.774	1.	0.774	0.	0.	– 19.683
Y3	– 0.175	0.	1.	0.	0.	– 4.438
Y4	0.199	0.	0.	1.	0.	16.554

In order to reduce the model to Y1 (supply) and to Y2 (demand) we have to operate a permutation of the columns corresponding to the endogenous variables for the variables Y3 and Y4 to be deleted at the beginning of the list. Thus:

Interchanged structural matrix

D_1:

	Y3	Y4	Y1	Y2	Y5	Y6
Y3	1.	0.	– 0.175	0.	0.	– 4.438
Y4	0.	1.	0.199	0.	0.	16.554
Y1	0.	1.	1.	– 1.	– 1.	0.
Y2	0.774	0.	– 0.774	1.	0.	– 19.683

The obtained semi-reduced form

$$D_2: \quad \begin{array}{c} \\ Y3 \\ Y4 \\ \dot{Y}1 \\ Y2 \end{array} \begin{array}{cccc|cc} Y3 & Y4 & Y1 & Y2 & Y5 & Y6 \\ - & - & - & - & - & - \\ - & - & - & - & - & - \\ - & - & 0.801 & -1. & -1. & -16.554 \\ - & - & -0.639 & 1. & 0. & -16.248 \end{array}$$

D_2 allows writing the two expressions of C since:

$$\begin{aligned} 0.801\ Y - C - (\bar{I} + \bar{G} + \bar{X}) - 16.554 &= 0 \\ -0.639\ Y + C \qquad\qquad\qquad - 16.248 &= 0 \end{aligned} \tag{VIII}$$

From the data given by Lafay (1972), $\bar{I} + \bar{G} + \bar{X}$ is therefore equal in 1968 to 199.746:

$$\begin{aligned} C^{(1)} &= 0.801\ Y - 216.3 \\ C^{(2)} &= 0.639\ Y + 16.248 \end{aligned} \tag{IX}$$

$C^{(1)}$ is representative of a total supply function, $C^{(2)}$ of a total demand function. This schematical description shows how the macroeconomic equilibrium is achieved. It can easily be proved that the model has one solution, since:

$$\det \begin{bmatrix} 1 & -0.801 \\ 1 & -0.639 \end{bmatrix} = 0.162 \tag{4.1}$$

Finding the equilibrium $C^{(1)} \equiv C^{(2)}$ is equivalent to operating the transfer to the ultimate reduced form expressed in Y, i.e.:

$$0.162\ Y^* - (\bar{I} + \bar{G} + \bar{X}) - 32.802 = 0 \tag{4.2}$$

This equation shows how slowly the procedure converges to the equilibrium.

(ii) Root-trees and calculation of determinants

The Hicks IS–LM model is described by (I) and specified by a list of variables and a matrix D_2 containing the set of structural coefficients:

Variables*: endogenous		(index)	: exogenous	(index)
Y : income	...	(Y1)	$\bar{G} + \bar{X}$: autonomous expenditures (public expenditure and exports)	... (Y7)
C : consumption	...	(Y2)	$\bar{M}_0$: money supply	... (Y8)
I : investment	...	(Y3)	1 : constant	... (Y9)
T : taxes	...	(Y4)		
M : imports	...	(Y5)		
r : interest rate	...	(Y6)		

* at current price

(a) The model can be reduced to two equations expressed in Y and C.

Initial structural matrix

	Y1	Y2	Y3	Y4	Y5	Y6	Y7	Y8	Y9
Y1	1.	– 1.	– 1.	0.	1.	0.	– 1.	0.	0.
Y2	– 0.798	1.	0.	0.798	0.	0.	0.	0.	–12.491
Y3	– 0.159	0.	1.	0.	0.	0.661	0.	0.	0.
Y4	– 0.182	0.	0.	1.	0.	0.	0.	0.	– 1.672
Y5	– 0.149	0.	0.	0.	1.	0.	0.	0.	– 1.840
Y6	– 0.194	0.	0.	0.	0.	1.	0.	0.489	0.

Semi-reduced form

	Y1	Y2	Y7	Y8	Y9
Y1	1.118	– 1.	– 1.	– 0.323	1.840
Y2	– 0.653	1.	0.	0.	–11.157

Two different expressions can be derived for C, as follows:

$$C^{(1)} = 1.118\ Y - (\bar{G}+\bar{X}) - 0.323\ \bar{M}_0 + 1.840 \qquad \text{(X)}$$
$$C^{(2)} = 0.653\ Y + 11.157$$

(b) The semi-reduction process of the model may also operate with Y and r and it provides the following representation of the IS–LM equilibrium:

	Y1	Y6	Y7	Y8	Y9
Y1	0.337	0.661	–1.	0.	– 9.317
Y6	– 0.194	1.	0.	0.489	0.

where

$$0.337\,Y + 0.661\,r - (\bar{G}+\bar{X}) - 9.317 = 0 \qquad \text{(XI)}$$
$$-\,0.194\,Y + r + 0.489\,\bar{M}_0 = 0$$

From (XI) two expressions of r can be derived, namely:

$$r^{(1)} = -\,0.510\,Y + 1.513\,(\bar{G}+\bar{X}) + 14.098 \qquad \text{(XII)}$$
$$r^{(2)} = 0.194\,Y - 0.489\,\bar{M}_0$$

(c) We reach the equilibrium value by reducing the model to one variable Y, thus:

$$0.465\,Y - (\bar{G}+\bar{X}) - 0.323\,\bar{M}_0 - 9.317 = 0$$

(d) We prove that the results obtained here in sections (a) and (b) can be read as a definite rooted-tree[11], with C as its root for (a) and r as the root for (b).

In order to determine how many partial graphs a graph considered G contains, these partial graphs being rooted-trees, we define:

$$B = (b_{ij})_{i,j=1,n} \qquad \text{with} \qquad b_{ij} = m_G^{+}(x_i, x_j) \qquad (4.3)$$

as the number of arcs of G from x_i to x_j and the diagonal matrix $D = (d_{ij})$ with:

$$d_{ij} \begin{cases} = 0 & \text{if } i \neq j \\ = m_G^{+}(X - \{x_i\}, x_i) & \text{if } i = j \end{cases} \qquad (4.4)$$

The matrix D−B is:

$$\begin{bmatrix} \sum_{i\neq 1} b_{i1} & -b_{12} & \cdots & -b_{1n} \\ -b_{21} & \sum_{i\neq 2} b_{i2} & \cdots & -b_{2n} \\ -b_{31} & -b_{32} & \cdots & -b_{3n} \\ -b_{n1} & -b_{n2} & \cdots & \sum_{i\neq n} b_{in} \end{bmatrix}$$

THEOREM (Bott, Mayberry, 1954 [12]): Let G = (X, U) be the graph of the associated matrix b_{ij} and $x_1 \in Y$; the number of rooted-trees with x_1 as a root which are partial graphs of G is equal to the determinant:

$$\Delta_1 = \begin{vmatrix} \sum_{i\neq 2} b_{i2} & -b_{23} & \cdots & -b_{2n} \\ -b_{32} & \sum_{i\neq 3} b_{i3} & \cdots & -b_{3n} \\ \hline -b_{n2} & -b_{n3} & \cdots & \sum_{i\neq 2} b_{in} \end{vmatrix} \qquad (4.5)$$

When C is taken as a root, the number of rooted-trees is given by the determinant:

$$\Delta_1 = \begin{vmatrix} 3. & -1. & -1. & -1. & -1. \\ -1. & 2. & 0. & 0. & 0. \\ 0. & 0. & 1. & 0. & 0. \\ -1. & 0. & 0. & 1. & 0. \\ 0. & -1. & 0. & 0. & 1. \end{vmatrix} = \begin{vmatrix} 1. & 0. & 0. & 0. & 0. \\ 0. & 2. & -1. & 0. & 0. \\ -1. & -1. & 3. & -1. & -1. \\ 0. & 0. & -1. & 1. & 0. \\ 0. & -1. & 0. & 0. & 1. \end{vmatrix} \qquad (2.22)$$

$$\Delta_1 = 1 \cdot \begin{vmatrix} 2. & -1. & 0. & 0. \\ -1. & 3. & -1. & -1. \\ 0. & -1. & 1. & 0. \\ -1. & 0. & 0. & 1. \end{vmatrix} \qquad (2.23)$$

We prove that in the general case of a matrix B of size n, we can compute this determinant by means of the same computation process as the one used to build the semi-reduced forms described in formula (3.3):

$$b_{ij}^{(p)} = b_{ij}^{(p-1)} \cdot \frac{b_{i1}^{(p-1)}\, b_{1j}^{(p-1)}}{b_{p-1\,p-1}^{(p-1)}}$$

We obtain $\Delta_n = b_{11}^{(1)}\, b_{22}^{(2)} \cdots b_{nn}^{(n)}$ for all the semi-reduced forms as the product of the associated factors.

For this application:

$\Delta_1 = 2 \times 2.5 \times 0.6 \times 0.668 = 2$ (integer)[13]

The two rooted-trees with C as a root are:

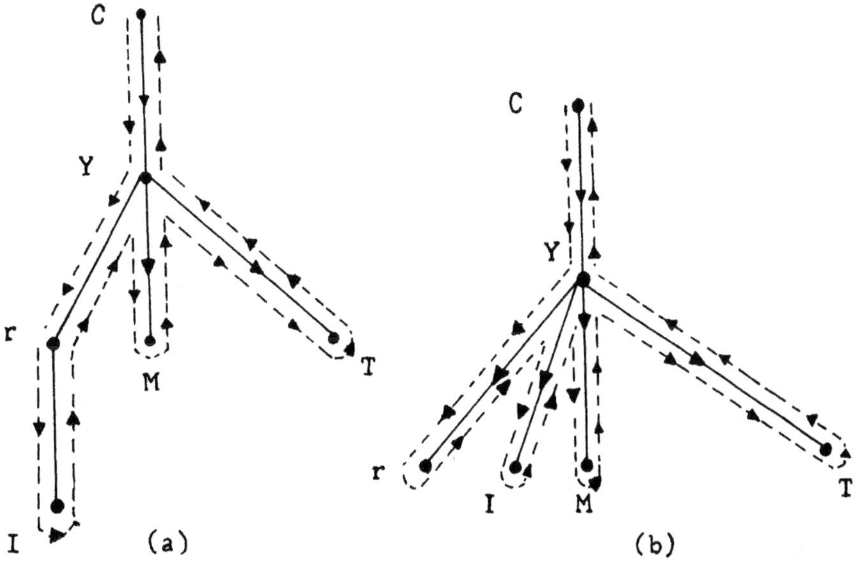

Figure 2.

The directed contour line indicates the ordering according to which the computations can be carried out.

$$\Delta_1 = \begin{vmatrix} 3. & -1. & -1 & -1 & -1 \\ -1. & 2. & 0. & 0. & 0. \\ -1. & 0. & 2. & 0. & 0. \\ 0. & -1. & 0. & 1. & 0. \\ -1. & 0. & 0. & 0. & 1. \end{vmatrix} = 2 \text{ (integer)} \qquad (4.8)$$

Therefore, the graph can have two rooted trees with r as their root:

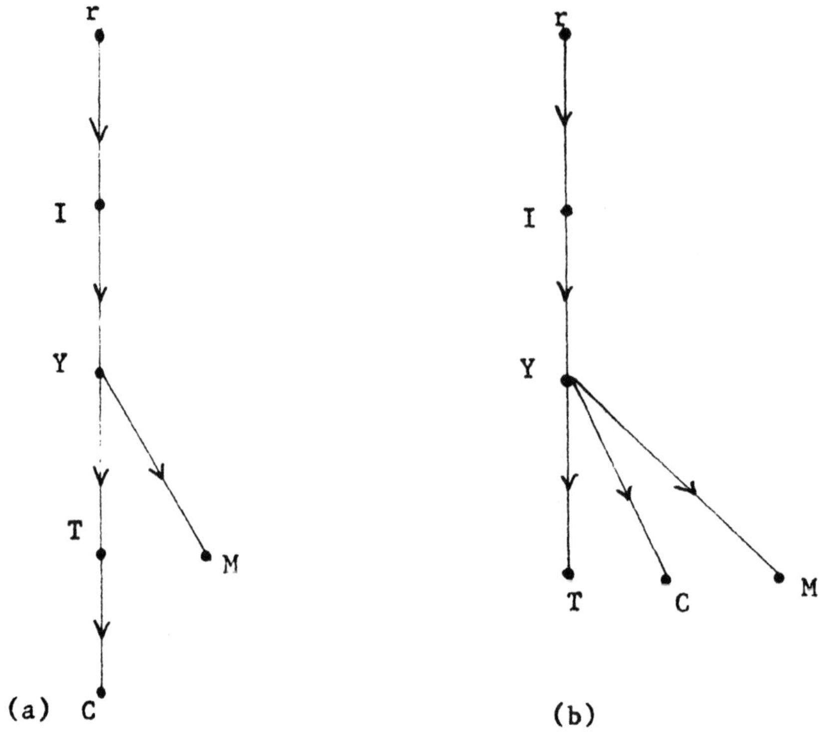

Figure 3.

(iii) Calculation procedure of final forms

The Samuelson oscillator is represented by the following equations and variables:

Equations

$$
\begin{aligned}
Y &= C + I + \bar{G} + \bar{X} - M \\
C &= b_1(Y-T)<-1> + b_0 \\
I &= b_4 Y <-1> + b_3 Y <-2> + b_2 \qquad\qquad \text{(XIII)} \\
T &= b_6 Y + b_5 \\
M &= b_8 Y + b_7
\end{aligned}
$$

$<i>$ specifies a lag of i periods

Variables*: endogenous		(index)	: lagged endogenous	(index)
Y : income	...	(Y1)	$Y\langle -1 \rangle$	... (Y6)
C : consumption	...	(Y2)	$Y\langle -2 \rangle$	... (Y7)
I : investment	...	(Y3)	$T\langle -1 \rangle$	... (Y8)
T : taxes	...	(Y4)	: exogenous	
M : imports	...	(Y5)	$\overline{G} + \overline{X}$: autonomous expenditures	(Y9)
			1 : constant	(Y10)

* at current price

The structural matrix is:

	Y1	Y2	Y3	Y4	Y5	Y6	Y7	Y8	Y9	Y10
Y1	1.	–1.	–1.	0.	1.	0.	0.	0.	–1	0.
Y2	0.	1.	0.	0.	0.	–0.813	0.	0.813	0.	–20.207
Y3	0.	0.	1.	0.	0.	–0.530	0.319	0.	0.	29.721
Y4	–0.178	0.	0.	1.	0.	0.	0.	0.	0.	– 3.155
Y5	–0.204	0.	0.	0.	1.	0.	0.	0.	0.	18.224

The equations of the general dynamic equilibrium are derived from the semi-reduced form expressed in Y and C, namely:

	Y2	Y1	Y6	Y7	Y8	Y9	Y10
Y2	1.204	–1.	–0.530	0.319	0.	–1.	11.497
Y1	0.	1.	–0.813	0.	0.813	0.	–20.207

Assume the following recurrent system:

$$-Y + 1.204C - 0.530\,Y\langle -1 \rangle + 0.319\,Y\langle -2 \rangle - (\overline{G} + \overline{X}) + 11.497 = 0 \qquad \text{(XIV)}$$

$$Y - 0.813\,Y\langle -1 \rangle + 0.813\,T\langle -1 \rangle - 20.207 = 0$$

Two straight lines can illustrate the properties of this model in the short term (without the lag effect): the first line represents total demand and shows a positive slope in the positive quadrant (C, Y) where C is the ordinate and Y the abscissa. The second line describes total supply as perpendicular to Y.

The final form of a model[14] is generally derived from its reduced form by eliminating the lagged values of all the endogenous variables (see Deleau and Malgrange (1978)) other than those explained by that equation. It is easily seen that the final form can be derived from a semi-reduction procedure of a dynamic model. The approach to compute the final form expressed in Y is therefore equivalent to the scanning of the semi-reduction process in Y. Let:

$$\begin{array}{c} \\ Y1 \end{array} \left[\begin{array}{c|ccccc} Y1 & Y6 & Y7 & Y8 & Y9 & Y10 \\ 1.204 & -1.343 & 0.319 & 0.813 & -1. & -8.710 \end{array}\right]$$

or

$$1.204Y - 1.343Y<-1> + 0.319Y<-2> + 0.813T<-1> - (\bar{G}+\bar{X}) - 8.710 = 0 \tag{4.9}$$

The endogenous term of the equation expressed in $T<-1>$ must be eliminated; since

$$T = 0.178\,Y + 3.155 \tag{4.10}$$

(4.9) becomes

$$1.204\,Y - 1.198\,Y<-1> + 0.319\,Y<-2> - (\bar{G}+\bar{X}) - 6.145 = 0$$

This recurrent equation whose order is two has a single characteristic such as, when postulating

$$L^{\theta}\,Y = <-\theta> \tag{4.11}$$

$$1.204 - 1.198\,L + 0.319\,L^2 = 0 \tag{4.12}$$

The discriminant of this equation is $\Delta = -0.101$. We deduce that the dynamics of Y is oscillatory weak $\Delta < 0$ and that the product of the roots is equal to $0.265 < 1$. The complex roots have the following modulus: $0.5143 < 1$.

(iv) Enlarged illustration

The integration of the monetary mechanism into Samuelso's model has been carried out by Lovell and Prescott[15]. The following example has been adapted from Lafay (1972).

Equations

$$\begin{aligned} Y &= C + I + \bar{G} + \bar{X} - M \\ C &= b_2(Y-T)<-1> + b_1\bar{M}_0<-1> + b_0 \\ I &= b_6Y<-1> + b_5Y<-2> + b_4r + b_3 \\ T &= b_8Y + b_7 \\ M &= b_{10}Y + b_9 \\ r &= b_{12}Y<-1> + b_{11}\bar{M}_0 \end{aligned} \tag{XV}$$

$<-i>$ represents a lag of i periods

Variables*: endogenous		(index)	: lagged endogenous		(index)
Y : income	...	(Y1)	Y<–1>	...	(Y7)
C : consumption	...	(Y2)	Y<–2>	...	(Y8)
I : investment	...	(Y3)	T<–1>	...	(Y9)
T : taxes	...	(Y4)			
M : imports	...	(Y5)	Exogenous		
r : interest rate	...	(Y6)	$\bar{M}_0$: money supply	...	(Y10)
			$\bar{M}_0$<–1>	...	(Y11)
			$\bar{G}+\bar{X}$: autonomous expenditures		(Y12)
			1 : constant	...	(Y13)

* at current price

The structural matrix is:

	Y1	Y2	Y3	Y4	Y5	Y6	Y7	Y8	Y9	Y10	Y11	Y12	Y13
Y1	1.	1.	1.	0.	1.	0.	0.	0.	0.	0.	0.	–1.	0.
Y2	0.	1.	0.	0.	0.	0.	–0.712	0.	0.712	0.	–0.307	0.	–19.611
Y3	0.	0.	1.	0.	0.	2.864	–0.315	0.163	0.	0.	0.	0.	– 4.539
Y4	–0.183	0.	0.	1.	0.	0.	0.	0.	0.	0.	0.	0.	– 1.360
Y5	–0.151	0.	0.	0.	1.	0.	0.	0.	0.	0.	0.	0.	– 1.039
Y6	0.	0.	0.	0.	0.	1.	–0.155	0.	0.	0.341	0.	0.	0.

The equations of the real dynamic equilibrium are computed from the semi-reduced form expressed in Y and C, as:

	Y1	Y2	Y7	Y8	Y9	Y10	Y11	Y12	Y13
Y1	1.151	1.	–0.129	–0.163	0.	0.977	0.	–1.	5.578
Y2	0.	1.	–0.712	0.	0.712	0.	–0.307	0.	–19.611

We derive (XVI):

$$1.151Y + C - 0.129Y\langle -1\rangle - 0.163Y\langle -2\rangle + 0.977\bar{M}_0 - (\bar{G}+\bar{X}) + 5.578 = 0$$

$$C - 0.712Y\langle -1\rangle + 0.712T\langle -1\rangle - 0.307\bar{M}_0\langle -1\rangle - 19.611 = 0 \qquad \text{(XVI)}$$

The equilibrium IS–LM on both the real and the monetary markets can be found by computing the semi-reduced form expressed in Y and r, such as:

	Y1	Y6	Y7	Y8	Y9	Y10	Y11	Y12	Y13
Y1	1.151	–2.864	1.207	–0.163	–0.712	0.	0.307	–1.	25.289
Y6	0.	1.	–0.155	0.	0.	0.341	0.	0.	0.

We derive (XVII):

$$1.151\,Y - 2.864\,r + 1.027\,Y<-1> - 0.163\,Y<-2> - 0.712\,T<-1>$$
$$+ 0.307\,\bar{M}_0<-1> - (\bar{G}+\bar{X}) + 25.189 = 0 \qquad \text{(XVII)}$$
$$r - 0.155\,Y<-1> + 0.341\,\bar{M}_0 = 0$$

We achieve the final form expressed in Y by continuing the semi-reduction process, hence:

	Y1	Y7	Y8	Y9	Y10	Y11	Y12	Y13
Y1	1.151	0.583	–0.163	–0.712	0.977	0.307	–1.	25.189

$$1.151\,Y + 0.583\,Y<-1> - 0.163\,Y<-2> - 0.712\,T<-1> + 0.977\,\bar{M}_0$$
$$+ 0.307\,\bar{M}_0<-1> - (\bar{G} + \bar{X}) + 25.189 = 0 \qquad (4.13)$$

For $T<-1>$ we substitute its structural expression, such as

$$T<-1> = 0.183\,Y<-1> + 1.360 \qquad (4.14)$$

We obtain:

$$1.151Y + 0.453\,Y<-1> - 0.163Y<-2> + 0.977\bar{M}_0 + 0.307\bar{M}_0<-1>$$
$$-(\bar{G}+\bar{X}) + 24.221 = 0 \qquad (4.15)$$

The characteristic equation is:

$$1.151 + 0.453\,L - 0.163\,L^2 = 0 \qquad (4.16)$$

giving $\Delta = -0.545$. The changing process of Y, as in the previous model, is oscillatory weak with $\Delta < 0$ and a product of the roots is $-0.142 < 1$. The complex roots give the following modulus: $0.3763 < 1$.

5. CONCLUSION

Generally, the importance of the semi-reduced forms, at an intermediate step of the model solving process, stems from the ease of implementation as well as from the possibility to discover the economic characteristics of the model. We have shown that their usefulness lies in the explanatory contribution and simplifications by means of reducing the system to a more controllable system such as a partial equilibrium on a given market or a general equilibrium of the IS–LM type: the discrete implementation of the parameters makes a synthetic reading of the economic mechanisms implicit in a model easier and the changing effects of the model can be probed through the play of the structural parameters contained in the semi-reduced form.

Four simple examples illustrate the relevance of the semi-reduction process presented here. Every model can be reduced to a total equilibrium, such as supply–demand, IS–LM. We can calculate the equilibrium value. We show the correspondencies with the operations carried out with the associated digraphs. In particular, certain ordering processes selected for the resolution are in fact just rooted-trees of a specific type determining the resolution sequence order[16]. The final form of the model, useful to investigate the dynamic properties of the model, can be derived from the ultimate semi-reduced forms (a single variable being left).

Finally, these exercises can be extended as we have shown, to the case of larger scale representations of models and non-linear ones (e.g. MINIMETRIC)[17]. It can be useful to reemphasise that every intermediate stage of the simplification process is, during the whole process, bound by the condition that the sub-systems considered be solvable (Wronskian non-zero value); this can be checked numerically, provided a certain kind of constraints is imposed on the parameters.

NOTES

This study, initiated by the author during his stay at DULBEA (Département d'Economie Appliquée) of Brussels University in 1980, with the collaboration of A. Dramais and R. Lommel of DULBEA, has further been developed as regards the definition of the project, the applications including the development of the first version of the computer program (FORTRAN) and the computation on C.D.C. computers.

For her contribution in the translation from French, I am also grateful to my wife, Claudine.

1) For example, Mazier (1978) reduces the system of equations he is analysing to two literal expanded equations translatable into a supply and demand relation the implementation of which with structural parameters provides in particular a complete explanation of the inflation mechanisms by means of the labour costs, profits, demand and credits.
2) The decomposability can be worked out by means of an optimisation scheme such as the one described by Fisher (1962) upon which some aggregation proedures are based: the aggregation of a model described by its final form is provided, at each level, by minimising a certain quadratic cost criterion which is

the variance of the endogenous variables (see W.D. Fisher (1962), 'Optimal Aggregation in Multi-Equation Prediction Models', *Econometrica,* Vol. 30, No 4, October, pp. 744-769 and (1966), 'Simplification of Economic Models', *Econometrica,* Vol. 34, No 3, July, pp. 563-584.

3) For a different approach to this question, see Keller (1970) and Deleau (1973), M. Deleau (1973), 'Une étude des méchanismes du modèle MINIFIFI', *Annales de l'INSEE,* No 12/13, pp. 159-213.
4) The pattern of this example was drawn from Lafay (1972). The feedback variables represent those used during an iterative process before computation: they correspond to a very significant behaviour; the technique using eigenvalues can help to reveal them. The consistency variables have values numerically equal, at the equilibrium position.
5) In this kind of representation, it is possible to operate an interesting distinction between the ex-ante effects upon the consistency variables and the ex-post effects upon the feedback variables (Deleau and Malgrange (1978)).
6) In order to standardise the equation system, we have to determine the 'left-hand' variables, e.g. consumption in the consumption function.
7) The representation is based on the assumption that two questions are solved beforehand: the standardisation of the equation system and the linearisation of the equations around a definite solution.
   - The standardisation can be understood as bi-partitioned graphs in which there is a maximum vertices matching where every associated vertex from the whole set of variables is the source of a single arc and in which every associated vertex from the whole set of equations is the sink of a single arc. (M. Gilli (1979), 'Etude et analyse des structures causales dans les modèles économiques', Université de Genève). The solution chosen here, which is not necessarily unique, corresponds to the one given by the model builder (see M. Boutillier (1982)).
   - The linearisation by tangential approximation or by simulations at a solution point or around a solution path leads us to achieve the matrix representation we were trying to find.
8) $a^{(p-1)}_{p-1\ p-1}$ specifies the pivot point of the change of basis; it is generally chosen as large as possible in modulus form in order to minimise the rounding off errors in solving linear equation systems, so that

   $a^{(p-1)}_{p-1\ p-1} = \mathrm{Max}_{i,j\ =\ p-1,-,n} \left| a^{p-1}_{ij} \right|$ according to the pivot operation

   (Gaussian method).
9) The present version of the fortran IBM compatible program is an amended version of the preceding program (improved inputs/outputs).
10) We have only changed the notations.
11) The rooted-tree is a tree whose orientation is such that every vertex, except one –the root– is found to be the end of a single arc.
12) R. Bott and J.P. Mayberry, Matrices and Trees, Economic Activity Analysis, John Wiley and Sons, New York, pp. 391-400.

13) The determinant is a measuring device of the spread of the rooted-tree from a pole over the structure (see Lantner (1974)). A FORTRAN-program is used to carry out these computations.
14) This expression was introduced by J. Tinbergen (1939), 'Statistical Testing of Business Cycle Theories, II; Business Cycles in the United States of America 1919-1932', Geneva.
15) M. Lovell and E. Prescott (1968), 'Money, Multiplier Accelerator Interaction and the Business Cycle', *Southern Economic Journal.*
16) The number of rooted-trees with a given root can be greater than shown in the examples developed here. We thus find a number of 42 partial rooted-trees with Y as their root (Y: income) in the MINIMETRIC model with 21 equations against 4 rooted-trees in the second model presented with monetary integration.
17) Numerous examples about model analysis can be found in the literature. I. and F.L. Adelman, in their survey of the Klein-Goldberger model dynamics, reduced the 22 equations model to a 4 equations one by algebraic substitutions (Adelman I. and F.L. (1959), 'The Dynamic Properties of the Klein-Goldberger Model', *Econometrica,* Vol. 27, No 4, p. 600). The usual calculation procedure makes the solving procedure of linear equation systems shorter by calculating the inverse matrices, since the computation time is a proportion of the matrix rank to the third power.

REFERENCES

Boutillier, M. (1982), '*Lecture des Modèles Macroéconomiques, recherche des bouclages',* Thèse de Doctorat 3ème Cycle, Université de Paris I.

Deleau, M. and P. Malgrange (1978), *L'analyse des Modèles Macroéconomiques Quantitatifs,* Economica, Coll., ENSAE/C.E.P.E., Economie et Statistique avancées, Paris.

Gilli, M. and E. Rossier (1979), 'Understanding Complex Systems', Cahier 79.12 du Département d'Econométrie, July 1979, Université de Genève.

Keller. A. and E. Valensi (1973), 'Une méthode d'étude structurelle des modèles économiques', *Publications Econométriques,* Vol. VI, Fasc. é. éd. Sirey, pp. 28-53, Paris.

Keller, A. (1970), *Etude structurelle de quelques Modèles Mathématiques de Prévision Economique à Court Terme,* Mémoire de Doctorat de Sciences Economiques, No. 1934, Université de Paris.

Keller, A. (1976), *Essai sur les structures comparées des modèles macroéconomiques de prévision: construction d'une typologie par l'étude des graphes associés et l'analyse factorielle,* Thèse pour le Doctorat d'Etat ès Sciences Economiques, Université de Paris I.

Lafay, J.-D. (1972), 'Ajustement de Modèles Macroéconomiques simples sur les données françaises (1950-1968)', *Revue d'Economie Politique,* No. 6, Novembre-Décembre, pp. 1135-1171.

Lantner, R. (1974), *Théorie de la Dominance Economique,* Dunod, coll. Cournot, Paris-Bruxelles-Montréal.

Mazier, J. (1978), 'La Macroéconomie appliquée', PUF, Coll. l'Economiste, pp. 215-222, Paris.

Rossier, E. (1980), *Economie Structurale,* Economica, Paris.

CHAPTER 7

THE DYNAMICS OF A DISCRETE VERSION OF A GROWTH CYCLE MODEL

R.A. Dana and P. Malgrange
University of Paris and CEPREMAP–CNRS, France

1. INTRODUCTION

Macroeconometric dynamic models are generally estimated and simulated with a discrete time basis although they often rest on continuous time theoretical models.

It is well known that discretisation of linear structures leads to some measurable bias depending on the time step and the chosen approximisation. For nonlinear structures the distorsion is far more complex and up to now there are no general results.

This paper investigates this problem in the case of a rather simple economic structure of growth cycles, which can be formalised by a dynamic two equations model, an accumulation equation and an equation of progressive adjustment to a disequilibrium.

The guinea-pig model we use in the following is Kaldor's 1940 model (Kaldor (1940) and (1971)), which, though now out of date, has generated a considerable amount of methodological interest because of its beauty and simplicity (e.g. Chang and Smyth (1971), Klein and Preston (1968), Torre (1977), Varian (1979)).

The paper is organised as follows. In section 2 we present a generalisation of the Kaldor theory and its continuous version. The discrete time model is developed in section 3. Section 4 is devoted to the generation of cycles. In section 5, we analyse the differences between the continuous time model and our own discrete version. We give a numerical example to illustrate certain aspects of the model.

2. THE CONTINUOUS TIME MODEL

Kaldor's model is a purely quantitative aggregate model, belonging to the 'multiplier-accelerator' family. In this model, it is assumed that the global supply of goods and services Y by firms has as its immediate counterpart an income distribution of equal amount and generates for consumers and firms a consumption demand C and an investment demand I. The consumption and investment are both assumed to be dependent only on Y and the capital K. It is further assumed that in the case where demand for goods differs from supply, the investment demand is satisfied in priority. The ex post household consumption is identically equal to Y−I and generally differs from C or symetrically ex post saving is equal to I and differs from ex ante saving Y−C. It is finally assumed that firms will gradually adjust supply Y to demand C+I according to a scheme of 'Keynesian quantitative tatonnement' (variation of production proportional to excess demand). This scheme may be formalised in the following well known very simply manner (see Chang and Smyth (1971)):

$$\begin{cases} I = I(Y,K) \\ S = S(Y,K) \\ \dot{Y} = \alpha(C+I-Y) = \alpha(I-S) \\ \dot{K} = I - \delta K \end{cases}$$

where α is the characteristic parameter for the speed of adjsutment of supply to demand and δ is the rate of depreciation of the capital. Kaldor (1940) and (1971) assumed that for a fixed value of capital the marginal propensities to invest and consume with respect to Y would increase for extreme values of the production, [1] so that the total marginal propensity to spend ($\partial C/\partial y + \partial I/\partial y$) is greater than one for average values of production (corresponding to an explosive multiplier mechanism) and less than one for higher or lower levels of production. He also assumed that net investment would be positive for high values of production and negative for low values of production. If the long term equilibrium $\dot{Y}=\dot{K}=0$ is located in the average area it may be unstable. On the other hand, the evolution will remain globally confined by the slack in demand.

In order to derive a model of growth cycles for the Kaldor theory, we introduce a specification in which the autonomous demand increases exponentially with time G_0e^{gt}. This leads to the following model:

$$\begin{cases} \dot{Y} = \alpha\,[I(Y,K) - S(Y,K) + G_0e^{gt}] \\ \dot{K} = I(Y,K) - \delta K \end{cases} \tag{2.1}$$

We will assume that I and S are homogenous of degree one in Y and K to obtain a stationary solution involving a constant rate growth path. Using a classical change of variable,

$$\begin{cases} k = Ke^{-gt} \\ y = Ye^{-gt} \end{cases}$$

we get the following system for the 'reduced variables':

$$\begin{cases} \dot{y} = \alpha(I(y,k) - S(y,k) + G_0) - gy \\ \dot{k} = I(y,k) - (g+\delta)k \end{cases} \tag{2.2}$$

We shall assume that there exists a unique fixed point (y^*,k^*) with $y^*>0$ and $k^*>0$.

We note that, at the equilibrium (y^*,k^*), the ratio of capital to output is determined by the second equation. It is independent of G_0 and α.

The following theorem is an adaptation of the central theorem of Chang and Smyth (1971). It shows that under some 'global' assumptions on I and S, and if the fixed point is unstable, the evolution of the system will be periodic. Let Z denote the following set of conditions:

there exists a unique ratio of output to capital, x_0 smaller than $x^* = y^*/k^*$ such that:

$I(x_0,1) - S(x_0,1) = x_0 g/\alpha$ and for

$x>x_0$ $xg/\alpha > I(x,1) - S(x,1)$

$x \to \infty$, $xg/\alpha - I(x,1) + S(x,1) \to \infty$ and

$$\frac{xg/\alpha - I(x,1) + S(x,1)}{x} \to \ell$$

Theorem 1: Let the following assumptions hold:

a) The funtions I and S are homogenous of degree 1, continuous in the non-negative orthant and of class C^2 in the positive orthant R^2_+.

b) There exists a unique fixed point strictly politive (y^*,k^*) satisfying $I'_{y*}>S'_{y*}>0$ and $\alpha(I'_{y*}-S'_{y*}) + I'_{k*} > 2g + \delta$, where $I'_{y*} = \frac{\partial I}{\partial y}(y^*,k^*)$ etc.

c) Z holds.

Then all trajectories starting from the positive orthant are either periodic or tend towards a periodic orbit.

Proof: The proof being classic, we only sketch it here.

Under the assumptions given above, it is possible to construct and invariant compact set Γ = (ABCDE), containing a unique fixed point which is a repeller. By the Poincaré-Bendixson theorem (see Hirsch and Smale (1974)), we conclude that limit sets of points in Γ are periodic orbits and there exists in Γ some limit cycle. Now the trajectories of points in the positive orthant eventually enter Γ and tend towards a periodic orbit (which is in Γ).

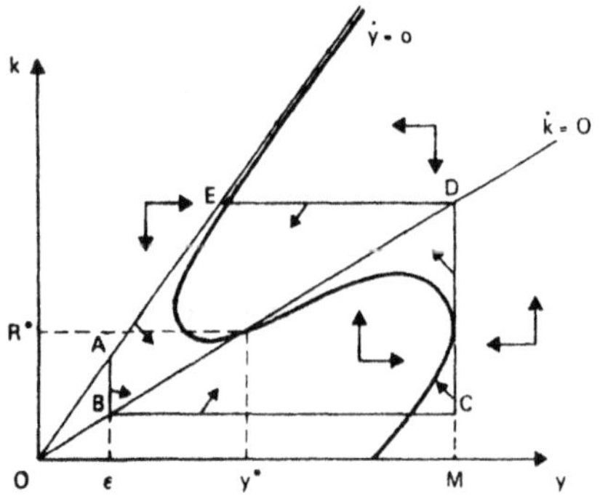

Figure 1.

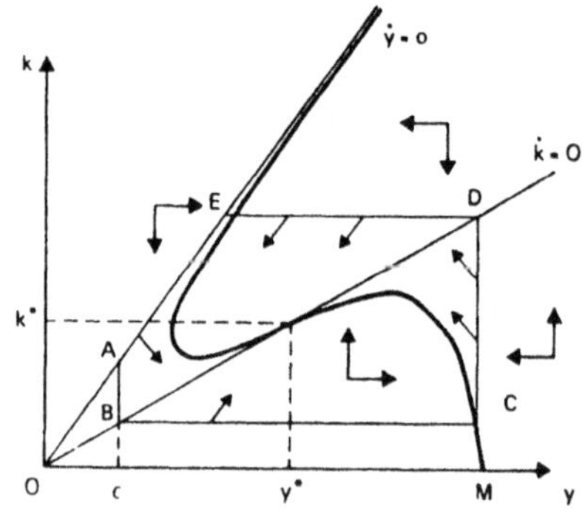

Figure 2.

A numerical example

For numerical purpose, we chose a linear consumption function and a S-shaped, 'logistic', investment function:

$$\begin{cases} S(Y,K) = sY \\ I(Y,K) = K\,\Phi(\frac{Y}{K}), \quad \text{with } I(Y,0) \equiv 0 \end{cases} \tag{2.3}$$

Φ is supposed to have the following form.

$$\Phi(x) = c + \frac{d}{1 + \exp(-a(vx-1))}$$

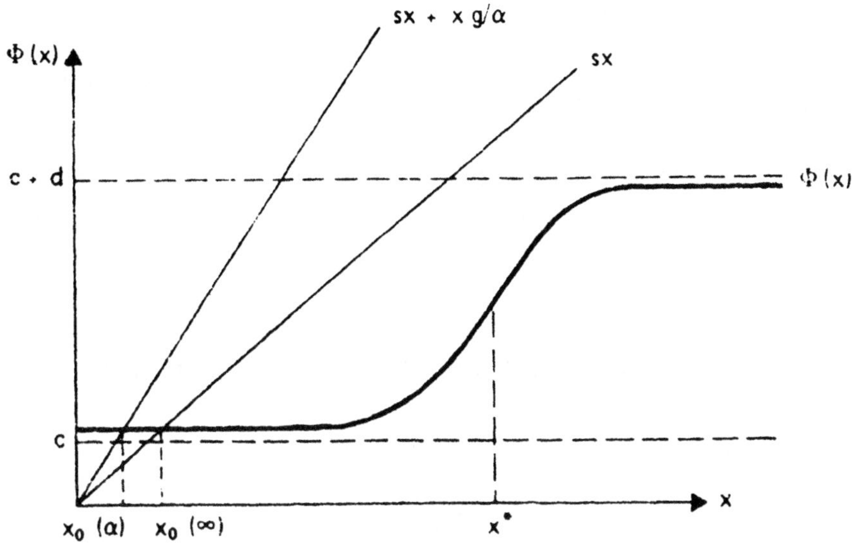

Figure 3.

The figures of model (2.3) are based on French quarterly data for 1960–1974, leading to the following results:

$$\begin{cases} I = K\left[0.01 + \dfrac{0.026}{1+\exp\left[-9\left(v\dfrac{Y}{K}-1\right)\right]}\right] \\ \\ S = 0.15\ Y \end{cases}$$

with $v = 4.23$, $\delta = 0.007$ and $g = 0.016$.

We arbitrarily chose $G_0 = 2$.

It can be checked that the system has a unique fixed point with positive coordinates $(y^*(\alpha), k^*(\alpha))$ where

$$k^*(\alpha) = \frac{\alpha G_0}{gx^* + \alpha(sx^* - (g+\delta))}, \quad y^*(\alpha) = x^* k^*(\alpha)$$

and x^* is the unique solution of the equation $\Phi(x^*) = g + \delta$.

I and S being homogenous, condition (b) depends only on x^* and holds for all values of $\alpha > \alpha_o$, with $\alpha_o = \dfrac{2g + \delta - I'_{k*}}{I'_{y*} - S'_{y*}} \cong 0.76.$

Conditions Z hold for all positive values of α, as can be seen from figure 3. x_o depends on α, its value is $\dfrac{0.01}{s+g/\alpha}$. When $\alpha \to \infty$, $x_o \to \dfrac{1}{15}$.

The phase diagram in the example looks as in figure 1 above. So for all values of $\alpha > \alpha_o$, all trajectories starting from the positive orthant tend towards a periodic orbit.

3. THE DISCRETE MODEL: INTRODUCTION AND A NUMERICAL EXAMPLE

We now give a discrete description of system (2.1) [2]

$$\begin{cases} Y_{t+1} - Y_t = \alpha[I(Y_t,K_t) - S(Y_t,K_t) + G_o(1+g)^t] \\ K_{t+1} - K_t = I(Y_t,K_t) - \delta K_t \end{cases} \tag{3.1}$$

As before, we shall assume that public expenditures grow at a constant rate. The investment and saving functions I(Y,K), S(Y,K) are still assumed to be homogeneous of degree 1, so that by using a standard change of variables $K = k(1+g)^t$, $Y = y(1+g)^t$, we obtain the following system for the 'reduced' variables:

$$\begin{cases} y_{t+1} = \dfrac{1}{1+g} [y_t + \alpha(I(y_t,k_t) - S(y_t,k_t) + G_o)] \\ k_{t+1} = \dfrac{1}{1+g} [k_t(1-\delta) + I(y_t,k_t)] \end{cases} \tag{3.2}$$

The dynamics of the model instead of being described by the autonomous differential system (2.2), $(\dot{y}, \dot{k}) = F_\alpha(y,k)$ is described by a mapping from R^2_+ intc R^2_+: $(y,k) \to T_\alpha(y,k)$ where $T_\alpha(y,k) = \dfrac{1}{1+g} [y + \alpha(I(y,k) - S(y,k) + G_o), k(1-\delta) + I(y,k)]$.

If (y,k) is the state of the system at time t, $T_\alpha(y,k)$ represents the state of the system one unit of time afterwards.

Note that the relation between systems (2.2) and (3.2) can easily be computed:

$$T_\alpha(y,k) = \frac{F_\alpha(y,k)}{1+g} + Id$$

We would like to study the asymptotic behaviour of the system. For this purpose let us recall a few classical definitions for dynamic systems in R^n (Hirsch and Smale (1974)).

A *discrete time dynamic system* is a C^1 map g from an open W of R^n into R^n. The *orbit* of a point x in W is the set:

$$O^+(x) = \{g^n(x), n \in N\}.$$

When g is a diffeomorphism, the *orbit* of x is $O(x) = \{g^n(x), n \in Z\}$.

The *ω-limit set* of x, $\omega_g(x)$ is defined by:

$$\omega_g(x) = \{y \in R^n, \quad n_i \to \infty \quad g^{n_i}(x) \to y\}$$

When g is a diffeomorphism, one can define similarly the *α-limit set* of x, $\alpha_g(x)$ by

$$\alpha_g(x) = \{y \in R^n, \quad n_i \to -\infty \, g^{n_i}(x) \to y\}$$

The *limit set* of x is the union of the ω-limit set and the α-limit set of x.

A bounded set A is an *attractor* for the map g if the following definitions hold:

a) there exists a neighbourhood invariant V of A such that $A = \bigcup_{t \geq 0} g^t(V)$.

b) One can choose a point x_0 in A such that, arbitrarily close to each other point in A, there is a point $x^t = g^t(x_0)$ for some positive t. (This indecomposability condition implies that A cannot be split into different attractors).

We shall say that A is a *strange attractor* [3] for g if A is an attractor but not a manifold (i.e. it is not locally homeomorphic to a subset of R^n). Numerous examples are given in Ruelle (1980). In general g is then *'sensitive to initial conditions'* [4]: the orbits of 'many' x (in the sense of Lebesgue measure) depend in a sensitive way on the choice of the initial point x, i.e. given x, one can find a y arbitrarily close to it whose trajectory will differ from it after some time.

One wants to study the limit sets in order to know the asymptotic behaviour of trajectories.

In the case of an autonomous differential equation in the plane, the Poincaré Bendixson theorem states that a bounded limit set is either a closed orbit or the union of equilibria and trajectories $\Phi_t(x)$ such that $\lim_{t\to\infty} \Phi_t(x)$ and $\lim_{t\to-\infty} \Phi_t(x)$ are equilibria.

Under the assumptions of section 2, the equilibrium point is totally unstable. Thus either all orbits are periodic or tend to periodic orbits.

It is known that this simple classification of limit sets does not apply to non-autonomous differential equations in the plane, nor to discrete dynamic systems (e.g. Ruelle (1980)).

Many diffeomorphisms in the plane have a 'strange' asymptotic behaviour; see for example Beddington et al. (1975), Curry and Yorke (1978). If one works with maps which are not invertible, as it is the case in our model (for high values of α), one can expect that some trajectories will be very complex, since even in dimension 1 many pathological examples are known.

This kind of phenomenon is very well known by physicists, chemists, biologists, ecologists (e.g. May (1976), Ruelle (1980)). Numerous models and examples have been studied. In economics, some examples have been investigated in one dimension (Benhabib and Day (1981), Stutzer (1980)). We would like to give an example to show that these chaotic phenomena can arise in a multiplier-accelerator model even under the strong assumptions of theorem 1.

The numerical model (2.3) was simulated over 500 periods, for values of α between 0.5 and 25. We chose initial conditions (y_0, k_0) close to the positive fixed point.

We observed five regimes when α varied.

1st Regime *'Steady state'* (Figures 4 and 5)

The trajectories spiral around a fixed point and converge towards it.

2nd Regime *'The periodic regime'* (Figures 6 and 7)

The trajectories spiral around an invariant curve. The movement is almost periodic and the period seems to vary regularly with α.

3rd Regime *'Choppy periodic regime'* (Figures 8 and 9)

There still exists an invariant curve and the movement is almost periodic but the production now oscillates and the oscillation grows with α.

4th Regime *'Intermittent chaos'* (Figures 10 and 11)

There exists an invariant domain and the trajectories circle around it. But here regular periods similar to what was observed in the previous regimes are followed by bursts of turbulence.

We tried to test 'sensitive dependence on initial conditions'; so we measured the impact of an error of 0.01%. Although we cannot say that the difference between two trajectories grows exponentially fast, two trajectories which start in the same neighbourhood rapidly lose any relationship to each other. So in this last regime computation of long range behaviour is seriously affected by small errors. This

Figures 4– 11

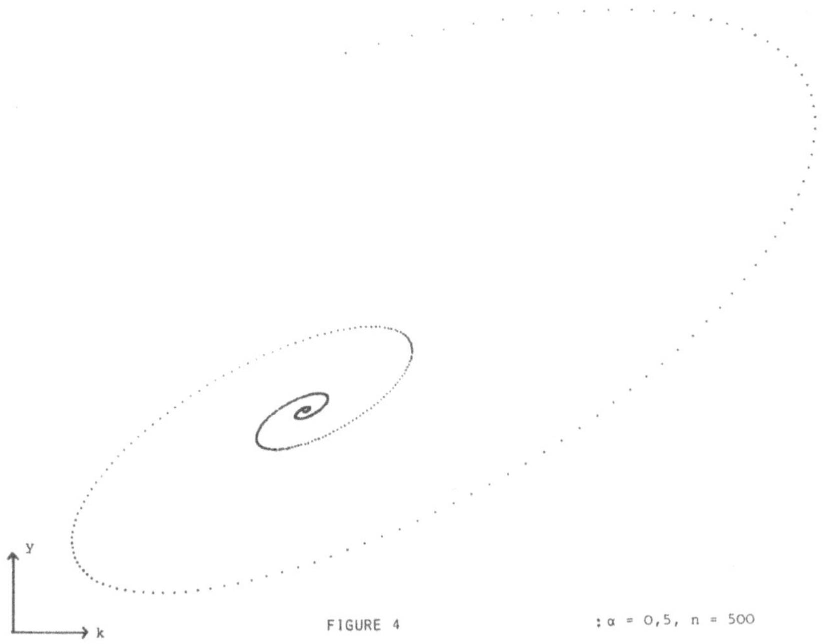

FIGURE 4 : α = 0,5, n = 500

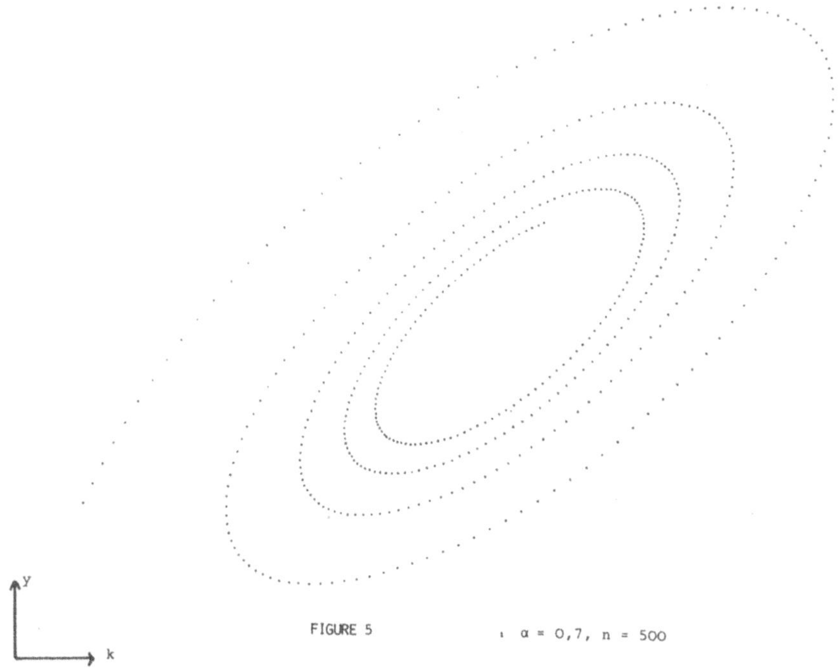

FIGURE 5 , α = 0,7, n = 500

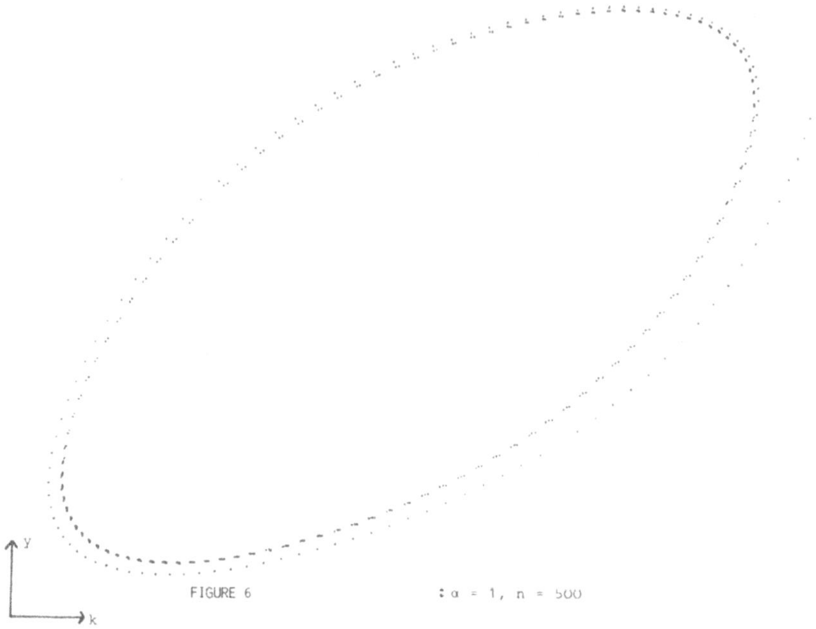

FIGURE 6 : $\alpha = 1$, $n = 500$

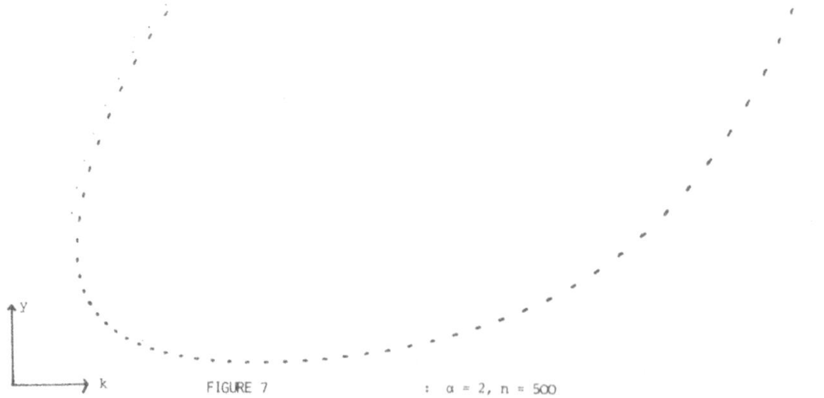

FIGURE 7 : $\alpha = 2$, $n = 500$

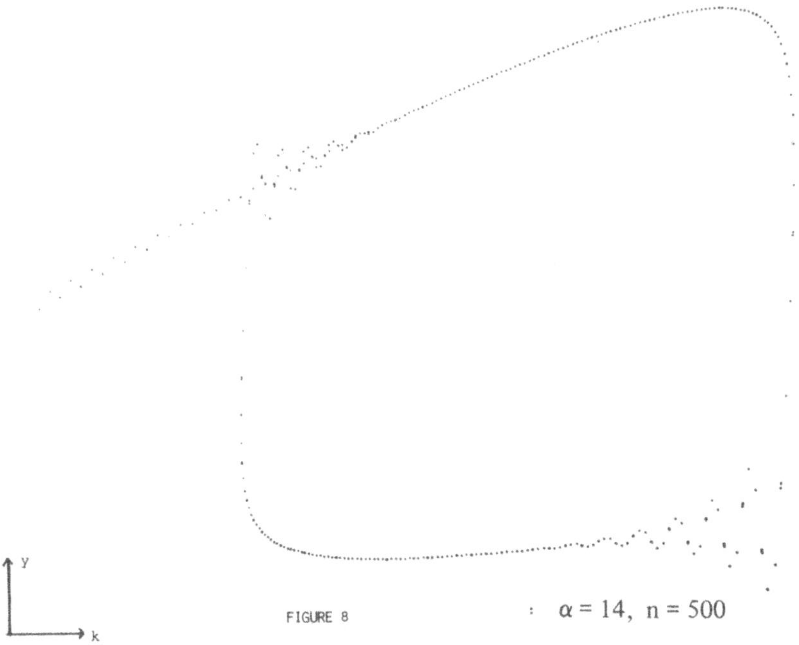

FIGURE 8 : $\alpha = 14$, $n = 500$

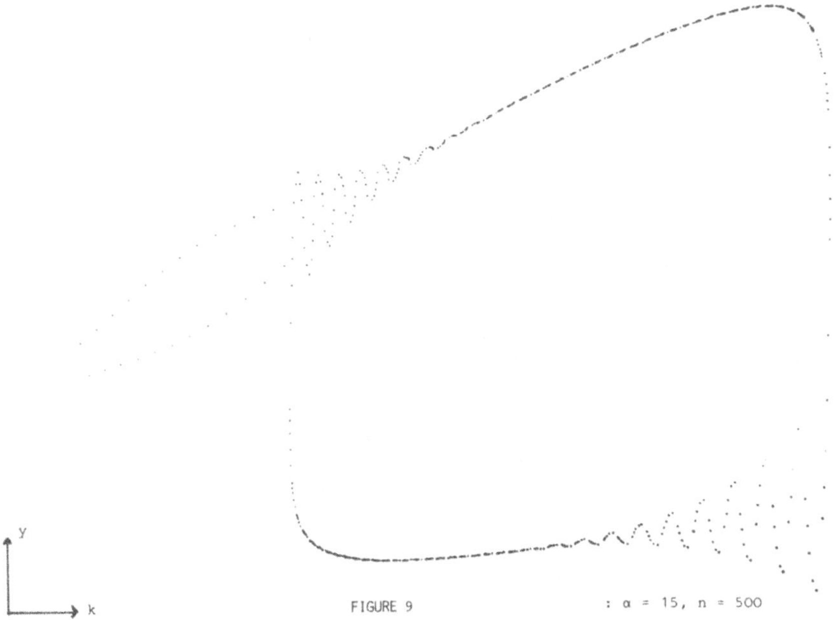

FIGURE 9 : $\alpha = 15$, $n = 500$

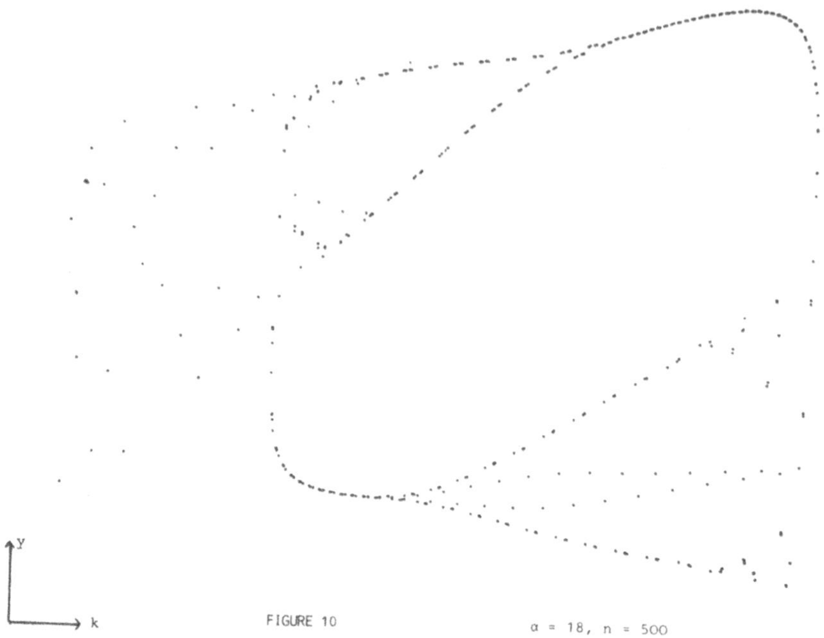

FIGURE 10 α = 18, n = 500

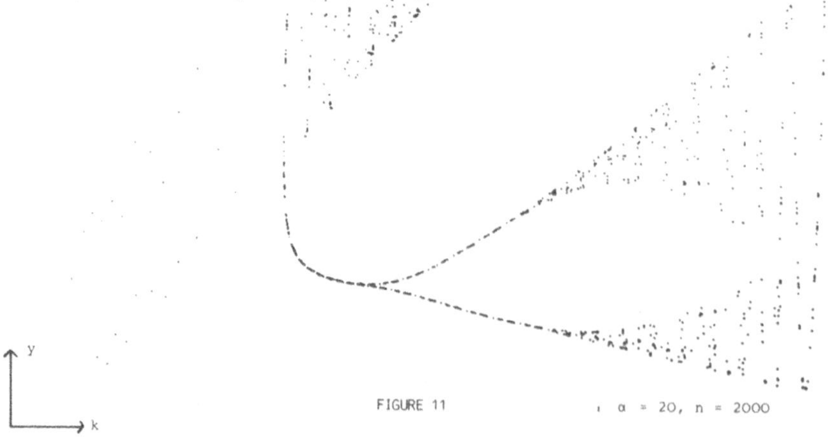

FIGURE 11 α = 20, n = 2000

should be contrasted with the previous regimes where two trajectories starting together will remain together.

5th Regime *'Divergence'*

Trajectories rapidly go to infinity when $\alpha > 20$.

To conlude this section, the above experiments show that it may be impossible to make 'accurate' forecasts. Although a trajectory may come close to its starting point after T periods of time, it is impossible to predict whether, during the next time interval T, the trajectory will be similar.

The best we can hope for is to characterise some features of the dynamics 'statistically' (i.e. most orbits tending to the attractor will spend the same proportion of time in its subsets).

4. THE DISCRETE MODEL: PERIODIC REGIME

4.1. General

This section summarises the mathematical basis which will allow us to interpret the generation of periodic behaviour.

Note on the figures that in regime 1, trajectories spiral towards the fixed point; then, in regime 2, they spiral towards an invariant curve. This phenomenon is called the 'Hopf bifurcation'. In effect, Hopf, in 1942, was the first to provide a theory of this phenomenon for differential equations, the idea going back to Poincaré. For discrete systems results are more recent (Ruelle (1977), Iooss (1979), Landford (1973)). We recall some ideas of the Hopf bifurcation (see Iooss (1979)):

The Hopf bifurcation

Let us consider a mapping f_α from an open set u of R^2 into R^2, of class C^k, $k \geqslant 6$. Let us suppose that for each α, f_α has a fixed point denoted here by $x(\alpha)$. Let A_α be the jacobian of f_α at $x(\alpha)$. Let A_α satisfy the following assumptions:

(H1) There exists an α_0 such that A_{α_0} has two conjugate eigenvalues λ_0 and $\bar{\lambda}_0$ with $|\lambda_0| = 1$, $\lambda_0 \neq \pm 1$, $\lambda_0^n \neq 1$ for $n = 1, 2, 3, 4$.

To ensure that the eigenvalues escape from the unit disc when α crosses α_0, we then assume that the so-called 'Hopf-condition' holds:

(H2) $\frac{d}{d_\alpha} \; |\lambda(\alpha)|_{\alpha = \alpha_0} > 0$

It is known that 'in general' a closed curve invariant for f_α bifurcates, from the fixed point, on one side of α_0. More precisely, it is possible to simplify f_α, after several changes of coordinates, so that the mapping f_{α_0}, in polar coordinates, takes the form:

$$(r, \varphi) \to (R, \Phi) \begin{cases} R = r(1-ar^2) + 0(r^4) \\ \Phi = \varphi + \theta_0 + 0(r^2), \text{ with } \theta_0 = \frac{1}{2\pi} \arg \lambda_0 \end{cases}$$

Let us further assume that:

(H3) $a \neq 0$

It can be shown by means of a fixed point argument in some appropriate space, that if H1, H2, H3 hold, there exists for each value of α in a right or left neighbourhood of α_0, an invariant curve for the mapping f_α, homeomorphic to a circle. At α_0 there is an exchange of the stabilities of the fixed point $x(\alpha_0)$ and the invariant circle. The following two cases are possible:

1) If $a > 0$, then the invariant curves exist and are attractive for $\alpha > \alpha_0$. For $\alpha \leqslant \alpha_0$ the fixed point is stable and unstable for $\alpha > \alpha_0$.

2) If $a < 0$, the invariant curves exist for $\alpha < \alpha_0$ and are repelling. For $\alpha < \alpha_0$ the fixed point is stable, and unstable for $\alpha \geqslant \alpha_0$.

4.2. The application of Hopf-bifurcation to the discrete Kaldor model

Let us consider again the system (3.2):

$$(y, k) \to T_\alpha(y, k) \text{ where}$$

$$T_\alpha(y, k) = \frac{1}{1+g} [y + \alpha(I-S+G_0), k + I - \delta k]$$

Let us suppose that the equation $I(x,1) = g + \delta$ has a unique solution x^*. Then T_α has a unique fixed point with positive coordinates $y^*(\alpha)$, $k^*(\alpha)$,

$$\begin{cases} k^*(\alpha) = \dfrac{\alpha G_0}{gx^* + \alpha(S(x^*,1) - g - \delta)} \\ y^*(\alpha) = x^* k^*(\alpha) \end{cases}$$

It is easy to see that $y^*(\alpha)$ and $k^*(\alpha)$ are C^∞ if α is greater than $gx^*/(g+\delta-S(x^*,1))$. Let A_α be the jacobian of T_α at the point $y^*(\alpha)$, $k^*(\alpha)$.

$$A_\alpha = \frac{1}{(1+g)} \begin{bmatrix} \alpha(I_y'^* - S_y'^*) + 1 & \alpha(I_k'^* - S_k'^*) \\ I_y'^* & 1-\delta + I_k'^* \end{bmatrix}$$

Since investment and saving are homogeneous functions of y and k the jacobian depends only on the ratio x^*.

The sum and the product of the eigenvalues are as follows:

$$P(\alpha) = \frac{1}{(1+g)^2} [1-\delta + I_k'^* + \alpha(-S_y'^*(1-\delta + I_k'^*) + (1-\delta + S_k'^*) I_y'^*)]$$

$$S(\alpha) = \frac{1}{(1+g)} [2-\delta + I_k'^* + \alpha(I_y'^* - S_y'^*)]$$

Since $P(\alpha)$ is a linear function of α, there exists a unique value α_0 such that $P(\alpha_0) = 1$ [5]

$$\alpha_0 = \frac{(1+g)^2 - (1-\delta + I_k'^*)}{(1-\delta + S_k'^*) I_y'^* - S_y'^*(1-\delta + I_k'^*)}$$

Thus let us make the following assumptions of Hopf bifurcation:

(H1) $S(\alpha_0)^2 < 4$

$\lambda(\alpha_0)^n \neq 1, \quad n = 2, 3, 4$

(H2) $\frac{dP_\alpha}{d\alpha}\Big|_{\alpha=\alpha_0} > 0$

Thus $(1-\delta - S_k'^*) I_y^* - S_y'^*(1-\delta + I_k'^*) > 0$

(H3) Condition H3 is very unattractive. It depends on the derivatives of the functions I and S at $y^*(\alpha_0)$, $k^*(\alpha_0)$ up to the order 3. We shall not express it here.

It is therefore possible to get an invariant curve in a Kaldor discrete model.

To conclude this section, the assumptions we made are 'local' ones and so are the results. We only get information on trajectories starting from a neighbourhood of the fixed point. Also we only know what will happen in a neighbourhood of the bifurcation value 'α_0'. However, a more profound theorem shows that the invariant curve persists for a bigger interval of α's (see Hirsch et al. 1977)). In our example it persisted up to the end of the third regime. Note that during regime 2, the restriction of T_α to the invariant curve is one to one, but not in regime 3.

5. THE DISCRETE MODEL: HIGH VALUES OF α

The purpose of this section is to analyse the properties of the model for higher values of 'α'. Since it was Kaldor's assumption, we will go back to his original explanation of the trade cycle and explore the differences between his model and ours. We show that in some cases, part of this theory can be used if a discrete adjustment is used instead of a continuous time adjustment.

Let us recall a few facts about Kaldor's theory. To simplify, we shall assume here that the saving function depends only on production. Kaldor assumed that for a fixed value of K, the function $Y \to I(Y,K)$ would have a floor-ceiling shape. He also assumed that, in the region of the cycle, the function $K \to I(Y,K)$ would be a decreasing function of K, and for a fixed value of capital K_0 the functions $Y \to I(Y, K_0)$ and $Y \to S(Y)$ would have three points of intersection (figure 12).

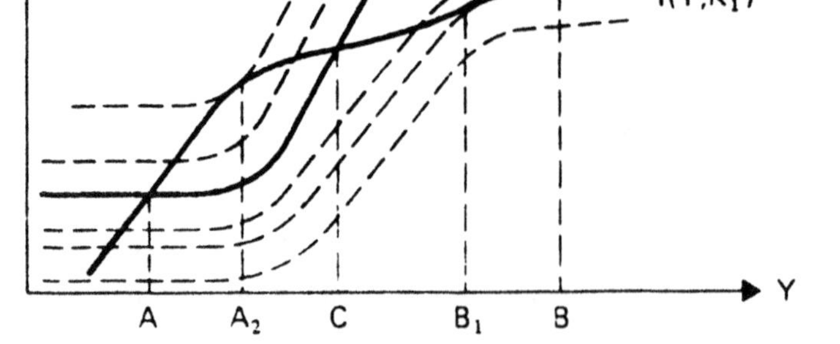

Figure 12.

Production was supposed to adjust according to the following continuous scheme:

$$\dot{Y} = \alpha(I(Y,K) - S(Y)), \tag{5.1}$$

with, for a fixed value K_0 of K, three equilibria, A and B stable, and C unstable.

His theory was that if one starts from a value of production close to B (resp. A), the production would tend to B (resp. A) very fast because of the high speed of adjustment. So production can be identified with one of the stable equilibria of (5.1). When production is high, investment is high and capital grows. Then investment decreases. The stable equilibrium B decreases, so Y decreases. C gets closer to B. This phenomenon goes on, says Kaldor, until a critical position is reached, for a value of K, K_1 such that $I(Y,K_1)$ and $S(Y)$ are tangential, and equilibrium B_1 is a 'saddle node'.

For values of K slightly larger than K_1, equation (5.1) has only one stable equilibrium at A. Production falls until it gets to A. When activity is low, net investment is negative, capital decreases, the investment curve shifts upwards. Equilibrium 'A' increases. Production slowly increases until a new critical position is reached for a value K_2 of K such that $I(Y,K_2)$ and $S(Y)$ are again tangential, and equilibrium A_2 becomes a saddle node.

For values of K lower than K_2, (5.1) has one stable equilibrium at B. Production shifts upwards and the cyclical movement is repeated.

As it has been shown by Varian (1979), Kaldor's cycle can be interpreted as an 'hysteresis' cycle. The set of fixed points of the 'fast dynamics',

$$M = \{(Y,K), I(I,K) - S(Y) = 0\}$$

has the shape of figure 13.

The upper and lower branches correspond to stable fixed points of the fast dynamics, the medium branch to unstable fixed points.

When the adjustment parameter 'α' is high, away from 'M', the vector field is almost vertical. So any solution moves quickly to the vicinity of M. In the upper plane, it follows M downwards and in the lower plane upwards. When a solution reaches a point where M has a vertical tangent, it jumps quickly to the other point of M on the vertical line. So there is a limit cycle PQRS which consists of two segments of M and two vertical lines. The velocity along a vertical segment is much larger than the velocity along a segment which follows M.

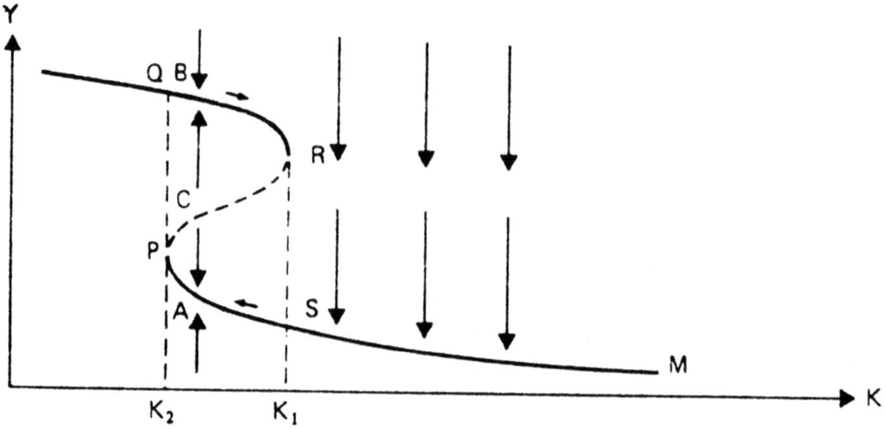

Figure 13.

Let us now suppose that the adjustment of supply to demand is discrete and fast. Suppose that the adjustment of production is represented by the following scheme:

$$Y_{n+1} = Y_n + \alpha (I(Y_n, K_0) - S(Y_n)), \tag{5.2}$$

for a fixed value of capital K_0.

Let us consider the map $T_{K_0}(Y)$: $Y \to Y + \alpha(I(Y, K_0) - S(Y))$.

It can easily be seen that the discrete adjustment (5.2) has the same equilibria $T_{K_0}(Y) = Y$ as (5.1). However, it does not have the same stable equilibria. (A fixed point Y_0 of the mapping $Y \to T_{K_0}(Y)$ is stable if $|T'_{K_0}(Y_0)| \leqslant 1$. On figure 14, A is stable, B and C are unstable).

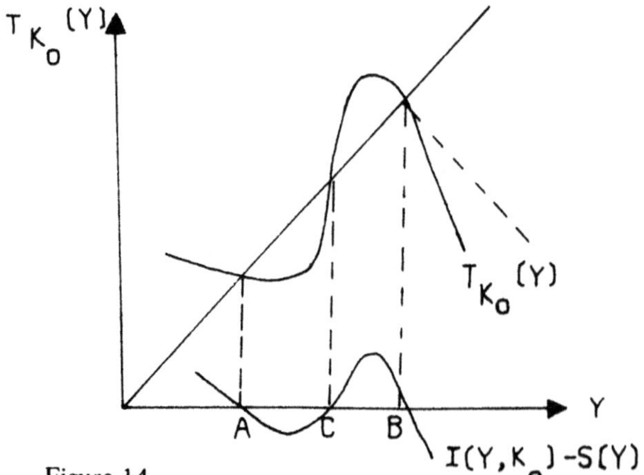

Figure 14.

Now what happens if firms start from a value of production close to B, if it is unstable? It is not possible to conclude as in the continuous case that production will tend to A, the stable position. The evolution of production will depend on the properties of the discrete dynamic system.

5.1 The case of the existence of an invariant domain

Let us first suppose that for all values of K considered there exists an interval $[\bar{Y}_0 \ \bar{Y}_1]$ invariant under the family of mappings $T_K(Y)$.

One-dimensional discrete dynamic systems are now fairly well understood. Considerable amount of work has been done on iterated mappings on the interval with one extremum and some regularity [6]; (see Collet and Eckmann (1980), and May (1976)).

A typical 'Kaldor map' (e.g. figure 14) has two extrema, one maximum and one minimum. Mappings similar to these have been studied in the biology literature (May (1981) and in physics to describe turbulent phenomena with intermittence (Arneodo et al. (1980), Pomeau and Manneville (1980)).

It is not our purpose to develop a complete theory of the attractors and bifurcations of these mappings. We just want to show that from the study of the one-dimensional system, we may expect various types of transitions for the two-dimensional system.

In what follows we study the properties of mappings $T_K(Y)$ for values of K such that they have three fixed points, focusing only on a couple of cases for which we are able to provide simulations.

Case 1 $\quad$ *$T_K(Y)$ has always two 'independent branches'*

Let us fix K to K_0.

Let C be the medium fixed point of $T_{K_0}(Y)$, D and E be such that $T_{K_0}(D) = T_{K_0}(E) = C$.

Let m_{K_0} be the minimum of $T_{K_0}(Y)$ and M_{K_0} its maximum. Let us suppose that $T_{K_0}(m_{K_0}) \in DC$ and $T_{K_0}(M_{K_0}) \in CE$. Then both intervals DC and CE are invariant under T. The theory of iterated mappings on the interval with one extremum can be used on each of the intervals DC and CE. The mapping T will be assumed to be sufficiently regular. Let $T_1 = G/DC$ and $T_2 = G/CE$. To study the attractor for T, it

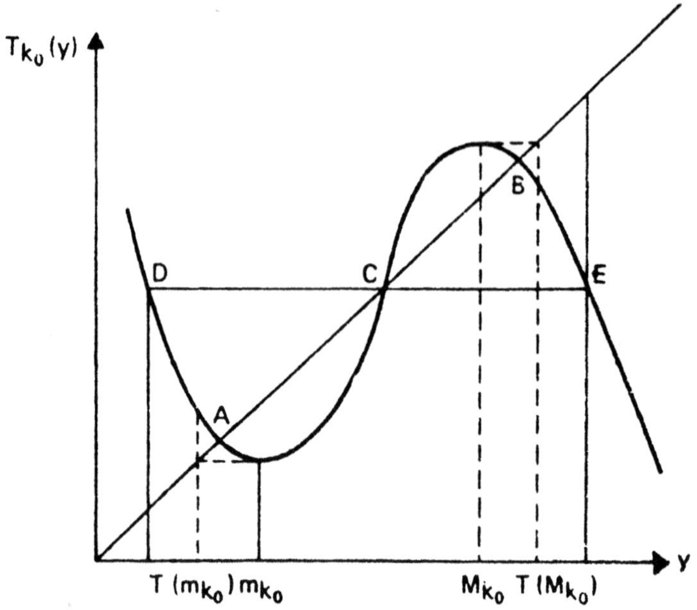

Figure 15.

suffices to study those of T_1 and T_2.

Only the following cases are possible: (e.g. Misiurewicz (1981)):

(i) T_1 has a stable periodic point, i.e. there exist $\bar{Y}$ and p such that $T_1^p(\bar{Y}) = \bar{Y}$ and $|T_1'^p(\bar{Y})| \leqslant 1$. It is known that almost every point in DC is attracted to the orbit of $\bar{Y}$ and m_{K_0} is attracted to the orbit of $\bar{Y}$. For regular families, the set of parameters K, such that T_1 has an attracting periodic orbit, is open. If p is sufficiently small, in an experiment, one observes p points neatly.

(ii) T_1 does not have a stable periodic orbit. There may exist probabilistic ergotic invariant measure absolutely continuous with respect to Lebesgue measure (p.i.a.m). For almost every x in the support of the measure, if ζ is the density of the measure and A a measurable set then

$$\lim_{n\to\infty} \frac{1}{n} \text{ card } \{k<n, f^k(x) \in A\} = \int_A \zeta(t)\,dt$$

In an experiment we observe a stochastic behaviour of orbits, with sensitive dependence on initial conditions. The set of T_1 for which K has an ergodic absolutely continuous invariant measure, has positive Lebesgue measure for most families.

(iii) There are values of K such that neither periodic attracting orbits nor p.i.a.m. measure exists for T_1. It is not known whether they can be experimentally observed.

The numerical model

To illustrate these ideas, let us consider our own model (system 3) which is only slightly different from Kaldor's.

Let us consider the mapping: $y \to T_k(y) = \frac{1}{1+g}\,[y+\alpha(I(y,k) - S(y,k) + G_0)]$

On figure 16 [7], we plot the family of mappings $y \to T_k(y)$ for $\alpha = 20$, $120 \leqslant k \leqslant 220$. It can easily be checked that the functions we consider, when they cross the diagonal three times, have two independent branches.

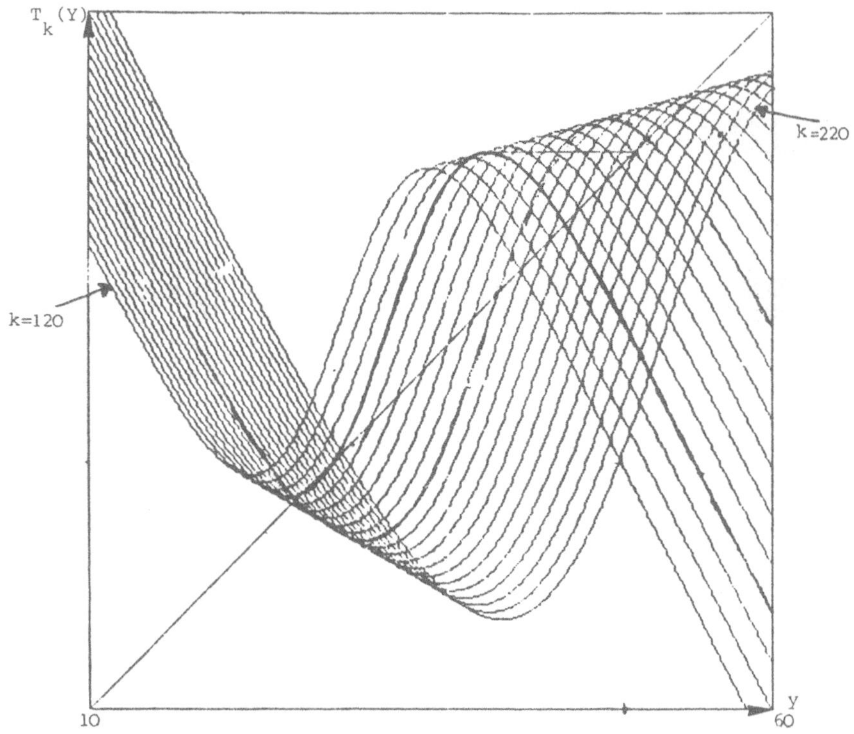

Figure 16.

Then, for each value of k, to know whether or not the map $y \to T_k(y)$ has a periodic orbit we have performed the following experiment.

We fix k and compute the critical points of $T_k(y)$. Then, for each fixed k, we plot on the vertical axis the images of the critical points waiting 500 iterations until we plot the first point. If $T_k(y)$ has a stable periodic orbit of low period, the iterates of some of the two critical points will be close to it. We then get figure 17:

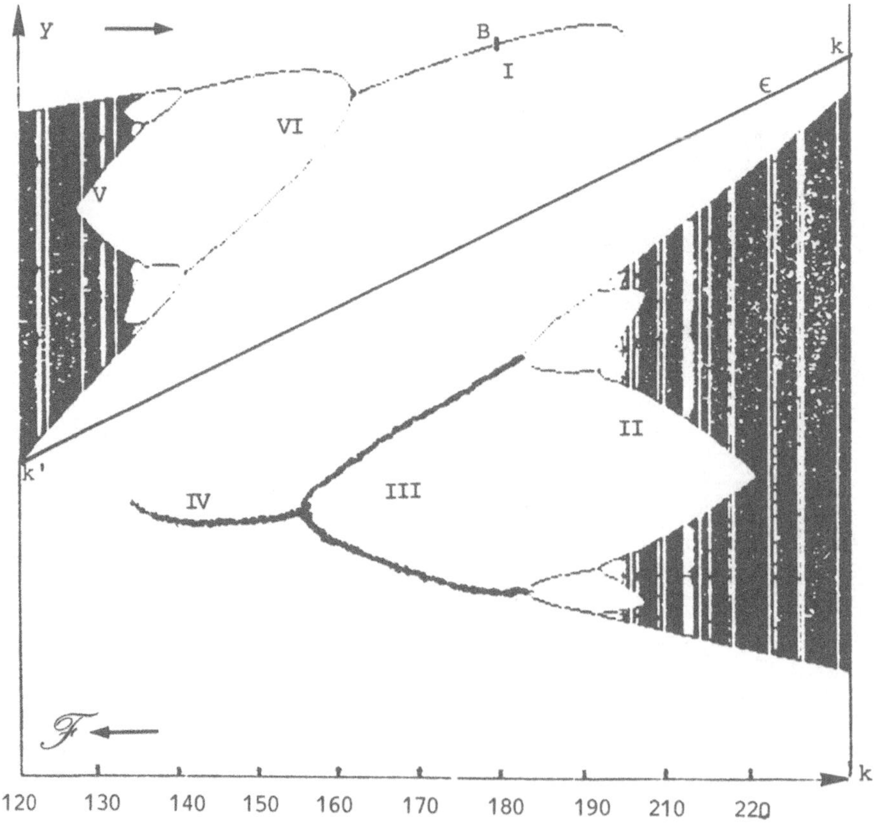

Figure 17.

We are now able to answer our initial question: what happens if, for a fixed value of k, we start close to B in the case it is an unstable fixed point? If $T_k(y)$ has a stable periodic point of low period, say 'n', we observe n values of production. Otherwise we observe a set of points on some interval.

Let us now consider the two-dimensional system, under the assumption that, having fixed k, we are in case 1.

Except for the values of k for which $T_k(y)$ has a stable fixed point, production varies on some interval. If the variations of production are not too large and if investment is not too sensitive to those variations then k will move fairly slowly compared to production. Then as in Kaldor's theory, it can be considered as a parameter of the model. Suppose that for 'high' values of production net investment is positive and for 'low' values of production it is negative.

Suppose one starts from a high value of production y_0 and a value of capital k_0 such that net investment is positive.

Then if $Y \to T_{k_0}(y)$ has a stable 'upper' fixed point as in region I of figure 17, production gets close to that point. Otherwise it oscillates (region (VI). It remains high so that net investment is positive. Capital thus increases slowly. Capital will continue to increase if y is sufficiently high. Suppose that for some value k_1 of k, $T_{k_1}(y)$ is almost tangent to the bisector.

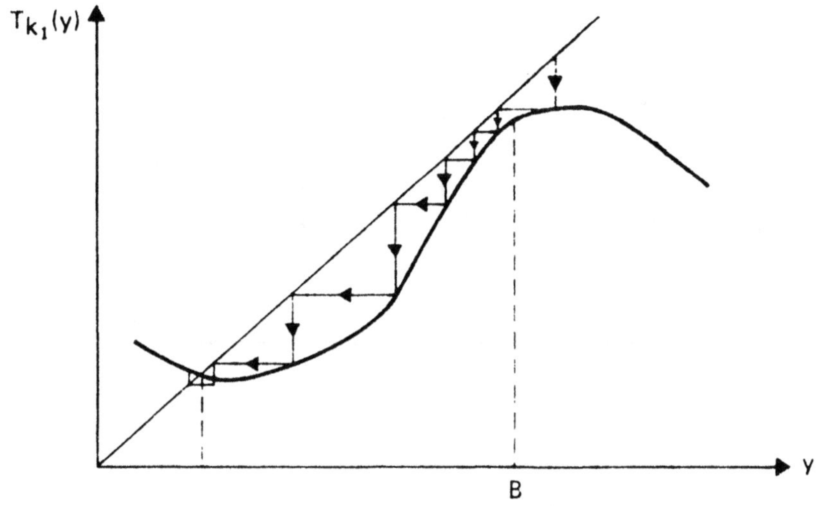

Figure 18.

Then production will decrease until it reaches the other branch and its pathologies. So again production will either oscillate or vary steadily according to the properties of the lower branch of the function $y \to T_k(y)$ (region II, III, IV).

When production has reached the lower branch, if net investment is too low, capital decreases, and will do so until a new ciritical position is reached for a value of capital k_2 such that $T_{k_2}(y)$ is almost tangent to the bisector.

Then production rises to the other branch. Capital will then increase since net investment is high ... and this pseudo-cyclical movement is repeated, capital being rather periodic and production being aperiodic.

Let us again stress the fact that it was assumed that, on each branch, variations of production were never important enough so as to change the sign of net investment and thus the evolution of capital. This is then a rather particular case. So we will present a case where the evolution of the variables are really unpredictable.

Case 2 An example of other possible behaviour

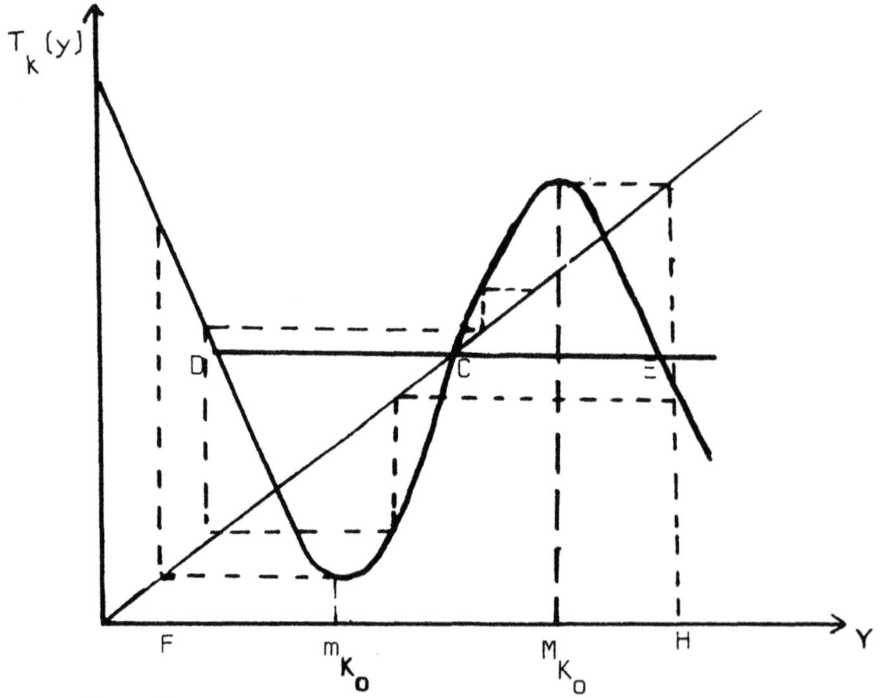

Figure 19.

In this case $H = T(M_{K_0}) \notin CE$, $T^2(M_{K_0}) \in DC$, $F = T(m_{K_0}) \notin DC$, $T^2(m_{K_0}) \in CE$. None of the fixed points are stable. None of the intervals DC and CE are invariant, but FH is invariant. As in the previous case, the mapping $Y \to T_k(y)$ restricted to FH may have periodic and aperiodic trajectories.

A theorem of Misiurewicz (1981) shows that almost every initial condition in CE has an iteration outside this interval before T is reached, thus enters DC and almost every initial condition in DC has an iteration outside DC, thus enters CE. So one can expect variations of production to be much larger than in case 1. Thus net investment may take positive and negative values. Then even if capital varies more slowly than production, the sign of its evolution is unknown. One loses the fairly regular behaviour of capital described in case 1.

We will illustrate this by an example.

Klein and Preston (1969) considered a discrete version of Kaldor's model, with a linear investment function I(Y,K) and a piecewise linear saving function, independent of K, S(Y). For high values of α, the following trajectories of (Y,K) are obtained (figure 20). The cyclical pattern is totally destroyed.

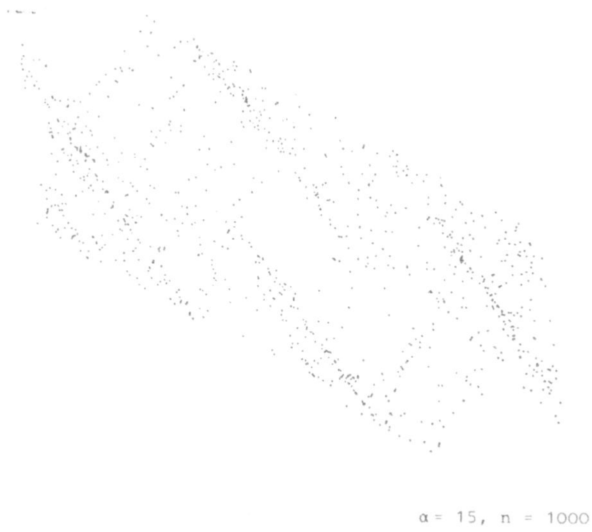

Figure 20.

The mappings $Y \to T(Y)$ are piecewise expanding, i.e. $|T_K'| \geq a > 1$, and there cannot be any attracting periodic orbit. It is known that in this case there exists an absolutely continuous invariant measure for T_K. Thus the long term behaviour of almost all points is stochastic, and the variations of production are large, inducing non-negligible variations of investment, and thus a rather chaotic behaviour of capital.

5.2 The case of divergence

For higher values of α and for a fixed value of K, there will not exist any invariant interval for the mapping $T_K(Y)$. In this case trajectories go to infinity, with high oscillations which are economically meaningless, K and Y becoming negative.

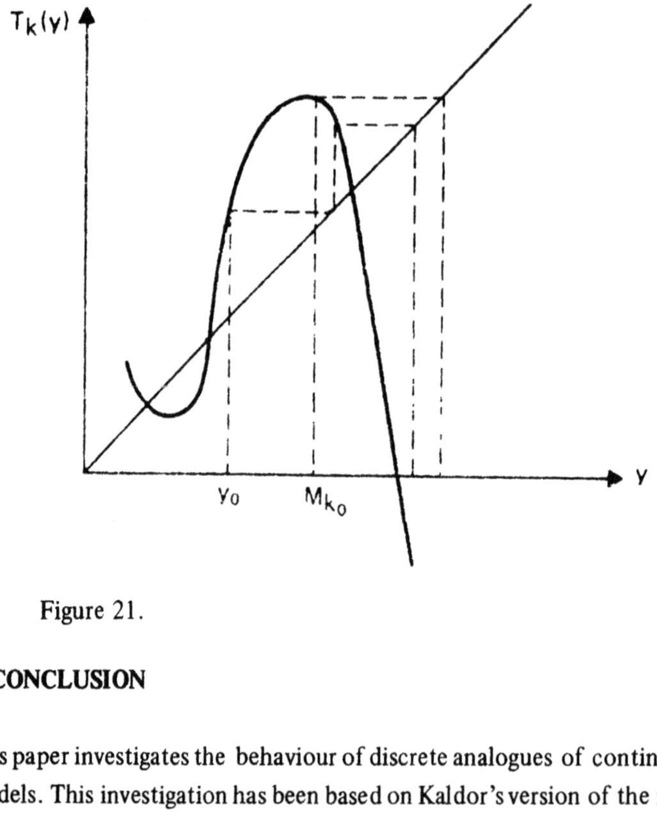

Figure 21.

6. CONCLUSION

This paper investigates the behaviour of discrete analogues of continuous time cyclic models. This investigation has been based on Kaldor's version of the non-linear multiplier-accelerator model.

We have shown that the continuous model and its discretisation have different qualitative properties, when the speed of adjustment of supply to demand is varied. In the continuous case trajectories will either approach a steady state or a periodic orbit or go to infinity. In the discrete case, other behavioural patterns are possible. In particular trajectories may fluctuate in an aperiodic, chaotic fashion. The deterministic discrete system may render predictions impossible since the evolution of the system may be sensitive to initial conditions.

To analyse what happens when the system becomes irregular we have focused on one equation of the model, corresponding to the 'fast dynamics'. We have shown that the conclusions depend on the properties of this equation.

It is known that when the dynamics is complex some regularities may become discernible by adopting some macroscopic representation of the chaotically evolving variables. So we hope that the use of ergodic theory will lead to some meaningful invariant quantities.

NOTES

We would like to express our appreciation to M. Herman and D. Rand who got us started on the subject and more particularly to A. Chenciner for his help during the preparation of the paper. We also benefited from a very stimulating conversation with Y. Pomeau and a discussion with C. Tresser.

The example we give was prepared by Chabert during his training period at the CEPREMAP in 1978.

1) See also Hicks (1950).
2) This type of description is usual in discrete models. It is not supposed to be a good mathematical discretisation of equation (2.1).
3) This definition is not at all universal and is still very controversial.
4) The definition we give here is Guckenheimer's (1979). Ruelle (1980) gives a different definition.
5) In the numerical example, we got $\alpha_0 = 0.73$ instead of 0.76 for the continuous case.
6) It is usually assumed that mappings have a negative 'schwarzian derivative', the schwarzian derivative of a mapping 'f' being defined by $S(f) = f'''/f' - 3/2(f''/f')^2$
7) Figures 16 and 17 were made with the help of C. Tresser, theoretical physicist at the University of Nice.

REFERENCES

Arneodo, A., P. Coullet and C. Tresser (1980), 'On the Existence of Hysteresis in a Transition to Chaos after a Single Bifurcation', *Journal Physique-Lettres*, 41, pp. 243–246.

Beddington, J.R., C.A. Free and J.H. Lawton (1975), 'Dynamic Complexity in Predator Prey Models Framed in Difference Equations', *Nature*, 255, pp. 55–58.

Benhabib, J. and R. Day (1981), 'Rational Choice and Erratic Behaviour', *Review of Economic*

Studies, 48, pp. 459–71.

Chang, W.N. and P.J. Smyth (1971), 'The Existence and Persistence of Cycles in a Non-Linear model: Kaldor's 1940 Model Re-examined', *Review of Economic Studies* 38, pp. 37–44.

Collet, P. and J.P. Eckmann (1980), *Iterated Maps on the Interval as Dynamic Systems*, Birkhauser, Cambridge.

Curry, J.H. and J. Yorke (1978), 'Computer Experiments with Maps on R^2', in: *The Structure of Attractors in Dynamic Systems*, Springer Verlag, New York, pp. 46–65.

Henon, M. (1976), 'A Two Dimensional Mapping with a Strange Attractor', *Communication in Mathematical Physics*, pp. 69–77.

Hicks, J.R. (1950), *A Contribution to the Theory of the Trade Cycle*, Clarendon Press, Oxford.

Hirsch, M., C. Pugh and M. Shub (1977), *Invariant Manifolds*, Springer Verlag, New York.

Hirsch, M. and S. Smale (1974), *Differential Equations, Dynamical Systems*, Academic Press, New York.

Iooss, G. (1979), *Bifurcation of Maps and Applications*, North Holland, Amsterdam.

Kaldor, N. (1940), 'A Model of the Trade Cycle', *Economic Journal*, 50, pp. 78–92.

Kaldor, N. (1971), 'A Comment', *Review of Economic Studies*, 38, pp. 45–46.

Klein, L.R. and R.S. Preston (1969), 'Stochastic Non-Linear Models', *Econometrica*, 37, pp. 95–106.

Landford, O. (1973), 'Bifurcation of Periodic Solutions into Invariant Tori' in Marsden, Mac Cracken (eds), *The Hopf Bifurcation and its Applications*, Springer Verlag, New York, pp. 206–18.

May, R. (1976), 'Simple Mathematical Models with Complicated Dynamics', *Nature*, 261, pp. 459–67.

May, R. (1981), 'Non-Linear Problems in Ecology and Resource Management', Lecture Notes for Les Houches Summer School on 'Chaotic Behaviour of Deterministic Systems'.

Misiurewicz, M. (1981), 'Maps of an Interval', Lecture Notes for Les Houches Summer School on 'Chaotic Behaviour of Deterministic Systems'.

Pomeau, Y. and P. Manneville (1980), 'Intermittent Transition to Turbulence in Dissipative Dynamic Systems', *Communication in Mathematical Physics*, 74, pp. 189–97.

Ruelle, D. (1980), 'Strange Attractors', *Mathematical Intelligentser*, Springer Verlag, New York, pp. 146–194.

Stutzer, M. (1980), 'Chaotic Dynamics and Bifurcation in a Macro-Model', *Journal of Economic Dynamics and Control*, 2, pp. 353-76.

Torre, V. (1977), 'Existence of Limit Cycles and Control in Complete Keynesian System by Theory of Bifurcations', *Econometrica*, 45, pp. 1457–66.

Varian, H.R. (1979), 'Catastrophe Theory and the Business Cycle', *Economic Enquiry*, 17, pp. 14–28.

CHAPTER 8

THE STRUCTURE OF RATIONAL EXPECTATIONS BEHAVIOUR IN ECONOMICS: AN EMPIRICAL VIEW

A.S. Brandsma and A.J. Hughes Hallett
Erasmus University, Rotterdam, The Netherlands

1. INTRODUCTION

In recent years many authors have proposed models of economic behaviour in which certain current endogenous variables react to rational (mathematical) expectations of future endogenous variables. Almost always the reasoning behind that specification is heuristic and the specified model correspondingly ad hoc. The purpose of this paper is to present a theoretical rationale for these expectations terms which is based on rational behaviour on the part of decision makers. We then look at some empirical consequences of such a specification in a typical macroeconometric model.

In his famous critique of policy making, Lucas argues that any systematic policy measures undertaken by the government can be anticipated by the private sector. Rational agents then have an incentive to respond by altering their own decisions so as to improve on their objectives; and that may in turn induce the government to adjust its actions, and so on. That implies that behavioural reactions must be conditioned on current expectations of future events because that is (in part) the conditioning information employed when making decisions in any dynamic system. But is model specification as simple as that? It is well known, for example, that optimal decisions for a dynamic system can usually be written as a feedback rule plus a term involving expected future exogenous events (Chow (1975)). So, while it is obvious that econometric models are improved by a rigorous specification of the expectations mechanism employed by the agents whose behaviour is being modelled, it is not obvious that expectations of future endogenous rather than exogenous variables is the correct way to do so – unless the endogenous expectations stand as proxies for other variables which cannot be measured accurately or directly. Even then, how is the specification of the existing rational expectations models arrived at? Why are certain future periods important, and others ruled out? Obvious examples here are inflationary expectations in the models of Sargent and Wallace (1975), or the expectations augmented Phillips curve models (a recent example is Minford and

Peel (1982)). Although one may accept the arguments for including such terms, one wants to know why a particular specification was chosen and what it depends on. As always, the trouble with heuristic models is the lack of precise behavioural theory, with the result that it is not possible to pin the corresponding maintained hypothesis down to exact and testable propositions on the coefficients or variables of the final model.

This paper argues that rational expectations models commonly arise because the economy develops as the outcome of a noncooperative and unrestricted game, where the decisions of one (or more) player(s) are not accurately observed. Examples might be competition between government, employers, and employees on the labour market; or the mutual dependence of trading nations; or speculators and producers in commodity markets; and so on. The decisions of one player may not be observed simply because they are not monitored or announced, but also because they become lost in some bargaining process or because the information is too confused to establish a reliable 'representative' value.

In what follows, sections 2-4 set out optimal decisions under uncertainty. Section 5 answers three questions:

a) In what form do the rational expectations terms appear in a structural econometric model?
b) What is the structure of such a model? and
c) What are the important components involved in the impact of the rational expectations terms?

In sections 6-9 we use those results to examine the quantitative significance of these rational expectations terms for policy analysis. We do this using a model of the labour market in the Dutch economy. Specifically we investigate

a) if these expectations really matter or whether the Lucas critique of policy making is quantitatively significant;
b) if these expectations imply that policies actually do become relatively or absolutely neutral (in the sense of Sargent and Wallace (1975)); and
c) how much information about the working of the economy is contained in the expectations process.

We must make clear, however, that we do *not* consider the estimation of the parameters in models with rational expectations terms.

2. NONCOOPERATIVE STRATEGIES

Consider a dynamic and noncooperative 2-player game involving m targets, y_t; n_1 instruments for player 1, $x_t^{(1)}$, and n_2 for player 2, $x_t^{(2)}$; and uncontrollable and uncertain variables s_t. Let the planning period contain discrete decision intervals t=1 .... T, and write $y'=(y_1' \ldots y_T')$; $x^{(i)'}=(x_1^{(i)'} \ldots x_T^{(i)'})$ for i=1,2; and $s'=(s_1' \ldots s_T')$. Suppose each player has ideal values $y^{(i)d}$ and $x^{(i)d}$ for his own decision variables, implying the policy 'failures' $\tilde{y}^{(i)} = y - y^{(i)d}$ and $\tilde{x}^{(i)} = x^{(i)} - x^{(i)d}$. The interests of each player can be represented by a loss function containing a known weighted sum of quadratic and linear deviations from his ideal values:

$$w^{(i)} = \tfrac{1}{2}\tilde{z}^{(i)\prime} Q^{(i)} \tilde{z}^{(i)} + q^{(i)\prime}\tilde{z}^{(i)} \qquad i = 1,2 \tag{1}$$

where $\tilde{z}^{(i)\prime} = (\tilde{y}^{(i)\prime}, \tilde{x}^{(i)\prime})$ and $Q^{(i)}$ is positive semi-definite and symmetric. Thus $Q^{(i)}$ may have rows and columns of zeros if player i ignores some targets in the game, but it has rank at least $n_i T$.

Noncooperation implies that each player unilaterally and selfishly maximises his self-interest, as represented by his objective function, subject to his perception of any constraints he may face. He takes no account of the objectives of any other decision makers, except in so far as an improvement in an opponent's expected achievements might further his own interests. Conflicts arise whenever the expected target outcomes depend on values of both $x_t^{(1)}$ and $x_t^{(2)}$. In that case, each player's optimal strategy depends on the strategy of the other player and cannot be determined by standard optimisation techniques applied to each instrument set $x_t^{(i)}$, $t=1...T$, independently. The optimal decisions for this competitive game are therefore a feasible pair $(x^{(1)*}, x^{(2)*})$ satisfying

$$\begin{aligned} & w^{(1)}(\tilde{x}^{(1)*}, \tilde{x}^{(2)*}) \leqslant w^{(1)}(\tilde{x}^{(1)}, \tilde{x}^{(2)*}) \\ \text{and} \quad & w^{(2)}(\tilde{x}^{(1)*}, \tilde{x}^{(2)*}) \leqslant w^{(2)}(\tilde{x}^{(1)*}, \tilde{x}^{(2)}) \end{aligned} \tag{2}$$

for all feasible $x^{(1)} \neq x^{(1)*}$, $x^{(2)} \neq x^{(2)*}$. Neither player has any incentive to deviate unilaterally from his own choice. So $x^{(1)*}$ and $x^{(2)*}$ constitute a Nash equilibrium solution.[1]

At any t, player i will have an information set, Ω_{ti}, comprising realised values of past variables in the system, expectations for future exogenous variables, and estimates of the objectives $w^{(1)}$, $w^{(2)}$, and of the economy's dynamic responses. Thus each player has the opportunity to recompute $x^{(1)*}$ and $x^{(2)*}$, conditional on his information Ω_{ti}, at each t. We define *open loop* decisions as $x_t^{(i)*} = g_{t,1}(\Omega_{1i})$ where $g_{t,1}(\cdot)$ are T optimal functions determined at $t=1$. *Closed loop* decisions are given by $x_t^{(i)*} = g_{t,t}(\Omega_{ti})$, where $g_{t,t}(\cdot)$ are determined optimally at t.[2] For section 3 we take $\Omega_{t1} = \Omega_{t2}$, but we consider players with differing information sets in section 4.

3. PRIVATE OPTIMAL DECISIONS

Each player faces a dynamic economic system of the form

$$y_t = f_t(y_{t-1}, x_t^{(1)}, x_t^{(2)}, e_t) \tag{3}$$

where e_t represents any noncontrollable exogenous influences. Hence the minimisation of $w^{(1)}$ and of $w^{(2)}$ is constrained by

$$y = R^{(1)}x^{(1)} + R^{(2)}x^{(2)} + s \tag{4}$$

where $R^{(i)} = \begin{bmatrix} R_{11}^{(i)} & & 0 \\ \vdots & \ddots & \\ R_{T1}^{(i)} & \cdots & R_{TT}^{(i)} \end{bmatrix}$ is a matrix of impact and dynamic multipliers such

that $$R_{tj}^{(i)} = \begin{cases} \partial f_t/\partial x_j^{(i)} & \text{if } t \geqslant j. \\ 0 & \text{otherwise} \end{cases} \tag{5}$$

The strictly causal nature of this economy is reflected in the block triangularity of $R^{(i)}$, i=1,2, which in practice would be evaluated from a structural model at suitable values of $x_t^{(1)}$, $x_t^{(2)}$ and e_t. Hereafter we assume that $R^{(1)}$ and $R^{(2)}$ are *known* matrices, in order to abstract from the complications of stochastic optimisation with parameter uncertainty.[3]

Once (4) has been constructed, any rows corresponding to nontargets can be deleted. Now, as far as player 1 is concerned, the restrictions on his choice variables are

$$\tilde{y}^{(1)} = R^{(1)}\tilde{x}^{(1)} + b^{(1)} \tag{6}$$

Player 2, on the other hand, has choice variables restricted by

$$\tilde{y}^{(2)} = R^{(2)}\tilde{x}^{(2)} + b^{(2)} \tag{7}$$

The quantities $b^{(1)} = R^{(2)}\tilde{x}^{(2)} + c^{(1)}$ and $b^{(2)} = R^{(1)}\tilde{x}^{(1)} + c^{(2)}$, where

$$c^{(i)} = s - y^{(i)d} + \sum_{j=1}^{2} R^{(j)}x^{(j)d} \tag{8}$$

for i=1 and 2, define the information required by each player in order to make his own decision. Hence the optimal decision for $x^{(1)}$ is structurally dependent on that for $x^{(2)}$, and vice versa. Indeed, if $x^{(j)}$ were fixed, the necessary conditions for an optimal decision by player i would be

$$\partial w^{(i)}/\partial \tilde{x}^{(i)} + (\partial \tilde{y}^{(i)}/\partial \tilde{x}^{(i)})' \; \partial w^{(i)}/\partial \tilde{y}^{(i)} = 0 \tag{9}$$

Inserting the relevant partial derivatives from (1) and (6) or (7), and then substituting for $\tilde{y}^{(i)}$, yields the optimal decisions

$$\tilde{x}^{(i)*} = -\left[G_0^{(i)'} Q^{(i)} G_0^{(i)}\right]^{-1} G_0^{(i)'} \left\{Q^{(i)}(\underset{\sim}{c}^{(i)} + \underset{\sim}{R}^{(j)}\tilde{x}_0^{(j)}) + q^{(i)}\right\} \tag{10}$$

where $G_0^{(i)'} = [R^{(i)'} : I]$ and $i \neq j$.[4] Player 1 would be correct to use (10) if it is true that his opponent will choose some value $x_0^{(2)}$ irrespective of the value finally chosen for $x^{(1)}$; i.e. if $\partial x^{(2)}/\partial x^{(1)} = 0$ although $\partial x^{(1)}/\partial x^{(2)} \neq 0$. If player 2 meanwhile undertakes a similar calculation, then the discrepancy between $x^{(2)*}$ and $x_0^{(2)}$ reveals the suboptimality of player 1's decision rule (and vice versa for player 2). Of course that kind of discrepancy can be eliminated by solving (10) for $x^{(1)}$ and $x^{(2)}$ simultaneously. But that will still yield suboptimal decisions because (9) and (10) continue to impose $\partial x^{(2)}/\partial x^{(1)} = 0$ on $x^{(1)*}$, and $\partial x^{(1)}/\partial x^{(2)} = 0$ on $x^{(2)*}$. Each player thus computes an optimal reaction to his opponent's decision, but ignores the counteractions of this opponent who is doing the same. Like in chess, it is obvious that each move must be selected conditionally on the rational current and future counter moves expected from one's opponent. The choice of $x^{(j)}$ is not fixed with respect to $x^{(i)}$ (and vice versa) and it is inconsistent to derive a decision rule for $x^{(i)*}$ which recognises $\partial x^{(i)}/\partial x^{(j)} \neq 0$ but assumes $\partial x^{(j)}/\partial x^{(i)} = 0$, while at the same time deriving a rule for $x^{(j)*}$ which allows $\partial x^{(j)}/\partial x^{(i)} \neq 0$ but assumes $\partial x^{(i)}/\partial x^{(j)} = 0$.

The necessary conditions for the optimal decisions defined by (2) are, in fact,

$$\partial w^{(i)}/\partial \tilde{x}^{(i)} + \left\{(\partial \tilde{y}^{(i)}/\partial \tilde{x}^{(j)}) \, \partial \tilde{x}^{(j)}/\partial \tilde{x}^{(i)} + \partial \tilde{y}^{(i)}/\partial \tilde{x}^{(i)}\right\}' \; \partial w^{(i)}/\partial \tilde{y}^{(i)} = 0 \tag{11}$$

for i=1,2 and j≠i. Excepting $\partial \tilde{x}^{(j)}/\partial \tilde{x}^{(i)}$, all the partial derivates required to evaluate (11) are again given by (1) and (6) or (7). The difficulty will be to evaluate $\partial \tilde{x}^{(j)}/\partial \tilde{x}^{(i)}$ and $\partial \tilde{x}^{(i)}/\partial \tilde{x}^{(j)}$ correctly. Indeed, since $\partial \tilde{x}^{(j)}/\partial \tilde{x}^{(i)}$ is generally a function of $x^{(i)}$ and $x^{(j)}$, (11) contains two sets of simultaneous equations which are nonlinear in the decision variables $x^{(i)}$ and $x^{(j)}$. So it is not possible to write down analytic expressions for the optimal decisions. But an interative search procedure can be devised to evaluate the decisions which satisfy (11). For example, if $\partial \tilde{x}^{(j)}/\partial \tilde{x}^{(i)} = D^{(j)}$ were known for j=1 and 2 we could solve (11) for i=1 and i=2 simultaneously to obtain $(x^{(1)*}, x^{(2)*})$:

$$\begin{bmatrix} \tilde{x}^{(1)*} \\ \\ \tilde{x}^{(2)*} \end{bmatrix} = - \begin{bmatrix} G^{(1)'} Q^{(1)} G_0^{(1)} & \vdots & G^{(1)'} Q^{(1)} \begin{bmatrix} R^{(2)} \\ \cdots \\ 0 \end{bmatrix} \\ \cdots\cdots\cdots & \vdots & \cdots\cdots\cdots \\ G^{(2)'} Q^{(2)} \begin{bmatrix} R^{(1)} \\ \cdots \\ 0 \end{bmatrix} & \vdots & G^{(2)'} Q^{(2)} G_0^{(2)} \end{bmatrix}^{-1} \begin{bmatrix} G^{(1)'} \left\{ Q^{(1)} \begin{pmatrix} c^{(1)} \\ \cdots\cdots \\ 0 \end{pmatrix} + q^{(1)} \right\} \\ \\ G^{(2)'} \left\{ Q^{(2)} \begin{pmatrix} c^{(2)} \\ \cdots\cdots \\ 0 \end{pmatrix} + q^{(2)} \right\} \end{bmatrix} \tag{12}$$

where $G^{(i)'} = \{(R^{(i)} + R^{(j)} D^{(j)})' \vdots I\}$ and $G_0^{(i)'} = (R^{(i)'} \vdots I)$. One obvious way of evaluating (12), when $D^{(1)}$ and $D^{(2)}$ are unknown, is to construct a fixed point between $(D^{(1)}, D^{(2)})$ and $(x^{(1)*}, x^{(2)*})$. Indeed an iterative scheme for searching such a point is already implied, since inserting any trial values $D_s^{(1)}$ and $D_s^{(2)}$ into (12) automatically generates new values for those policy reaction matrices. With $D_s^{(1)}$ and $D_s^{(2)}$ inserted, (12 can be rearranged as

$$\begin{bmatrix} I & -D_{s+1}^{(1)} \\ \\ -D_{s+1}^{(2)} & I \end{bmatrix} \begin{bmatrix} \tilde{x}_{s+1}^{(1)} \\ \\ \tilde{x}_{s+1}^{(2)} \end{bmatrix} = \begin{bmatrix} F_{s+1}^{(1)} c^{(1)} + k_{s+1}^{(1)} \\ \\ F_{s+1}^{(2)} c^{(2)} + k_{s+1}^{(2)} \end{bmatrix} \tag{13}$$

where, for i,j=1 and 2, and i≠j,

$$D_{s+1}^{(i)} = - \left[G_s^{(i)'} Q^{(i)} G_0^{(i)} \right]^{-1} G_s^{(i)'} Q^{(i)} \begin{pmatrix} R^{(j)} \\ \cdots \\ 0 \end{pmatrix} \tag{14}$$

and $(F_{s+1}^{(i)} \vdots k_{s+1}^{(i)}) = -(G_s^{(i)'} Q^{(i)} G_0^{(i)})^{-1} G_s^{(i)'} \left\{ Q^{(i)} \begin{pmatrix} I \\ \cdots \\ 0 \end{pmatrix} \vdots q^{(i)} \right\}$ with

$G_s^{(i)'} = \left\{ (R^{(i)} + R^{(j)} D_s^{(j)})' \vdots I \right\}$. That means we can attempt to evaluate $(x^{(1)*}, x^{(2)*})$ by constructing a fixed point satisfying (11), say $(D_*^{(1)}, D_*^{(2)})$ and $(x^{(1)*}, x^{(2)*})$ using (13) and (14). We can be sure that such a fixed point exists because a Nash equilibrium solution exists for any nonzero sum game with conves objectives and strategy sets.[5] Indeed if (1) and (4) respectively contain quadratic and linear functions of $x^{(1)}$ and $x^{(2)}$, then the associated optimal decisions are unique.[6] But beyond this strictly linear-quadratic configuration, experimenting with different starts, $D_1^{(1)}$ and $D_1^{(2)}$, will be necessary to identify globally optimal decisions.

However, it is straightforward, if tedious, to derive an expression for player i's decisions in each step of (13). Equation (13) actually implies[7]

implies [7]

$$x^{(i)}_{s+1} = -\left\{G^{(i)\prime}_{s} Q^{(i)}\left[G^{(i)}_{s} - \binom{R^{(j)}}{o}(D^{(j)}_{s+1} - D^{(j)}_{s})\right]\right\}^{-1} G^{(i)\prime}_{s}\left\{Q^{(i)}\binom{I}{o}\cdot\right.$$

$$\left.\cdot\left[c^{(i)} + R^{(j)}(F^{(j)}_{s+1} c^{(j)} + k^{(j)}_{s+1})\right] + q^{(i)}\right\} \tag{15}$$

for i,j=1,2 and i≠j.

The optimal decisions, $x^{(1)*}$ and $x^{(2)*}$, generated by $D^{(1)}_{*}$ and $D^{(2)}_{*}$ (assuming that the iteration (14) is sure to locate those values) will therefore be given by the optimal decision for a single independent player attempting to minimise $w^{(i)}$ constrained by

$$\tilde{y}^{(i)} = (R^{(i)} + R^{(j)} D^{(j)}_{*})\tilde{x}^{(i)} + d^{(i)}_{*} \tag{16}$$

for i,j=1,2 and i≠j; where $d^{(i)}_{*} = c^{(i)} + R^{(j)}(F^{(j)}_{*} c^{(j)} + k^{(j)}_{*})$, and $F^{(j)}_{*}$, $k^{(j)}_{*}$ are defined in (14), when evaluated using $D^{(j)}_{*}$. This result follows because (15), when evaluated at $D^{(i)}_{*}$ and $D^{(j)}_{*}$, reduces to (10) with $R^{(i)} + R^{(j)} D^{(j)}_{*}$ replacing $R^{(i)}$ and $F^{(j)}_{*} c^{(j)} + k^{(j)}_{*}$ replacing $x^{(j)}$. Moreover $x^{(1)*}$ and $x^{(2)*}$ now satisfy the necessary conditions (11) exactly; and (15), evaluated at $D^{(1)}_{*}$ and $D^{(2)}_{*}$, implies that they also satisfy the sufficient conditions for the minima defined at (2).

But the nonlinearity of the key iterative process (14) is such that it cannot be shown to always converge on any fixed points, let alone on the required $(D^{(1)}_{*}, D^{(2)}_{*})$ values. So it is not certain that (13) and (14) will always construct the optimal decisions which satisfy (9). However, it is always possible to modify the search for $(D^{(1)}_{*}, D^{(2)}_{*})$ so that the associated steps in $x^{(1)}_{s+1}$ and $x^{(2)}_{s+1}$ are forced 'downhill', and ultimately onto $(x^{(1)*}, x^{(2)*})$. One way to do this is to replace

$$D^{(i)}_{s+1} \text{ by } \gamma_i D^{(i)}_{s+1} + (1-\gamma_i) D^{(i)}_{s} \tag{17}$$

where $0<\gamma_i<1$ is a scalar chosen to ensure a downhill step,

$$w^{(i)}(\tilde{x}^{(1)}_{s+1}, \tilde{x}^{(2)}_{s+1}) \leqslant w^{(i)}(\tilde{x}^{(1)}_{s}, \tilde{x}^{(2)}_{s}) \tag{18}$$

for i=1 and 2, in (2). Evaluation of $\partial w^{(i)}/\partial\gamma_i$ will indicate an appropriate γ_i value. There are many other possibilities. We have not attempted to define a computationally efficient algorithm here because (11) converts the dynamic optimisation into an extended static form, so that, in principle, any of the standard fixed point algorithms for constructing general equilibria could be employed. The purpose of the

$D_s^{(i)}$ iterations is to suggest new directions in the search for optimal decisions. [8]

4. UNCERTAINTY AND HETEROGENEOUS INFORMATION

Additive uncertainty can now be treated in the conventional manner by applying the certainty equivalence theorem to (16):

$$\min_{x^{(i)}} \left\{ E_{ti}(w^{(i)}) | \tilde{y}^{(i)} - (R^{(i)} + R^{(j)}D_*^{(j)})\tilde{x}^{(i)} - d_*^{(i)}) = 0 \right\} =$$
$$\min_{x^{(i)}} \left\{ w^{(i)} | \tilde{y}^{(i)} - (R^{(i)} + R^{(j)}D_*^{(j)})\tilde{x}^{(i)} - E_{ti}(d_*^{(i)}) = 0 \right\} \tag{19}$$

for i,j=1,2 and i≠j and where $E_{ti}(.) = E(\cdot|\Omega_{ti})$ denotes a conditional expectation. Certainty equivalent decisions are therefore obtained by using both $E_{ti}(c^{(1)})$ and $E_{ti}(c^{(2)})$ to construct each $E_{ti}(d_*^{(i)})$ in a reformulation of (10):

$$\tilde{x}^{(i)*} = -(G_*^{(i)\prime} Q^{(i)} G_*^{(i)})^{-1} G^{(i)\prime} (Q^{(i)} \begin{pmatrix} E_{ti}(d_*^{(i)}) \\ \hline 0 \end{pmatrix} + q^{(i)}) \tag{20}$$

for i=1 and 2, and $G_*^{(i)\prime} = \left[(R^{(i)} + R^{(j)}D_*^{(j)})' \,\vdots\, I \right]$.

5. THE STRUCTURE OF THE RATIONAL EXPECTATIONS MECHANISM

In the Lucas critique of policy making, systematic decisions undertaken by the government can be anticipated by the private sector. Rational agents respond by altering their own decisions. This has two unfortunate consequences; (a) the original policy measures will be invalidated, since they are based on a false (pre-change) assumption of the private sector's behaviour, and (b) the economy's expected responses (and the target outcomes in particular) will change from those just used to condition the government's policy calculations.

Evidently the opportunity exists for recomputing this pair of decisions sequentially, and eventually an equilibrium may be achieved in which the government's assumptions about the private sector agree with what the private sector now believes to be the optimal response to the policies just computed by the government. But there are obviously two ways of trying to reach that situation. The government can itself attempt to solve for its own optimal policies jointly with the private sector's rational responses. That involves locating the Nash equilibrium solution in (2) directly, and it corresponds to removing consequence (a) of the previous paragraph. This was done in section 3. Alternatively, the government may condition its decisions correctly by accounting *fully* for the consequences of its actions (which appear directly through the economy's responses, and indirectly through the private sector's responses which in turn affect the economy again). This may be done by including the associated rational expectations of future endogenous variables among the determinants of current economic behaviour before taking any decisions. That corresponds to removing consequence (b) of the previous paragraph. This section shows how those rational expectations terms appear in a dynamic model such as (3), and thereby exposes the structure of the constraints which the government must satisfy if it is to condition its decisions correctly.

Consider the development of the targets in response to the jointly dependent decisions which constitute the game solution given at (2). Suppose player 1 is the government and that, for the moment, there are no random variables in the problem. Using the fact that $D_*^{(i)} = F_*^{(i)}R^{(j)}$, we can insert $R^{(1)}\tilde{x}^{(1)} = \tilde{y}^{(1)} - b^{(1)}$ in the lower part of (13) to eliminate $\tilde{x}^{(1)}$. The only difficulty with the resulting expression for $\tilde{x}^{(2)*}$ is that $b^{(1)}$ is also a function of $\tilde{x}^{(2)*}$. But the existence of a model linking y and $x^{(1)}$ implies that latent computed values (expectations) for future endogenous variables will always be available to the government. Therefore substitute $R^{(2)}\tilde{x}^{(2)*} + c^{(1)}$ for $b^{(1)}$, then solve the expression obtained for $\tilde{x}^{(2)*}$ and insert the result into (4). Sorting out terms now yields

$$y_t = \sum_{j=1}^{t} R_{tj}^{(1)} x_j^{(1)} + \sum_{j=1}^{t-1} K_{tj} y_{t-j} + \sum_{j=0}^{T-1} K_{t,t+j} y_{t+j} + k_t \tag{21}$$

where $K = R^{(2)} \left[I + F^{(2)} R^{(2)} \right]^{-1} F^{(2)}$ and

$$k_t = \sum_{j=1}^{T} K_{tj} \left[c_j^{(2)} - s_j - \sum_{i=1}^{T} (R_{ji}^{(1)} x_i^{(1)d} + R_{ji}^{(2)} x_i^{(2)d}) \right] + s_t + \sum_{j=1}^{T} R_{tj}^{(2)} x_j^{(2)d} \tag{22}$$

We have writtern K_{tj}, $K_{t,t+j}$ and k_t as, respectively, the $(t,j)^{th}$ and $(t,t+j)^{th}$ submatrices of K and the tth subvector of k, all partitioned with respect to time.

Next we abandon the assumption if bi random variables. We can repeat the steps above conditional on the government's information set at each stage, Ω_{t1}, as a consequence of the certainty equivalence theorem which was applied tot he implicit game at (19). We finish up with

$$y_t = \sum_{j=1}^{t} R_{tj}^{(1)} x_j^{(1)} + \sum_{j=1}^{t} K_{tj} y_{t-j} + \sum_{j=0}^{T-t} K_{t,t+1} y_{t+1\,|t} + k_{t\,|t} \qquad (23)$$

where $y_{t+j\,|\,t} = E(y_{t+j}\,|\,\Omega_{t1})$. Finally $k_{t\,|\,t}$ is k_t with $c_{j\,|\,t}^{(2)} = E(c_j^{(2)}\,|\,\Omega_{t1})$ and $s_{j\,|\,t} = E(s_j\,|\,\Omega_{t1})$ replacing $c_j^{(2)}$ and $s_j^{(2)}$ in the first two terms only ($j \geq t$). Conditional expectations appear only in the first two terms of $k_{t\,|\,t}$ because the realisation of y_t is determined by an $x^{(1)*}$ which is chosen conditionally on $E_{t1}(x^{(2)*})$, and vice versa for $x^{(2)*}$. Hence the government's elimination of $x^{(2)*}$ is conditioned on Ω_{t1}. But the residual uncertainty still determines the realisation of y_t, which therefore depends directly on the stochastic events in s, the fixed (implemented) values of $x_j^{(1)}$ and $x_j^{(2)}$ ($j \leq t$), and current expectations of the future.

Thus, in the government's view, the targets appear to evolve as a function of its instruments, a reformulation of the dynamic structure, the impacts of (partly expected) external events, *and* rational expectations of the future endogenous variables. Since rational decisions by other agents are fully accounted for in the behaviour described by (23), a full solution of that model can provide evaluations for $y_{t+j\,|\,t}$ and thus the proper set of constraints to be applied in the government's policy selection procedure.

However, the government may be unable or unwilling to gather enough accurate information of the quantities $Q^{(2)}$, $R^{(2)}$, $z^{(2)d}$ and $E_{t2}(s)$ used by other agents in order to compute K and k correctly. In that case the government might estimate the coefficients of (23) directly from observations on the relevant variables. The point here is that the construction of (23) provides a theoretical justification for models containing rational expectations of future endogenous events; it specifies in detail the structure of such a rational expectations process; and it describes the behavioural responses which must be satisfied if decisions are to be protected from the Lucas critique.

6. AN EMPIRICAL PLANNING MODEL

The Dutch Central Planning Bureau makes policy recommendations to the government by means of central economic plans which are prepared on an annual basis. A macroeconomic forecast (the central projection) is prepared, assuming unaltered policies apart from those policy changes which are officially announced at the moment when the computation is made. Socially and politically feasible changes are then considered as policy alternatives. At each stage government officials, representatives of employers' and workers' organisations, and economic experts are consulted. The policy recommendations are generated using the Vintaf-II model which was developed by the Dutch Central Planning Bureau in the early seventies and which has been revised several times since then. [9] This is an annual model of 130 equations and the version we used includes a rudimentary monetary sector.[10] For the purposes of this exercise it has been linearised around the central projection for 1976–80 (for details see Brandsma, Hughes Hallett and Van der Windt (1984)). That linearisation conforms to the description surrounding equations (3) and (4) above.

The model can be divided in six interdependent blocks. The first block represents the supply side of the Dutch economy. It contains a vintage type production system with fixed technical coefficients between investment, capacity production and capacity employment per vintage. Because of the indirect measurements of capacity production, capacity employment and the stock of physical capital, this section of the model introduces one set of uncertainties facing government planners due to events on the labour market. The second block provides a conventional determination of effective demand. Domestic demand mainly depends on disposable income, while relative prices are important determinants of foreign trade. Confrontation of the production capacity with effective demand gives the utilisation rate of the capacity which in its turn is an explanatory variable in the equation for prices, imports and exports, and investment.

The third block determines wages and prices. Prices are determined by wage and import costs per unit of output together with foreign competitive prices. The wage equation implies full compensation for prices and for rises in labour productivity. This equation of course represents activity in the labour market, and directly, or indirectly through prices, it transmits any uncertainty over the effectiveness of incomes policies to other sectors of the economy. The Phillips-curve effect and a term expressing the pressure of social security charges and personal taxation complete this equation and it will be described in more detail below.

The fourth block describes the social security system in which the number of unemployed people plays an important role. The government sector (the fifth block) is less important because government expenditure and government employment are treated as exogenous. Tax revenues are modelled in a very simple way.

The monetary sector is the final block. It consists of an equation for base-money in which the balance of payments is the key variable. In its turn base-money is an explanatory variable in the equations of consumption– and investment expenditure. The structure of the model is set out in tabular form in the appendix.

7. ECONOMIC POLICY AND WAGE BARGAINING

It is generally accepted, at least in the Netherlands, that economic policies should aim at the following five objectives:

- acceptable economic growth;
- an equitable income distribution;
- a minimum unemployment rate;
- a balance of payments equilibrium; and
- a stable price level.

However, government plans published during the period 1976–80 suggest that economic growth was considered as more or less exogenous, while restraining the budget deficit has replaced the balance of payments as the most binding constraint on the political feasibility of economic policies. From a medium term plan presented by the government in 1978 we take the following target values:[11]

- a reduction of unemployment to no more that 150,000 man-years (which corresponds to 3.5% of the working population);
- the decrease of inflation to 2 or 3% a year;
- the improvement of the rate of return for firms;
- the constraint that the budget deficit of the government should be no higher than 4 or 5% of net national income in the medium term.

A rather rough quantification of the third objective was formulated in terms of a decline of 1%-point a year of the wage share in income. In addition, the plan foresaw zero real wage growth above an autonomous component of 1%.

Although originally extremely controversial, a consensus has now grown up among policy makers and their advisors that wage moderation would be the economic panacea, especially by improving international competitiveness and the rate of return for firms. Because of this, the government has exerted some downward pressure on wages, directly intervening, where necessary, in the wages negotiated at a national level. But these interventions seem never to have had more than a marginal effect on the overall outcome of the wage bargaining process. This implies labour unions anticipated, and discounted, the government's future interventions. Hence $W_t = f(W_{t+1|t}, U_{t+1|t} \ldots)$ if W_t = the money wage and U_t = unemployment, just as in the Lucas critique. This means that wage policy is only an indirect instrument in the hands of the government, and is different in this respect to government expenditures, taxes, and the control of the money supply by the central bank.

On the other hand, several channels exist, or may be created, by which the government can influence wage formation. Reducing government wages, or threatening to do so, increases potential supply on the labour market. Real wage resistance may be partly broken by tax measures. Job creation and reductions in labour time are both negotiable with labour unions and employers against a wage cut, and so on.

It is important to recognise the role played here by expectations of government policies in the wage bargaining process, and the repercussions which the resulting wage claims have on the effectiveness of government measures. Both with respect to the implied bargaining process and the generation of expectations, the wage equation which was supplied as part of the Vintaf-II model is not very sophisticated. In addition, the Central Planning Bureau excludes the Phillips curve effect from all model simulations whenever the level of unemployment reaches a value larger than 3% (Knegt et al. (1978)). Unfortunately, this condition applies to the whole planning period 1976–80. But, even if the traditional Phillips curve itself fails to hold or undergoes structural shifts when unemployment passes a certain threshold, that does not imply unemployment suddenly has no impact on wage settlements. On the contrary, if unemployment is rising, changes in unemployment continue to exert a very significant effect on the wage changes claimed and negotiated. This effect is demonstrated by Brandsma and Van der Windt (1983), who replace the constant of the Phillips curve by

$$\psi(u) = -2.5(1-e^{-2u}) \tag{24}$$

when $u \geq 0$ is the change in the unemployment rate. This function could have been incorporated directly in an amended version of the Vintaf model. But for two reasons we chose to introduce elements of bargaining and expectations via a dynamic game framework instead. First, rational expectations of wage earners (the 'private sector' of section 5) are likely to incorporate projections of the model which are officially published, and thus they should be based on the same model as used by the government for planning purposes. Secondly, these projections may in practice have the character of judgemental forecasts and the game framework leaves room for investigating the effects of expectations other than those generated by the model itself (cf. (20) in section 4). Notice also that a model incorporating (24) would induce discontinuities (depending on $u>0$ or $u \leq 0$) in the optimal decision rules.

The optimising behaviour of wage earners, whether or not represented by labour unions, which underlies the estimated wage equation in Brandsma and Van der Windt (1983) is an amended version of the real wage resistance hypothesis of Hicks (1975). It was formulated by Batchelor and Sheriff (1980) as the reluctance of workers to accept real wage increases that are less than the growth of labour productivity. The desired values of wage earners, implied by the game, are therefore equal to the projected growth of labour productivity for the period 1976–80 at the time of the negotiations. But when unemployment is rising that value is reduced by –2.5%, being the maximum downward shift of the Phillips curve implied by (24). Following Brandsma, Hughes Hallett and Van der Windt (1983), the trade-off between real wage increments and increasing unemployment can then be described, in terms of the objective function (1) for wage earners (i=2) as

$$\frac{\partial w^{(2)}/\partial y_1}{\partial w^{(2)}/\partial y_2} = \frac{\psi'[\tilde{y}_1 Q_{11}^{(2)}]}{\tilde{y}_2 Q_{22}^{(2)}} \tag{25}$$

where $\psi' = \partial y_2/\partial y_1$ denotes the partial derivative of real wage changes to changes in unemployment. If labour unions are concerned with the number of their rank and file who will become unemployed in the near future, as was supposed in the derivation of (24), $y_1^{(1)d} = y_{1,t-1}$ and the derivative ψ' may be evaluated at $\tilde{y}_1$. From (24) and (25) it then follows that a balanced trade-off requires the restriction

$$Q_{11}^{(2)} = -5(\tilde{y}_1/\tilde{y}_2)e^{-2\tilde{y}_1} \cdot Q_{22}^{(2)} \tag{26}$$

in the preference function of wage earners.

Thus we arrive at the specification of the policy problem faced by the government in confrontation with the rational expectations of wage earners in the private sector which is given in table 1. The penalties on deviations from unaltered policy for the government reflect the short term (political or admininstrative) inertia of those policy instruments. For instance, numerous pressure groups hamper the retrenchment of public expenditures, the central bank opposes an increase of the money supply, and higher taxes encourage tax evasion. On the other hand, additional wage claims are penalised, among other things, for the loss of jobs, cash and goodwill involved in potential strikes. Note, however, that instrument penalties are not a prerequisite for estimating the effect of rational expectations in (23). Even if the instrument part of $Q^{(2)}$ is zero, so that labour unions have a free hand in claiming wages, the matrix K in (21) only becomes singular if $D_s^{(1)} = 0$ in (14) for player 2. This would imply that labour unions take absolutely no account of the possibility of government reactions to their actions.

Table 1. The policy problem

(a) Government:

target variable	symbol	desired value	priority 1976–80
price level (of consumption)	P	< 2% a year	(1., 1., 1., 1., 1.)
wage share in income	S	– 1% a year	(1., 1., 1., 1., 1.)
unemployment rate	U	<3.5% each year	(1., 1., 1., 1., 1.)
budget deficit	D	<4.5% of NNI	(1., 1., 1., 1., 1.)
real wages	R	<.75% a year	(1., 1., 1., 1., 1.)
instrument		**benchmark value**	
government expenditures	G	unaltered policy	(1., 1., 1., 1., 1.)
money supply	B	unaltered policy	(1., 1., 1., 1., 1.)
direct taxes on wages	T	unaltered policy	(1., 1., 1., 1., 1.)

(b) Labour:

target variable		desired value	
unemployment	U	no change	(.77,.14,.01,.01,.01)
real wage per wage earner	R	8.5%–2.5%=6.5%	(1., 1., 1., 1., 1.)
instrument		**benchmark value**	
wage claim	WCL	no extra claim	(1., 1., 1., 1., 1.)

8. DECOMPOSING THE RATIONAL EXPECTATIONS MECHANISM

8.1 The structural importance of expectations

For the purpose of calculating the effects on the target variables of the government of (rational) expectations held by wage earners about (optimal) government policies, we rewrite (23) for i=1 and t=1 as

$$y_1 = R_{11}^{(1)} x_1^{(1)} + \sum_{j=1}^{T} K_{1j} y_{j|1} + k_{1|1} \tag{27}$$

If we assume that the information sets Ω_{t1} and Ω_{t2} contain the same information about noncontrollable and uncertain variables, it is easily seen that

$$k_{1|1} = s_1 + R_{11}^{(2)} x_1^{(2)d} - \sum_{j=1}^{T} K_{1j} y_j^{(2)d} \tag{28}$$

The rational expectations term of (27) may then be simplified to

$$f_1 = \sum_{j=1}^{T} K_{1j}(y_{j|1} - y_j^{(2)d}) \tag{29}$$

Tables 2 and 3 set out sample columns from K_{1j}, j=1...T, evaluated for the policy problem which was defined in table 1. These figure show the impact of the expected 1976–80 outcomes for unemployment and real wages on current (1976) targets.

Table 2. The column of K_{1j}, j=1 ...T, corresponding to the expectations of the unemployment rate, $E(U_j|\Omega_{11})$.

Year	1976	1977	1978	1979	1980
j =	1	2	3	4	5
P	– 0.088	– 0.026	0.000	0.000	0.000
S	– 0.071	– 0.021	0.000	0.000	0.000
U	– 0.028	– 0.008	0.000	0.000	0.000
D	– 0.011	– 0.003	0.000	0.000	0.000
R	– 0.112	– 0.033	0.000	0.000	0.000

Table 3. The column of K_{1j}, j=1 ...T, corresponding to the expectations for wage rate growth, $E(R_j|\Omega_{11})$.

j =	1	2	3	4	5
P	0.452	– 0.178	– 0.125	– 0.044	0.020
S	0.364	– 0.143	– 0.100	– 0.035	0.016
U	– 0.146	– 0.057	– 0.040	– 0.014	0.006
D	– 0.057	– 0.022	– 0.016	– 0.006	0.002
R	0.579	– 0.228	– 0.160	– 0.056	0.025

The results show that rising expectations for the unemployment rate have negative but highly damped effects on the government's target variables. These impacts actually go in the desired direction for each of those targets.Higher expectations of wage rate growth in the immediate and near future also have effects in the desirable direction. It is interesting to note that an anticipated additional 1% growth of real wages has a greater impact than an expected increment of the unemployment rate of equivalent size. More than half of the difference between an initially anticipated real wage increase and the government's target for that variable is discounted predominantly through the effects that the anticipated anti-inflation measures would have on P. The other target variables are affected in the order S, U, D. Furthermore, the greater the lead the smaller the effects of expectations. For $E(R_j|\Omega_{11})$, j=1...T, this reflects the time pattern of the multipliers, while the fact that the effects of $E(U_j|\Omega_{11})$ fade out so rapidly after a one-year lead (j=2) is largely due to the functional form of (24) which is insensitive to differences in unemployment rates if the (predicted) change in unemployment is already high.

8.2 The dynamic impact of expectations

The figures in table 3 suggest that the impact of the rational expectations components can be substantial, and that it may vary for different targets and different lead periods. It would be useful to have some indication of the impact of the expectations mechanism as a whole on the targets over the interval [1, T]. That can be done by comparing the model's characteristics and performance with and without taking the expectations terms into account, to give a quantitative measure of the role played by expectations, and of the seriousness of the Lucas critique, in policy problems. There are two items of interest here: (a) how do expectations affect policy effectiveness (the policy multipliers determine the ability to steer an economy); and (b) are predictive failures larger or systematically biased when expectations are ignored? To answer these questions, we stack (21) over t=1 ... T

$$y = R^{(1)}x^{(1)} + Ky_{|1} + k_{|1} \tag{30}$$

where $y_{|1}$ and $k_{|1}$ are partitioned similarly to y. Now

$$y_{|1} = (I-K)^{-1}R^{(1)}x^{(1)} + (I-K)^{-1}k_{|1} \tag{31}$$

But $(I-K)^{-1}R^{(1)} = R^{(1)} + R^{(2)}D_*^{(2)}$, which therefore evaluates the target-instrument multipliers while accounting *fully* for the expected rational decisions of wage earners. We compare the impact multipliers of G and T in table 4; the money supply instrument had no current effects.[12] Although in principle noncausality is present (cf. Brandsma and Hughes Hallett (1982)), the relevant elements of $(I-K)^{-1}R^{(1)}$ were quantitatively unimportant in this exercise.

Table 4. The impact multipliers of the government with and without rational expectations.

	G		T	
	with	without	with	without
P	0.050	0.047	0.006	0.024
S	– 0.046	– 0.049	0.053	0.068
U	– 0.031	– 0.032	0.014	0.020
D	0.095	0.095	– 0.068	– 0.066
R	– 0.008	– 0.012	0.051	0.075

The immediate impact of policies has been weakened by the expectations process, although no signs are reversed. It is clear that the multipliers of T are much more affected than those of G. Indeed, this is to be expected as taxes play a direct role in wage negotiations and there is the obvious possibility of offsetting the anticipated burden of taxes through wage claims. Indeed, the automatic indexing of wages in the Dutch economy means that wage earners have the ability to make their claims in terms of *real disposable* wages, with the result that taxes (whether direct or indirect) are almost completely neutralised as an anti-inflation instrument. Although this is predictable as an institutional fact, the failure to account for the consequences of the expectations generated by such predictions leads to policies which are computed on the assumption that taxes are 4 times more effective in controlling inflation than they really are.

Similarly the predictability of tax policy implies that about half of its impact on unemployment and incomes policy will be offset by wage earners' reactions to its anticipated consequences. On the other hand, government expenditure has very little immediate impact on labour's objectives and hence its impacts are discounted only slightly through expectations; the inflationary impact is increased slightly, and the incomes policy impact adjusted down, by reactions in the labour market.

8.3. Predictive performance and expectations

Alternatively we can measure the importance of the expectations process in terms of the projections of the targets implied by the model with and without rational expectations terms. The government's central projection for 1976–80 has been made without expectations terms; i.e. (4) and a fixed information set covering $x^{(2)}$ in addition to $x^{(1)}$ and s. This projection is taken as a benchmark. The projections generated by the same model and information set but allowing for rational expectations effects in place of $x^{(2)}$ (i.e. using (27)) are given in the first column of table 5. These figures are deviations from the original central projection. The impact of the expectations process is quite marked; predicted inflation, the wage share, and the real wage rate, have to be revised up by some 1 or 2%, and unemployment by 0.5%. On the other hand, nonrational expected values paint a rather worse picture. If one takes the expectations model but accepts the official central projection as the appropriate expectations of the future, we get the predictions in the last column of table 5. If instead the official projection is used for all expected values, except unemployment and real wages which are projected either on a 'no change' basis or 'equal changes' basis from 1976–80, then we get the two middle columns of table 5. The three right hand columns therefore indicate the sensitivity of an expectations model to different 'errors' in forming expectations.

Table 5. Projections for 1976 using the expectations model (27) but different expected values.

	Rational Expectations	Equal changes $(\Delta U_t=\Delta U_{t-1}, R_t=R_{t-1})$	No changes $(\Delta U_t=0, \tilde{R}_t=0)$	Government's Projection
P	1.52	1.34	4.52	4.94
S	1.22	1.08	3.64	3.97
U	0.49	0.43	1.46	1.60
D	0.19	0.17	0.57	0.62
R	1.95	1.71	5.80	6.33

It is clear that accurate rational expectations cause the least disturbances and that the expectations of U_t and R_t are the only ones which matter here. Moreover, labour unions (among others) have frequently complained that the Central Planning Bureau has 'systematically underestimated the economy's prospects', and Bomhoff (1980) has produced some evidence that official forecasts are systematically biased towards the government's desired values. Table 5 shows that failing to allow for the effects of (rationally) anticipated outcomes on current targets would tend to produce exactly the same results. Although this systematic bias might be a deliberate attempt by the government to influence wage negotiations (as Bomhoff argues), it is more likely to be due to a systematic neglect of the expectations mechanism when making model projections since unions with rational expectations would foresee (and discount) these interventions. If the government realised that, they would not risk being found out; and, even if they were, it would already have been allowed for in the unions' strategy. Indeed, the latter explanation is just an instance of the Lucas critique at work.

9. AN EVALUATION OF POLICY ALTERNATIVES AND FORECASTING BEHAVIOUR

The structural model of the rational expectations mechanism (31) produces optimal policies for the government, which are, of course, different from those which do not account for the anticipations of the private sector. Both types of 'optimal' policies are presented in table 6, where the latter is referred to as the policy alternative since this is the policy to be considered by the government if it attempts to control wages despite union reactions. It turns out that potential wage claims force the government to resort to even more retrenchment, coupled with higher taxes, and some money creation. Experience shows that this is exactly how governments react. It also reflects the fact that the government's instruments are relatively more effective for removing the budget deficit if rational expectations are taken into account (table 4).

Table 6. The open loop policies of the government (a) with, and (b) without, rational expectations.

(a) rational expectations

	1976	1977	1978	1979	1980
G	−3.20	−2.75	−1.88	−1.42	−0.18
B	0.79	0.96	0.60	0.77	0.00
T	0.95	1.06	0.81	0.62	−0.64

(b) policy alternative

	1976	1977	1978	1979	1980
G	−2.67	−2.22	−1.52	−1.23	−0.14
B	0.68	0.81	0.42	0.63	0.00
T	0.57	0.89	0.70	0.57	−0.64

The effects of the policy alternative and the rational expectations policy on the target variables of the government are compared to the central projection and to the realisations in figure 1. Although not treated as a target variable, we included production growth because it is both an important indicator of the economy's behaviour as well as an accumulator of prediction errors in the model. The pictures on the left show that the forecasting performance of the central projection is rather bad and that the policy alternative has, except for the budget variable, only slightly favourable effects on the target variables. Moreover, the inclusion of rational expectations terms has rather little effect on forecasting performance. However, this conclusion changes somewhat if we look at the revised projections, using the original model, after the first year policies $x_1^{(i)}$, i=1,2, have been applied. To see as to how far the first year revisions may be explained by the policies which either do or do not take account of rational expectations, the corresponding deviations are compared on the right hand side of figure 1. The first policy calculations (based on the 1976 information set), which account for rational expectations, are much closer to the revised nonrational expectations policies (based on the 1977 information set) than they are to the nonrational expectations policies based on the 1976 information. This result shows that policy recommendations from a rational expectations model react to predicted outcomes in such a way as to (partly) offset any anticipated target failures. A nonrational expectations model cannot provide this capability.

The revisions in production growth forecasts are, both absolutely and in their development over time, better explained with than without rational expectations. The same is true for unemployment and budget deficit figures. With some exceptions, the values and shape of the remaining curves are more in favour of accepting the rational expectations hypothesis than rejecting it. It should not be forgotten, however, that these results are derived from a model which is estimated without explicit allowance for rational expectations. Moreover, while it is generally recognised that the wage equation is central to the character of this model, we noted earlier that it is incompletely specified with regard to the Phillips curve effect. In the literature, this sometimes stands for unanticipated inflation and other information errors. The differences between the rational expectations effects and the projection revisions for real wages in figure 1 suggest that the performance of the model may improve from including an augmented wage equation directly. With this reservation, we may conclude that the revisions in the predictions with the model are partly explained by the neglect of rational expectations, and that the inclusion of anticipations reduces the variance of these revisions.

10. CONCLUSION

The analysis of the rational expectations mechanism in a realistic planning exercise for the Dutch economy in the period 1976–80 reveals that the implications of the Lucas critique are less important than the impacts of projections of endogenous variables into the future would suggest. Furthermore, these predictions are sensitive to the type of process which generates the expectations; i.e. they depend on whether any mechanical (predetermined) elements are at work in the expectation mechanism. It may therefore be that rational expectations are important for long run growth models and long run equilibrium models. But they appear to have rather less influence in the short run and in decision making problems.

In this exercise the new target-instrument multipliers did not change the qualitative nature of the policy recommendations. However, the forecasting behaviour of the model did deteriorate somewhat, although there was support for the hypothesis that the inclusion produces more consistent longer term model forecasts than their exclusion. If these results are found to hold in other situations (e.g. Gilbert, Hughes Hallett and Ghosh (1984)), then restricted rational (a mix of mechanical and rational) expectations would be the appropriate formulation.

Figure 1. Actual and predicted values under different assumptions about the policies or the government: unaltered policy (CP), optimal without rational expectations (the policy alternative) and optimal under a rational expectations regime. In the accompanying right hand side pictures: the deviations from the central projection compared with the revised projection given the implemented policy of 1976.

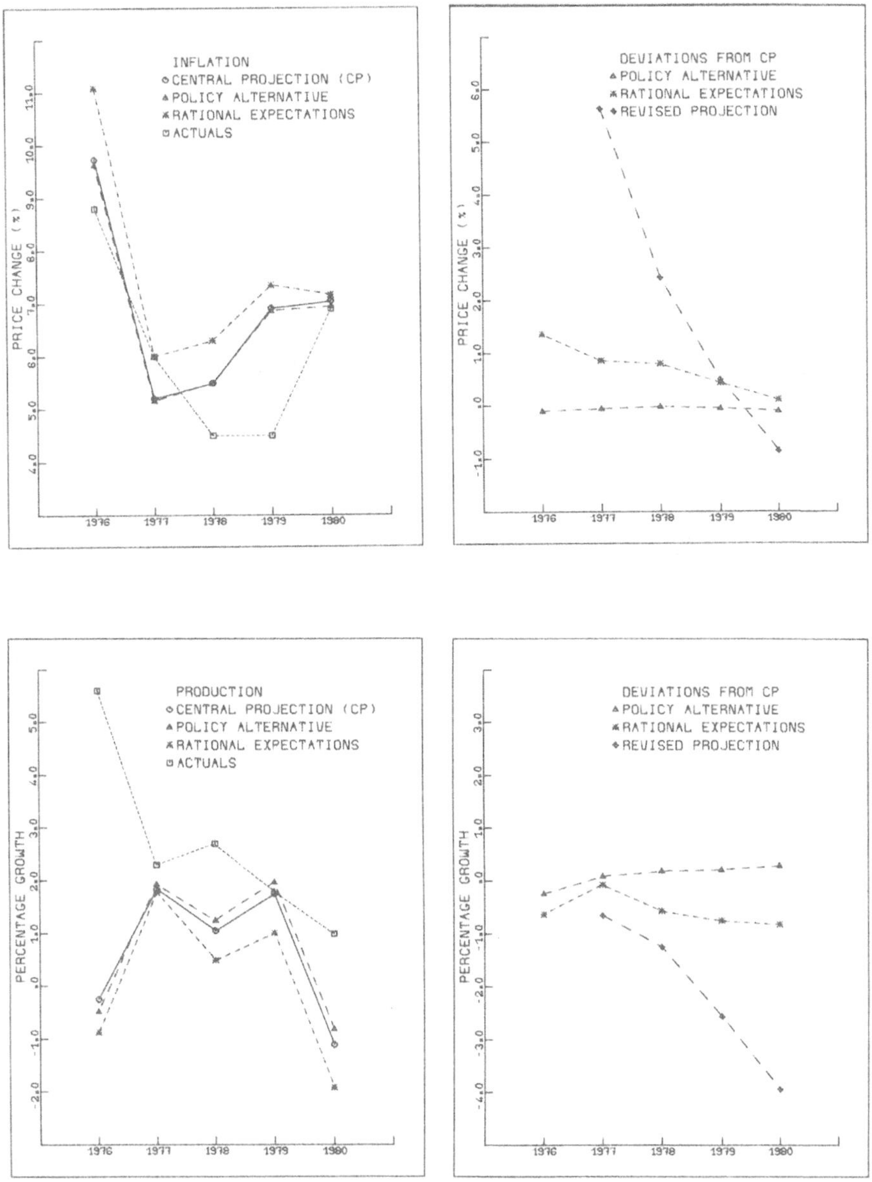

Figure 1 (continued)

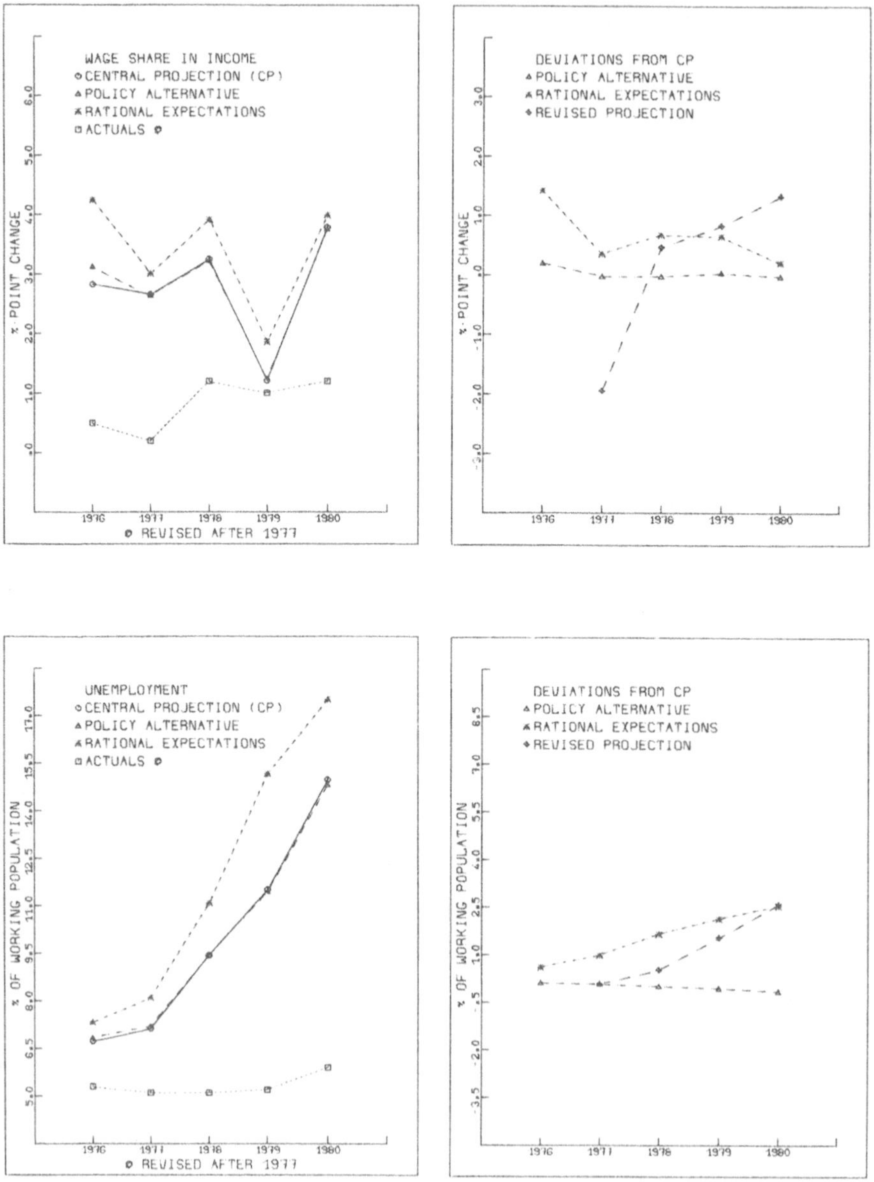

Figure 1 (continued)

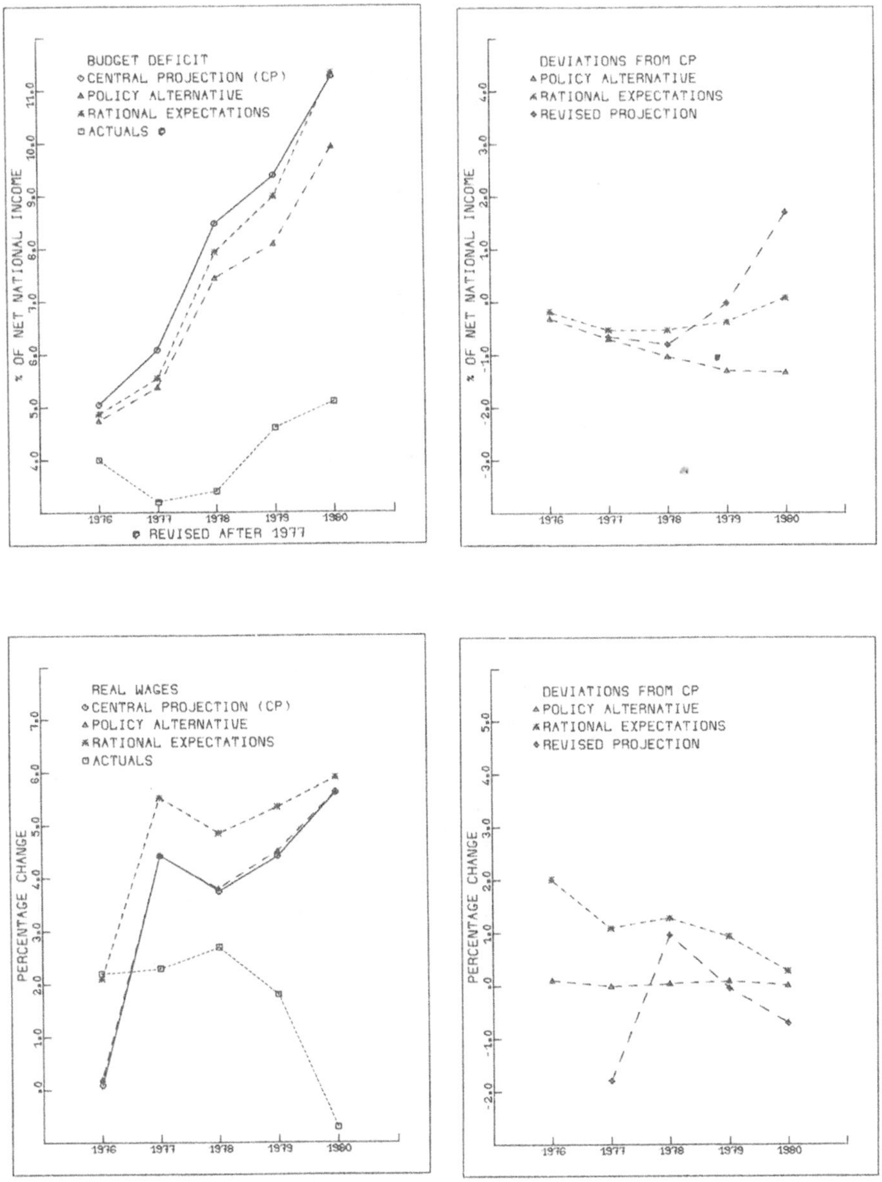

APPENDIX

EQUATION	DEFINITION	COMMENTS
Block I: Supply		
(1) $cap = cap(i, \upsilon)$	cap : capacity production i : investment	The supply side of the model contains a vintage type production system with fixed technical coefficients between investment, capacity and capacity-employment per vintage. The age of the oldest vintage is determined by real wages.
(2) $\upsilon = \upsilon(1, p_y)$	υ : age of the oldest vintage 1 : wage rate	
(3) $a = a(cap, q)$	p_y : price of production a : employment	
(4) $a_s = a_s(pop, 1/p_c, w)$	a_s : labour supply w : unemployment	Poplulation, real wages and unemployment (representing the discouraged worker effect) are the important elements in the labour-supply equation.
(5) $w = a_s - a$	p_c : price of consumption q : rate of capacity utilisation	
(6) $q = y/cap$	y : production pop : population	

EQUATION	DEFINITION	COMMENTS
Block II: Product demand		
(7) $y = c + i + g + x - m$	y_d : disposable income o_s : operating surplus of the economy	Domestic demand mainly depends on disposable income, while relative prices are important determinants of foreign trade. Confrontation of production capacity with effective demand gives (see block I, (6)) the utilisation rate of the capacity which in its turn is an explanatory variable in the equations for imports and exports, investment and prices.
(8) $c = c(y_d, B)$	c : consumption i : investment	
(9) $i = i(o_s, q, B)$	x : exports m : imports	
(10) $x = x(m_w, p_x/p_x', q)$	g : government material expenditure p_x : price of exports	
(11) $m = m(y, p_m/p_y, q)$	p_m : price of imports p_x' : price of competing exports B : base-money	
Block III: Wages and prices		
(12) $p_i = p_i(1, p_m, q)$	p_i : several prices (i=consumption, investment, etc.)	Prices are determined by wage and import costs per unit of output. The wage equation implies full compensation for prices and increases in labour productivity. The Phillips curve effect and a term expressing the pressure of social security charges and personal taxation complete this equation.
(13) $1 = 1(p_c, y/a, T_1, P, w)$	T_1 : direct taxes on wages P : premiums social security	
(14) $1_g = 1_g(1)$	1_g : government wage rate	

EQUATION	DEFINITION	COMMENTS
Block IV: Social security system		
(15) $U = U(w, 1)$	U : social benefits households	This block is a simple description of the social security system, in which the wage rate (as the price) and the number of unemployed people (as the volume) play an important role.
(16) $P = P(U)$		
Block V: Government		
(17) $T_j = T_j(Y_j)$	T_j : several taxes (j=wages, indirect, etc.) a_g : government employment Y_j : the relevant tax base F : government financing deficit	The government sector is less important because government expenditure and government employment are treated as exogenous. A confrontation of revenues and expenditures gives the financing deficit of the government.
(18) $F = F(T_j, g, 1_g, a_g)$		
Block VI: Monetary sector		
(19) $B = B(E, F)$	E: balance of payments	The monetary sector consists of an equation for base-money in which the balance of payments is the key variable; In its turn the base-money is an explanatory variable in the equations of consumption and investment expenditure. The monetary base bears 10% of the financing of a deficit.

Notes:

i) The Vintaf-II version was published in Central Planning Bureau (1977); the vintage concept being based on Den Hartog and Tjan (1976). The monetary sector was added by Knoester and Van Sinderen (1983).

ii) The variables in the main text follow by obvious definitions from this scheme; the symbols do not always correspond.

NOTES

1) In other words, the competition between players is completely unrestricted, and no simplifying assumptions are made. So we do not consider Cournot or Stackelberg games here (but see Hughes Hallett and Rees (1983)).
2) A pure feedback rule, $x_t^{(i)*} = g_{t,1}(\Omega_{ti})$, is not necessarily closed loop.
3) These issues are investigated extensively elsewhere; e.g. Kendrick (1981) and references therein.
4) Sufficient conditions for its optimality and existence are guaranteed by the positive semi-definite $Q^{(i)}$ with rank at least n_iT. This decision rule is essentially that developed by Theil (1964).
5) See Aubin (1979), p.271, theorem 1; Friedman (1977), theorem 7.3.
6) See Aubin (1979), p. 271.
7) Invert the partitioned matrix of (13) in terms of $R^{(1)}$, $R^{(2)}$, $D_s^{(1)}$ and $D_s^{(2)}$; then multiply out and manipulate the result to produce (15), reinserting the definition of $D_{s+1}^{(j)}$ in (14) to do so.
8) Further details of this dynamic game solution will be found in Brandsma, and Hughes Hallett (1982) and Hughes Hallett (1983).
9) See Den Hartog and Tjan (1976) or Central Planning Bureau (1977).
10) Knoester and Van Sinderen (1983).
11) Bestek '81 (1978).
12) This result supports the arguments of Sargent and Wallace (1975), but it does not generalise to any other dynamic multipliers.

REFERENCES

Aubin, J.P. (1979), *'Mathematical Methods of Game and Economic Theory'*, North Holland, Amsterdam.

Batchelor, R.A. and T.D. Sheriff (1980), 'Unemployment and Unanticipated Inflation in Postwar Britain', *Economica*, 47, pp. 179–92.

Bestek '81 (1978), 'The Main Features of Medium Term Financial, Social and Economic Policy', Government Printing Office, The Hague (in Dutch).

Bomhoff, E.J. (1980), *'Inflation, the Quantity Theory, and Rational Expectations'*, North Holland, Amsterdam.

Brandsma, A.S. and A.J. Hughes Hallett (1982), 'The Impact of Noncausality on Noncooperative Strategies for Dynamic Games', *Economic Letters*, 10, pp. 9–15.

Brandsma, A.S. and N. Van der Windt (1983), 'Wage Bargaining and the Phillips curve: A Macroeconomic View', *Applied Economics*, 15, pp. 61–71.

Brandsma, A.S., A.J. Hughes Hallett and N. Van der Windt (1983), 'Optimal Control of Large Nonlinear Models: An Effficient Method of Policy Search Applied to the Dutch Economy', *Journal of Policy Modelling* (forthcoming).

Brandsma, A.S., A.J. Hughes Hallett and N. Van der Windt (1984), 'Optimal Economic Policies and Uncertainty: the Case against Policy Selection by Nonlinear Programming', *Computers and Operations Research* (forthcoming).

Central Planning Bureau (1977), 'A Macro-model for the Dutch Economy in the Medium Term (Vintaf II)', Occasional Paper No. 12, The Hague (in Dutch).

Chow, G.C. (1975), *Analysis and Control of Dynamic Economic Systems,* John Wiley & Sons, New York.

DenHartog, H. and H.S. Tjan (1976), 'Investment, Wages, Prices and the Demand for Labour: a Clay-Clay Vintage Model for the Netherlands', *De Economist,* 124, pp. 32–55.

Friedman, J.W. (1977), *Oligopoly and the Theory of Games,* North Holland, Amsterdam.

Gilbert, C.L., A.J. Hughes Hallett, and S. Ghosh (1984), *The Econometrics of Stabilising Speculative Commodity Markets,* Oxford University Press, Oxford (forthcoming).

Hicks, J.R. (1975), 'What's wrong with Monetarism', *Lloyds Bank Review,* 118, pp. 1–13.

Hughes Hallett, A.J. (1983), 'Optimal Strategies for Dynamic Games and the Incentive to Co-operate', *International Journal of System Science,* 14, pp. 179–200.

Hughes Hallett, A.J. and H.J.B. Rees (1983), *Quantitative Economic Policies and Interactive Planning,* Cambridge University Press, Cambridge and New York.

Kendrick, D.A. (1981), *Stochastic Control for Economic Models,* McGraw-Hill, New York.

Knegt, L., A. Knoester, R.S.G. Lenderink and N. Van der Windt (1978), 'Macro-economic policy and Vintaf-II: a sensitivity analysis', in W. Driehuis and A. van der Zwan (eds.), *A critical review of economic policy making,* Stenfert Kroese, Leyden/Antwerp (in Dutch).

Knoester, A. and J. van Sinderen (1983), 'Economic Policy and Employment', in A. Maddison and B.S. Wilpstra (eds), *Unemployment: a Dutch Perspective,* Ministry of Social Affairs and Employment, The Hague.

Kydland, F.E. and E.C. Prescott (1977), 'Rules rather than Discretion: the Inconsistency of Optimal Plans', *Journal of Political Economy,* 85, pp. 472–79.

Lucas, R.E. (1976), 'Econometric Policy Evaluation: a critique', in K. Brunner and A.H. Meltzer (eds.), *The Phillips Curve and Labour Markets,* Carnegie-Rochester series on Public Theory, North-Holland, Amsterdam.

Minford, P. and D.A. Peel (1982), 'The Microfoundations of the Phillips Curve with Rational Expectations', *Oxford Economic Papers,* 34, pp. 449-51.

Sargent, T.J. and N. Wallace (1975), 'Rational Expectations, the Optimal Monetary Instrument, and the Optimal Money Supply Rule', *Journal of Political Economy,* 83, pp. 241–54.

Theil, H. (1964), *Optimal Decision Rules for Government and Industry,* North Holland, Amsterdam.

CHAPTER 9

THE DISEQUILIBRIUM THEORY IN MACROECONOMIC MODELS: A SMALL-SCALE MODEL

D. Bureau, D. Miqueu and M. Norotte
Ministry of Economics and Finance, Paris, France

1. INTRODUCTION

Today the advances made in research on temporary fixed-price equilibria have made it a proven fact that macroeconomic theory can be founded on microeconomic bases. Globally, this research is at present concerned with either theoretical work aiming at enlarging the framework of the 'three-goods model', or else it deals with often complex econometric means used to estimate the various disequilibrium regimes at work in the economy. The object of the small-scale model described here is not to present new theoretical contributions to the disequilibrium theory, nor does it set out to provide 'disequilibrium' estimates of structural parameters. It has been developed in order to:

- show that there is a *simple* means of simulating the various regimes of disequilibrium models and thus explain in a *pedagogical* manner both the static and dynamic operation of this kind of model;
- establish a link between this summarising presentation as encountered in recent work on disequilibrium and some of the studies on the structure and specification of traditional macroeconomic models.

As to the first point, the small-scale model employs the usual formulations of disequilibrium theory: time is envisaged as a succession of elementary periods during which prices remain fixed; the agents are unaware of their future environment and anticipate it basing their observations on the state of the economy and its past evolution. For each period quantities are adjusted by quantitative rationing. (Benassy (1976), Grandmont (1976), Grandmont and Laroque (1976)).

Prices are revised in the interperiod and stocks reevaluated, thereby generating the system's dynamics. On the goods markets, it is assumed that price revisions occur in a framework where for each product there are several firms in monopolistic competition. This assumption is consistent with that of a short term fixed-price adjustment (Drazen (1980)), and will suffice to define the dynamics of prices and investment. The important point is that the model of the firm is ***unique***, and can describe ***several*** disequilibrium situations: to the various short term equilibria of the small-scale model correspond specific price and investment equations, yet derived from the same intertemporal profit maximisation programme of firms.

As to the second point, the building of small-scale models is certainly no new invention. Whereas until now this type of tool was above all used to improve our understanding of 'large models' (Deleau et al. (1983)) by reducing their size so as to keep only their main mechanisms, the small-scale model presented here should rather be seen as the extension of a theoretical model. It will therefore be interesting to observe the similarity between certain dynamic regimes of the model and those presented by macroeconomic models: in the specific case of Keynesian underemployment numerical simulations indeed reproduce the same economic mechanisms as those in operation in econometric models (Artus and Muet (1980)).

In the first section the general structure of the model is presented. The second section deals with the optimisation programme of the firm from which all its short term effective demands – including investment – and the model's price equations are derived. Finally, the third section is concerned with reflation simulations: the first one, in a Keynesian regime, shows the similarity with empirical models; the others illustrate the links which should exist between short term adjustment disequilibria and dynamic equations in this type of model.

2. STRUCTURE OF THE MODEL

2.1. General points

Six goods are considered:

- the first two are produced in the domestic market by the corresponding sectors but may also be imported. Good 1 is a capital good whereas good 2 is a consumer good;
- labour is supplied by the households and consumed by two productive sectors;
- securities finance the sectors. By definition a bond corresponds to a revenue of 1 F for each period indefinitely. Letting r be the rate of interest, the bond price is therefore 1/r;
- money, whose price is 1, is used to carry out all transactions.

There are five agents:

- national productive sectors S_1 and S_2 corresponding to aggregates producing products 1 and 2. As factors of production, these firms use their capital, labour and imported goods. They modify their stock of capital through investments and can finance themselves by issuing bonds;

- households selling their labour and consuming goods 1 and 3;
- to the government who consumes goods 2 and 3, is aggregated the bank system which buys the securities issued by the firms. It can finance itself by creating money (ΔM).

Compared to the accounting framework selected by empirical small-scale models, the main difference is the distinction between three products. This choice was imposed by the theoretical assumptions of disequilibrium theory: if only one aggregate good had been considered, it would have been necessary to specify the rationing scheme between investment and consumption in case of excess demand, that is to say make explicit how a firm allocates the aggregate commodity between intermediate consumption and investment. It seems to be more relevant to define the problem in terms of allocation of factors of production between sectors, which is why several goods have been distinguished.

No attempt is made in this article to describe the behaviour of all the agents; this would indeed be very tedious. The description will therefore be limited to the behaviour of the producers, as they are central to the model. For the other equations, we will limit our comments to the following remarks:

- the behaviour of households is in keeping with the basic set up in the disequilibrium theory: their demands derive from a Cobb Douglas type utility function limited to one period; the variables are their consumption of goods 1 and 3, and their savings. Labour is exogenous;
- the evolution of wages is governed by a growth rate Phillips type equation.

In all the simulations presented, the external supply for the different goods is unlimited. The same applies for the supply of credits, the interest rate being exogenous (except for the variants on credit limitation presented later). Foreign demand depends on competitiveness under constant elasticity.

Finally it should be mentioned that the simulations are made around a steady growth path and that with respect to the theoretical system described below, an investment adjustment cycle has been introduced in order to obtain acceptable dynamic characteristics.

2.2. The periodisation

The model clearly distinguishes between what is realised in the short term, in which each elementary period is characterised by a fixed-price equilibrium, and what is realised between two periods and defines the dynamics (figure 1).

- in the *intraperiod*, the prices are fixed and the correspondence between agents'

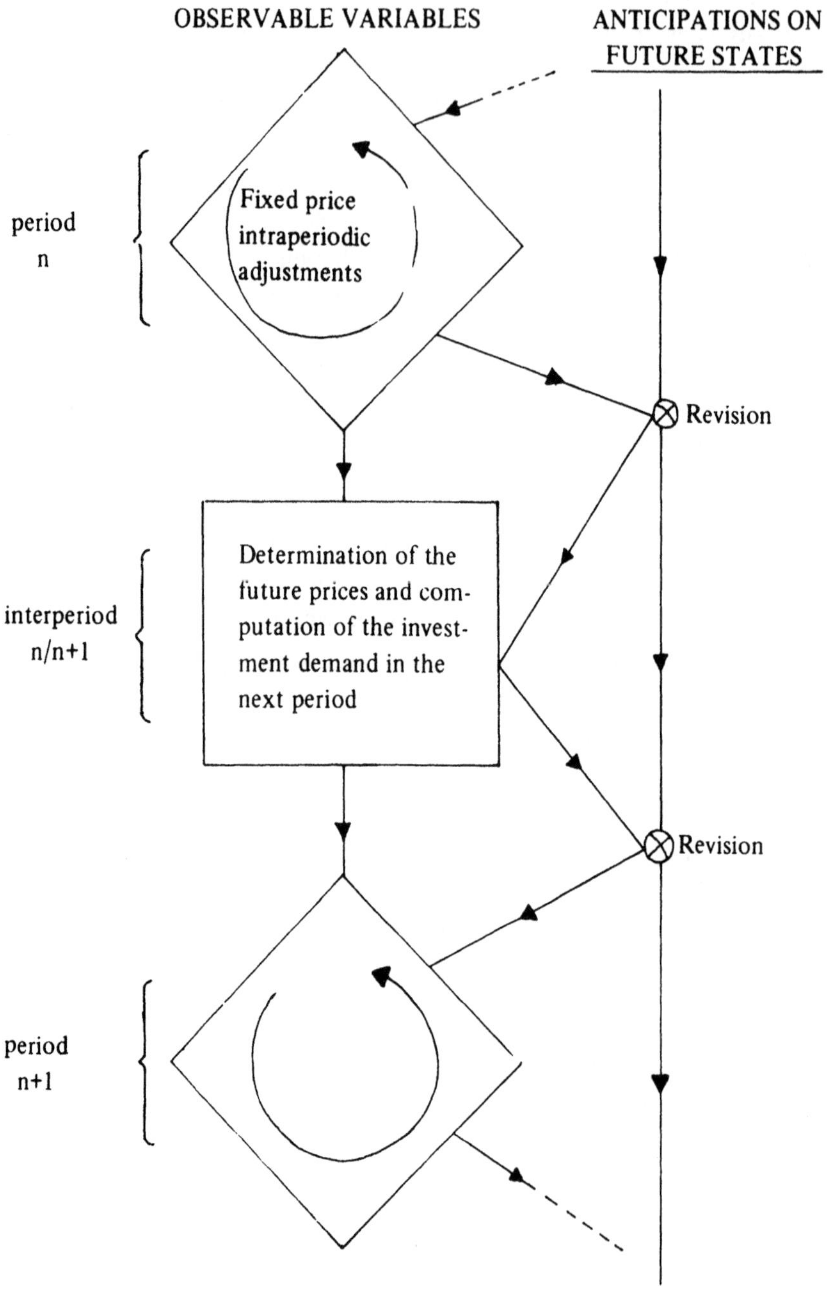

Figure 1. Overall scheme.

supplies and demands in all the markets is sought by a 'tatonnement process' on quantities as described by Benassy (1974): for each good, other than money, the agents' demands derive from the maximisation of their objective function, given the quantitative constraints they perceive for all the goods excluding the one under consideration; if the demands expressed by the agents are not compatible, a rationing scheme defines the allocations; each agent derives the quantitative constraints he will take into account to make his subsequent demands from the analysis of the comparison of expressed demands and allocations. The final equilibrium is a fixed point in the process represented by the following scheme:

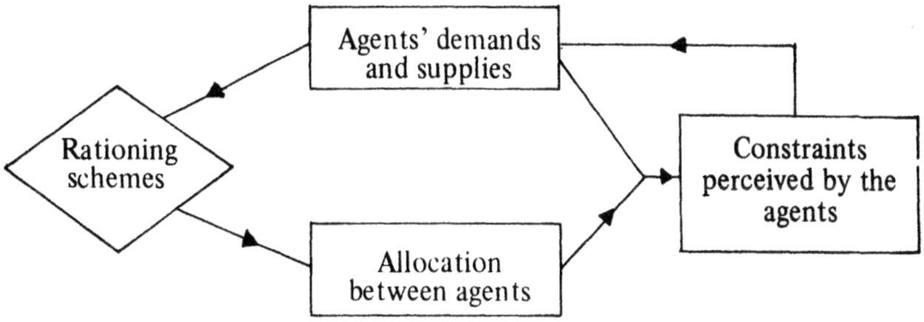

In this scheme, money is considered as a means of exchange: no quantitative constraint is perceived in this market and the monetary allocation realised is simply determined by Walras' law.

Concerning allocations, the model can either use a queue rationing scheme, or a scheme based on market shares fixed a priori. In the latter case, an iterative procedure is used following the classical rule of voluntary exchange according to which the sign of the transaction is kept and no agent exchanges more than he desires.

A theoretical study of this model (convergence of the algorithm, unicity of equilibria, etc.) would have gone beyond the scope of this article. This deficiency is not too bothersome given that the model's objective is not so much to move from zone to zone but rather to analyse various regimes both in a static and in a dynamic context. Thus, in the simulations presented the type of disequilibrium which is to be studied, is defined a priori. For these regimes, corresponding to the economic disequilibria mentioned in the literature, the algorithm implicit resolution structure is in general quite clear. In this sense the algorithm is just a practical means of implementing several resolution structures within the same framework.

- in the *interperiod* the investment made is integrated in the capital and firms fix their prices for the forthcoming period. In addition the variables considered as being fixed to the subsequent interperiod adjustment are then determined, i.e. the vector of supplies and demands from government and foreign countries, the amount of the monetary transfers between agents.

3. THE PRODUCERS

In this section we will show how all the equations usually relating to the behaviour of firms (production, demand for production factors, investments, prices) can be derived from a unique and consistent set of assumptions. This approach will enable us to state what ties should exist between the type of short term equilibrium which is attained and the price and investment equations.

For this purpose we will describe the behaviour of a representative firm, but it should be borne in mind that the model only holds if several firms coexist under monopolistic competition. This section is organised as follows: the first paragraph defines the notation and the constraints the firm faces; the second paragraph deals with all the effective demands the firm makes during the short term adjustment; and the last one analyses how the firm modifies its prices from period to period. Finally we will conclude with a few remarks on the situation of classical unemployment.

3.1. Notation and constraints of the firm

Notation: the lower indices refer to the time period; for the short term adjustment, the notional demands (supplies), effective demands (supplies) and quantitative constraints are respectively expressed as $\tilde{d}$, $\bar{d}$, $\bar{\bar{d}}$. The asterix x* refers to an anticipated value.

The production function: The technical constraints are represented by a Cobb Douglas production function with constant returns to scale. With the usual notation for capital (K), labour (L), production (Q) and technical progress (υ), we have:

$$\begin{cases} Q_t \leqslant a_t K_t^{a} L_t^{1-a} \\ a_t = a_0(1+\upsilon)^t \end{cases}$$

The perceived demand curve: This curve expresses the firm's anticipation for future periods of the link between the demand it will meet and the price P it will fix. We express this as $Q = Q^*(P/P^*)^{\epsilon}$. The elasticity value ϵ can be related to the real operation of the economy in a situation of monopolistic competition between firms. Q* and P* represent the firm's anticipations of the future economic environment. We will assume that they are related to the past values of Q and P in terms of autoregressive schemes (on these two points see Bureau (1982)).

3.2. The formulation of effective demand

To determine its effective demand during the short term adjustment, the firm performs a computation limited to two periods: the period designated as period 1 for quantity adjustments presently implied, and the subsequent period designated as period 2. Its aim is to determine the supplies and demands concerning current operation, as well as its demands for investment goods during this adjustment.[1] In this programme, the prices and capital available in period 1 are fixed. The environment of period 2 –including quantitative constraints– is anticipated. In addition it is taken that these anticipated values are not revised during period 1 quantitative adjustment iterations. As we will see, the firm's intertemporal programme is composed of elements referring to the current operation and elements concerning investment demand. This demand mainly arises from the anticipations on period 2 since this investment will not be integrated in the stock of capital until after the adjustment of period 1.

Let $\Pi_1 = P_1Q_1 - w_1L_1$ and $\Pi_2 = P_2Q_2 - \overset{*}{w}_2L_2 - \overset{*}{C}_2K_2$ be the profits in periods 1 and 2, I be the investment and Cr the credits. The programme is then:

$$\text{Max } \Pi_1(1+r) + \Pi_2$$

subject to the following constraints:

a) the production function:

$$Q_t \leqslant aK_t^{a}L_t^{1-a}, \qquad t = 1,2$$

b) 'attonnement' quantitative constraints:

$$Q_1 \leqslant \bar{\bar{Q}}_1,\ L_1 \leqslant \bar{\bar{L}}_1,\ I_1 \leqslant \bar{\bar{I}}_1,\ Cr_1 \leqslant \bar{\bar{Cr}}_1$$

c) anticipated quantitative constraints:

$$Q_2 \leqslant \overset{*}{Q}_2(P_2/\overset{*}{P}_2)^{\epsilon},\quad L_2 \leqslant \overset{*}{L}_2$$

d) stock-flow adjustment:

$$K_2 = K_1(1-\delta) + I_1$$

e) investment financing:

$$P_1^1 I_1 \leqslant \Pi_1 + Cr_1$$

with P_1^1 the price of good 1 in period 1.

The solution of this programme calls for several remarks:

1. $C = (r - \dot{p}^1 + \delta)P^1 = jP^1$.

This formulation assuming a perfect capital market may be criticised. The use of a synthesised index of the cost of capital was nevertheless adopted because this is common practice and simplifies the formulation of the problem.

2. This formally unique problem in fact groups together several programmes, determining the types of dynamic and static regimes at work in the economy, depending on the saturation or non-saturation of certain quantitative constraints. Finally it should be recalled that in keeping with the principle chosen, the programme determining the demand for each good is obtained by relaxing the quantitative constraint in the market under consideration.

3. The control variables are Q_1, L_1, Cr_1, I_1 in period 1 and Q_2, L_2, P_2, K_2 in the following period. But the object of this programme is only to determine the effective demands (supplies) $\bar{Q}_1, \bar{L}_1, \bar{Cr}_1, \bar{I}_1$. The variables Q_2, L_2, P_2 and K_2 are therefore to be considered as shadow variables which will be modified once the anticipations have been revised. It was, however, essential to introduce them at this stage as control variables in order to ensure the logical consistency of the programme: since firms are the agents setting prices, the latter must necessarily be computed simultaneously to any production plan.

4. This programme can be split into two subprogrammes, one being related to the operation under way, and the other concerning the determination of the notional investment I_1. Indeed, the only constraint linking the variables of period 1 and 2 is the financing constraint (e). If $\tilde{K}_2$ is the capital desired for period 2, independently from this constraint, the effective investment demand is then the lower of the desired investment or the investment which can be financed.[2]

$$\bar{I}_1 = \text{Min}\left\{\frac{\Pi_1 - \bar{\bar{Cr}}_1}{P_1^1} , \tilde{K}_2 - (1-\delta)K_1\right\}$$

It is therefore in the firm's interest to maximise Π_1, since any increase in Π_2 eases the financing constraint and hence increases Π_2. The two subprogrammes to be considered are therefore:

- the operation under way. The firm maximises its short term profit Π_1, under the quantitative constraints of the intraperiod adjustement (b) and its production function. The resulting behaviour is that of a usual three-goods model (Benassy (1976), Malinvaud (1977)).

– determination of the notional investment $\tilde{I}_1$. By this term we mean the investment corresponding to the capital $\tilde{K}_2$. This is the solution to the programme maximising Π_2 under the technical constraint (a) of the production function (with constant returns to scale on this horizon) and the quantitative constraints (c). It has to be noted that the product market constraint, represented here by the perceived demand curve, will always be saturated: otherwise the firm could increase its prices without changing its production, which would increase its profit, previously therefore not at its maximum. Since firms set their prices by making use of the perceived demand curve, no situation comparable to that of classical unemployment (constraint on profitability), can be envisaged for this programme whereas it will be possible to extend the situation of Keynesian unemployment (constraint on product markets) or repressed inflation (constraint on available employment).

This process can therefore be schematically represented as follows:

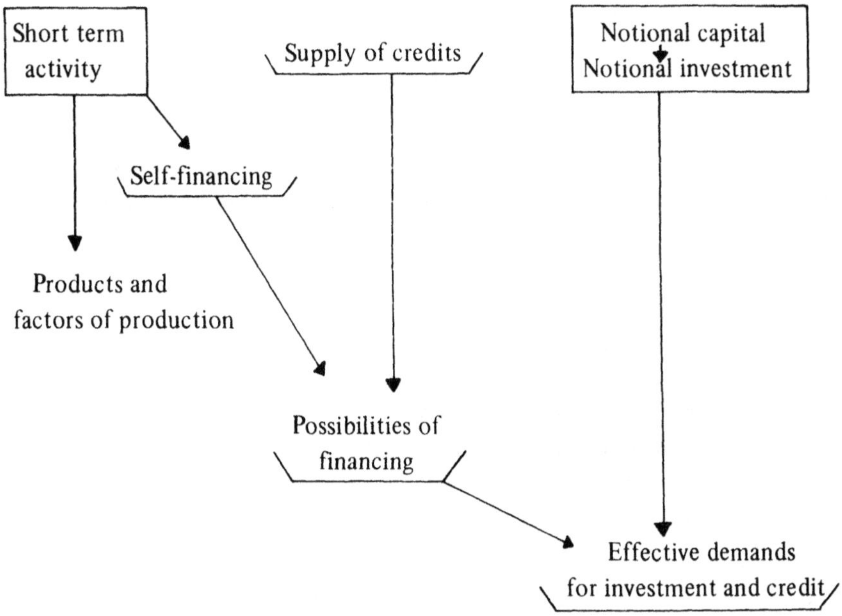

3.3. Price setting

The programme the firm solves in the interperiod 1–2 to determine the price P_2 of the forthcoming period is formally identical to that which concerned period 2 in the previous programme. It amounts indeed to the maximisation of the firm's profit under anticipated constraints. It differs from the previous programme only with respect to two points:

- the capital available for this period is now known so that the term C*K disappears from the objective function;
- whereas the anticipations for period 2 were not revised, while quantity adjustments iterations were made, it is now necessary for the firm to revise them and to integrate the results of the previous period.

Thus if the firm's expectations and desired investment were realised, price P_2 would be identical to the price which had been calculated previously. On the contrary, it is clear that if this is not the case, either because demand turned out to be lower than expected or because the firm had to face a rationing of its investment demand, then the price it will choose will be different from that predicted initially.

The programme the firm solves in the interperiod to determine the prices P_2 is therefore (if index 2 of the period is omitted to simplify the notation):

$$\begin{cases} \text{Max } \Pi = pQ - w^* L \\ \quad Q \leqslant aK^{a}L^{1-a} \\ \quad Q \leqslant Q^*(P/P^*)^{\epsilon}, \qquad L \leqslant L^* \end{cases}$$

The control variables are the quantities Q, L and the price P. As in the programme which determined the notional investment, no situation comparable to that of classical short term unemployment, will have to be considered.

3.4. On classical unemployment

As the prices are set by firms on the basis of the demand curve, the firms are left with surplus production capacity which is all the greater as the competition they meet is weaker. Therefore, for the price and investment programmes there is no situation comparable to that of classical unemployment. In the short term, the problem is slightly more complex because the demand curve which is used to take these decisions has been anticipated. The result therefore depends on the quality of the expectations concerning the capacities set aside by firms: although it is highly unlikely, an adjustment in classical unemployment is therefore possible. The question of interest concerns the mechanisms by which this situation can be left. Given what has been stated, two mechanisms may intervene:

- price setting: firms revise their expectations for each period; the creation of classical unemployment generates inflation. Indeed, when the perceived demand curve is modified, firms increase their prices to restrain demand to the level of their available capacities;

- investment: it is known that with a constant returns to scale production function if sufficient equipment is used and if the selling price exceeds the marginal cost, as it is the case in oligopolistic conditions, then any level of demand can be satisfied.

To illustrate these mechanisms a simulation was carried out whereby an increase in the expenditures for consumer goods was applied to an economy initially under Keynesian unemployment, and such that the demand for consumer goods exceeded domestic supply during the first year.

In this simulation the following sequences can be seen (see figure 2):

- in the first period, the firms manufacturing consumer goods cannot satisfy demand; this leads them to increase their prices and their demand for investment; this demand is then higher than the notional supply of sector 1, and between the second and the sixth period a situation of classical unemployment is observed; subsequently, only the consumer goods sector remains within the limits of the production capacities. This continues up to the ninth period, when Keynesian unemployment resumes, essentially as a result of the increase in capital. A high degree of inflation is indeed observed until the Keynesian zone is reentered, but due to the wage adjustments, the W/P ratio is scarcely modified as time passes: prices do not rake part in reabsorbing the disequilibrium.

As such the analysis is very global and the assertion that classical unemployment is unlikely could be weakened in a more complex model, especially if the assumption made concerning the role of the foreign sector were less favourable.

- in this simulation it was entirely due to imports that the investment could be made, as they compensated for the limits in domestic supply. With a stringent trade constraint, this mechanism could not have occurred and the equilibrium would therefore have remained in the classical unemployment zone. The main effect of the reflation would then have been to generate inflation. On the contrary, the consequences of inflation on exports was not taken into account, otherwise the exogenous demand would not have been maintained in volume: the increase in public expenditure would have been partially compensated by a decrease in exports. Prices would then have helped to reabsorbe the disequilibrium;
- in the theoretical model a high rate of substitutability between domestic products and imported goods has not been envisaged: in this case of a competitive sector it is clear that national producers may find themselves in a situation of classical unemployment.

Figure 2: Transition from classical unemployment to Keynesian unemployment (deviations as percentages)

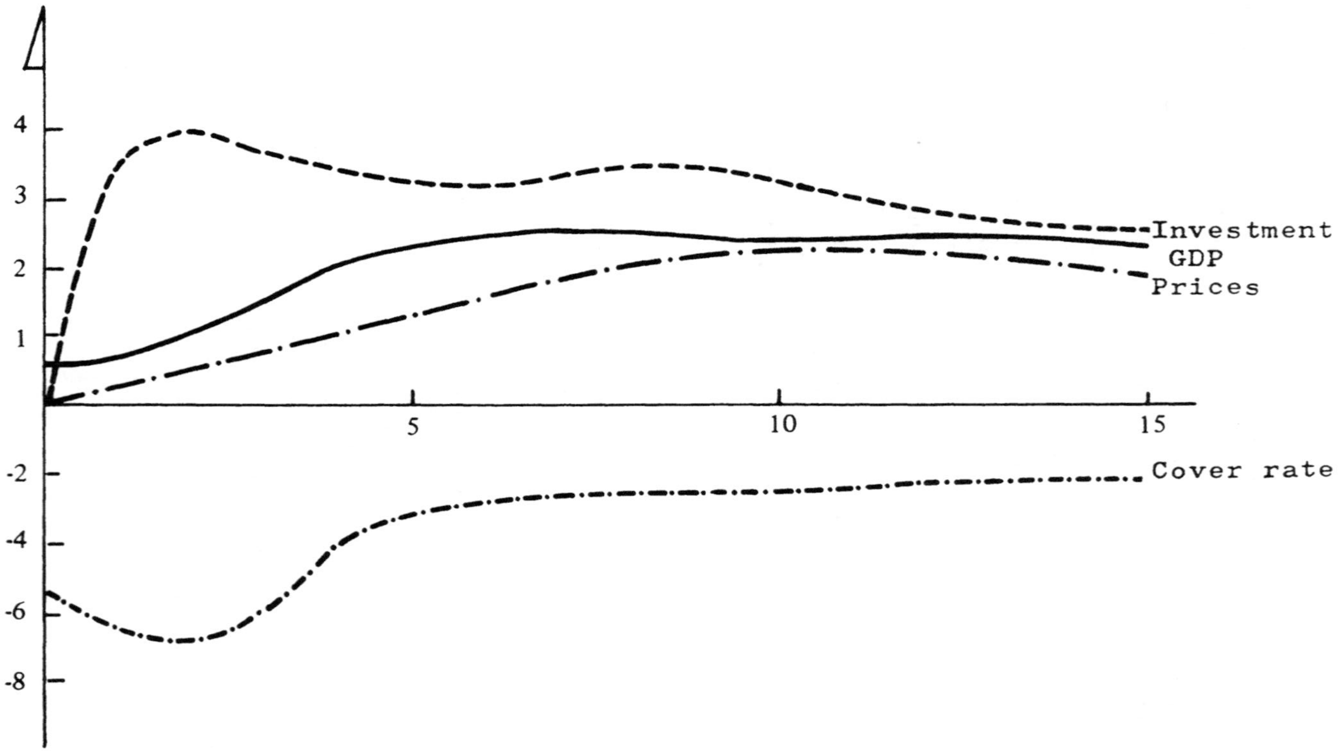

4. SIMULATIONS

The fundamental characteristic of the model is the link it establishes between the dynamic equations of prices and investment and short term adjustment disequilibria. In one sense price evolution can be said to depend on past disequilibria observed in markets, but the link is an indirect one since it is expressed via the constraints anticipated by agents in their optimisation behaviour.

We will therefore consider dynamic regimes corresponding to Keynesian unemployment of repressed inflation; however, it is to be noted that more complex situations than these pure regimes may also arise: if, for example, firms anticipate a constraint on employment supply, and thereby sufficiently increase their prices and investment, it may turn out that the short term solution for the forthcoming period is determined ex post by demand (Keynesian zone) and not by employment (repressed inflation zone). Thus the fundamental character of a situation (in the example, repressed inflation) may therefore appear only in the dynamic equations (prices and investment equations), the corresponding static adjustments being Keynesian. It therefore appears that in the analysis of the type of regime at work in an economy, equal importance must be granted to its dynamic equations as to the nature of the static equilibrium.

4.1. The Keynesian regime

By Keynesian regime we understand the regime corresponding to the case when demand is the only constraint met by firms both in the short term and in the long term. The price and investment equations are therefore the following:

– the notional investment is derived from the notional capital in the following period[3] by the relation:

$$\tilde{K} = \frac{Q^*}{a} \left(\frac{1-a}{a} \frac{w^*}{c^*} \right)^{1-a} \left(\frac{P}{P^*} \right)^{\epsilon}$$

where P is a function of the long term marginal cost:

$$P = \frac{1}{a(1+1/\epsilon)} \left(\frac{w^*}{1-a} \right)^{1-a} \left(\frac{c^*}{a} \right)^{a}$$

The last term has a value 1 if the firm does not anticipate a discrepancy between the reference price and its long term price, which is in particular the case in the solution of steady growth. The other two terms are well known: the term Q^* corresponds to the 'accelerator' effect; the second term results from the fact that the relative cost of production factors has been taken into account.

– The price equation represents an adjustment cycle between the trend price and a 'desired' price based on the marginal cost using a profit margin $1/(1+1/\epsilon)$, which ensures that the firm makes a profit:

$$P = (\hat{P})^{\mu}(P^*)^{1-\mu} \quad \text{with} \quad \mu = \frac{1-a}{1-a-a\epsilon}$$

where $$\hat{P} = \frac{1}{1+1/\epsilon}\,\frac{w^*}{(1-a)Q^*}\left(\frac{Q^*}{aK^a}\right)^{\frac{1}{1-a}}$$

These equations and those of short term adjustments are the traditional ones in neo-Keynesian models. This can be illustrated by a reflation simulation.

This simulation consists in a maintained increase in budgetary expenditure, fixed as 1% of the GDP, with reference to the steady growth path. The supply of employment is still sufficient for the short term adjustment to be Keynesian and for the constraint on employment available not to be anticipated. The mechanisms used are then very comparable to those selected in empirical models (Artus and Muet (1980)).

In the short term, the reflation is amplified by the multiplier mechanism. The well known accelerator-multiplier interaction mechanism can then be observed. After a few years, the role of the Phillips relation becomes decisive. Indeed the decrease in unemployment induces increase in purchasing power, whence durable inflation due to wage costs. External demand then decreases, which progressively diminishes the beneficial impact reflation had on the level of employment. Finally it is observed that these increases in purchasing power, entailing a modification in relative costs of factors of production, modified their composition since, at the end of the period the production is slightly higher than that of the reference simulation made with less employment (see figure 3).

There is, however, a major difference between this model and the macroeconometric models with respect to the formalisation of tension-variables (i.e. rate of capacity utilisation, treasury difficulties, rate of unemployment) whose fundamental role in the dynamics of macromodels is well known.

In these models the tensions are mere variables (with a status identical to that of prices or production) in an equation whose specification is never questioned. On the contrary, in the model presented here, the tensions appear indirectly in the form of the saturation of certain constraints and thus lead to a complete change in the specification. The difference is therefore between a unique equation 'modulated' by tension factors in traditional models, and a set of alternative equations describing a 'pure' behaviour consistent with such or such a regime in the case of our model. Two specific examples illustrate these mechanisms in our model:

- a constraint on the anticipated employment supply leads to the use of so-called 'repressed inflation' price and investment equations: in these equations the capital-labour relative cost term has disappeared;
- similarly, if firms are rationed on the credit market, the profit term becomes the determinant in the investment equation via the financing constraint.

4.2. Repressed inflation

This term which is used to refer to the division into zones in the three-goods model, is not suitable since the price equations will entail the development of demand inflation. Constrained by its production capacities, the firm increases its prices with respect to the reference price in order to force demand down to the physically attainable level, i.e.

$$P = P^* \left[\frac{aK^{a} (\bar{\bar{L}}^{*})^{1-a}}{Q^*} \right]^{1/\epsilon}$$

As for notional investment, the programme is slightly more complicated since the firm must choose between an increase in prices and an increase in production capacities. Indeed, by making use of the demand curve, the firm can also end up with an allocation of production factors which is not optimal with respect to their anticipated costs,

$$\tilde{K} = \hat{K}(P/P^*)^{\epsilon}$$

with

$$\begin{cases} \hat{K} = \left[\dfrac{Q^*}{a(\bar{\bar{L}}^{*})^{1-a}} \right]^{1/a} \\ P = (P^*)^{\lambda} \left[\dfrac{1}{1+1/\epsilon} \dfrac{c^*\hat{K}}{aQ^*} \right]^{1-\lambda} \end{cases} \quad \text{and} \quad \lambda = \frac{\epsilon(a-1)}{q+(a-1)\epsilon}$$

Figure 3: Pure Keynesian situation (deviations as percentages)

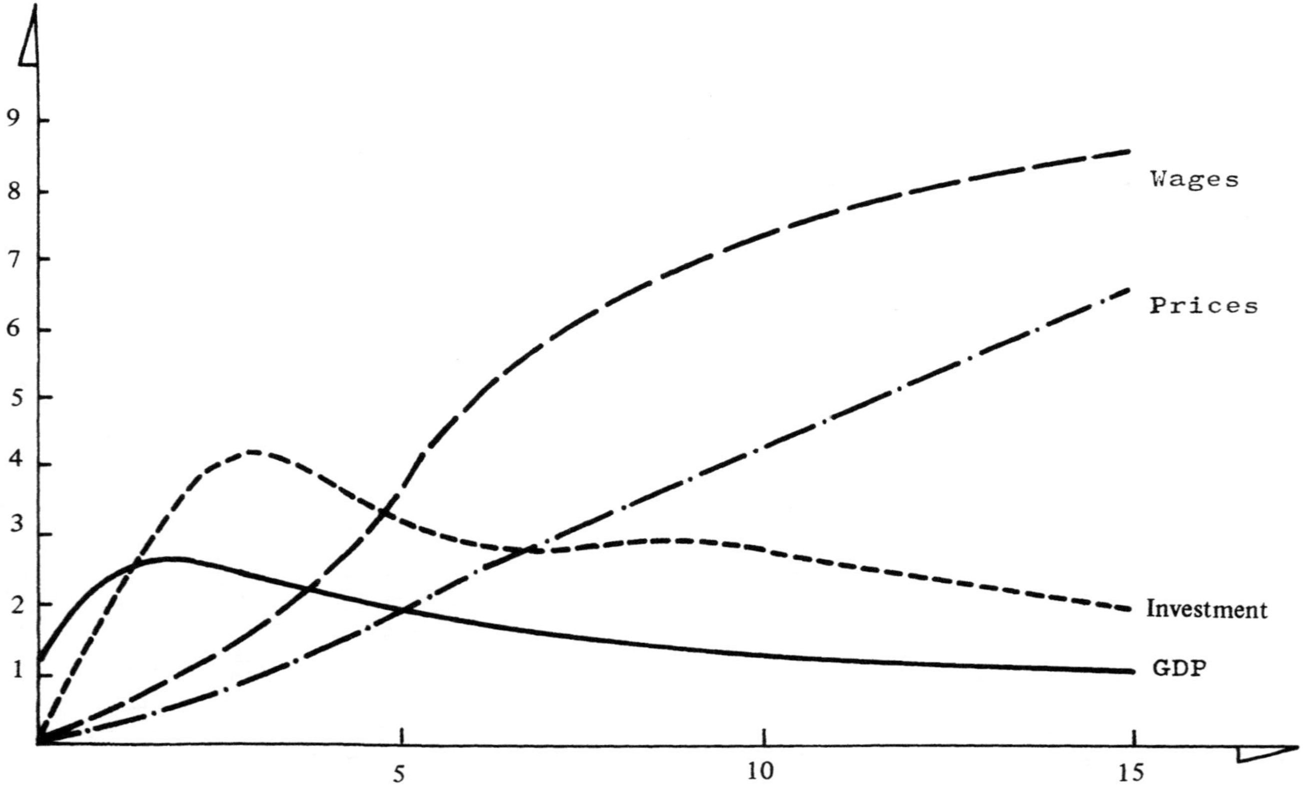

These mechanisms can be made explicit by means of a reflation variant (figure 4) in this situation. Its definition requires an explicit rationing scheme in the labour market: this concerns an allocation according to the market shares of each sector on the reference path. In addition the external supply of goods 1 and 2 will be sufficient for demand to be met. In the short term, reflation therefore does not modify domestic production, but causes a deterioration of the trade balance to the corresponding level. To compare this simulation in the short term with the previous one, the budgetary reflation was fixed at 1.7% of GDP, which in the absence of the multiplier mechanism yields an identical effect in both variants for the demand for good 2. The investment injected to compensate for labour deficiency is nevertheless lower than that observed in the Keynesian simulation, since firms prefer to raise their prices rather than to satisfy demand. This demand inflation is thus the main result. The level of inflation is comparable to what it was in Keynesian reflation yet arises from opposing mechanisms: here it is the lack of production factors which is the cause, wages merely following by indexation; on the contrary, in the previous case, the increases in purchasing power were at the origin of the price changes.

Figure 4: Full employment (deviations as percentages)

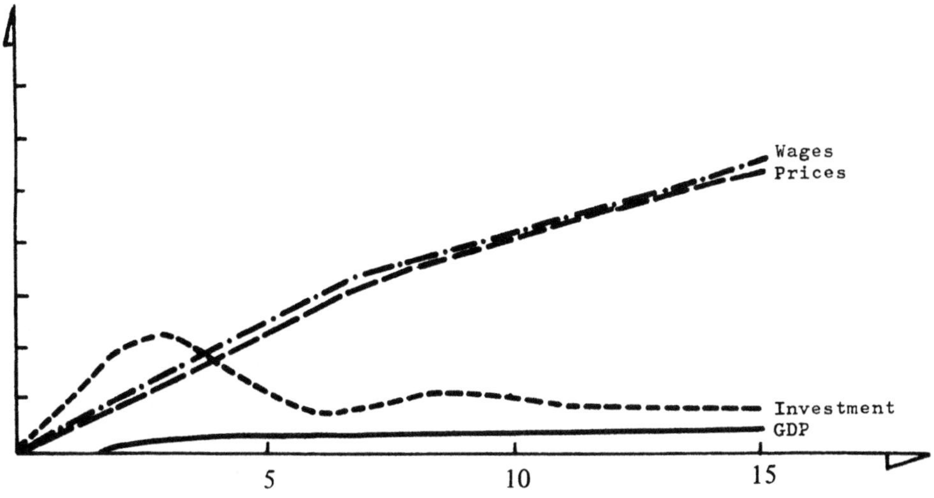

4.3. Two simulations with credit limitations

The aim of these two simulations which do not provide an exhaustive treatment of the subject is to show what this type of tool can contribute in fields where empirical models often have their limits. Firstly, they require a brief outline of how the supply of credits and the rate of interest are determined. The modelling is inspired from the work on indebted economies (Lévy Garboua (1978)) and assumes that the banks have a monopolistic behaviour: the latter maximises their profit under the constraint of a perceived demand curve and an institutional constraint on the credit supply. Given that profit is the difference between revenue and the re-financing and management costs, the following programme is obtained for very simple specifications of the different terms:

$$\text{Max } (r-\mu r_f-g)Cr \qquad \text{(profit)}$$

$$Cr \leqslant Cr^* \exp(-(r-r^*)/\epsilon) \qquad \text{(perceived constraint)}$$

$$Cr \leqslant \overline{\overline{Cr}} \qquad \text{(credit limitation constraint)}$$

with r being the interest rate and r_f the re-financing rate. In the absence of a credit limitation constraint, this formulation implies a rate of interest integrating a margin rate ($r=\mu r_f+g+\epsilon$) and an unlimited credit supply. In the presence of this constraint, making use of this demand curve simply leads to writing $\overline{\overline{Cr}} = Cr^* \exp(-(r-r^*)/\epsilon)$. If the effect of the anticipated credit limitation measured by $m^* = Cr^*/\overline{\overline{Cr}} - 1$ is weak, $r = r^* + \epsilon m^*$ to the first order approximation. The interest rate then increases as the credit limitation becomes more stringent. Completed by these equations, the model presents interesting features for studying credit limitation.

- the general framework of disequilibrium models provides an approach to deal with this problem as a rationing of supply on the credit market, which immediately raises the question of which rationing scheme is to be applied;
- the derivation of the agents' behaviour from general optimisation programmes provides consistency with the global set up. Indeed, modifications in the agents' environment automatically lead to transformations in behaviour, but the latter is always related to the same reference microeconomic framework.

The credit limitation variants consist in limiting credit supply in each period to 99% of the credits allocated in the reference simulation. In order to make this constraint effective, it is assumed that firms cannot find the lacking financial resources on foreign markets.

The direct mechanisms intervening in macroeconomic equilibrium are therefore the following:

- limitation of investment: when a sector is constrained on the credit market, its effective demand for investment goods is simply its financing capacity;
- an increase in the rate of interest as a result of the use of the credit demand curve by banks. This increase reduces firms' notional demand for investment. But in the simulations made it remains insufficient to slacken the credit limitation constraint.

In the short term, the main macroeconomic mechanisms arise from a decrease in activity, amplified by the multiplier effect.

At this horizon, the effect on prices is debatable since our small-scale model does not include an employment adjustment cycle. Thus prices do not increase as they would in an empirical model where a decrease in activity implies a short run increase in unit labour costs and therefore prices.

In the medium term, the depression is reinforced by the reduction in the increases in purchasing power (Phillips effect) and the decrease in self-financing which increases the severity of credit limitation.

But these phenomena are no longer the only ones exerting influence, and the global result depends on the impact of the decrease in investment on productivity. The latter indeed acts directly on production but also indirectly through the multiplier and prices. From this point of view the rationing scheme used to allocate credits is decisive.

To illustrate this point, two extreme schemes are used:

- in the first variant the consumer goods sector is served. It therefore effectively makes its notional investment (see figure 5);
- in the second variant the investment goods sector is served. This provides this sector with a higher level of productivity than the previous variant, and therefore a lower price. Because total investment in volume is determined as the ratio of the firms' financing capacities to the prices of sector 1, this variant is therefore much less depressing (see figure 6).

In fact, in the first simulation the two depression mechanisms envisaged below are put into use, i.e. a cumulative decrease in investment volume and a decrease in purchasing power gains, amplified by the Keynesian multiplier. Correspondingly this simulation is disinflationary due to the Phillips relation.

On the contrary, in the second simulation the initial depressing effect diminishes over time: productivity in sector 1 is high, which maintains the level of investment, and employment increases due to the necessity to substitute labour for the lacking capital. As for prices, the effects are weak: at the beginning, real wages decrease with the increase in unemployment but this effect diminishes as time passes; the prices of consumer goods increase due to the decrease in productivity. This reduces

Figure 5: Credit limitation. Producers of non-rationed consumer goods.

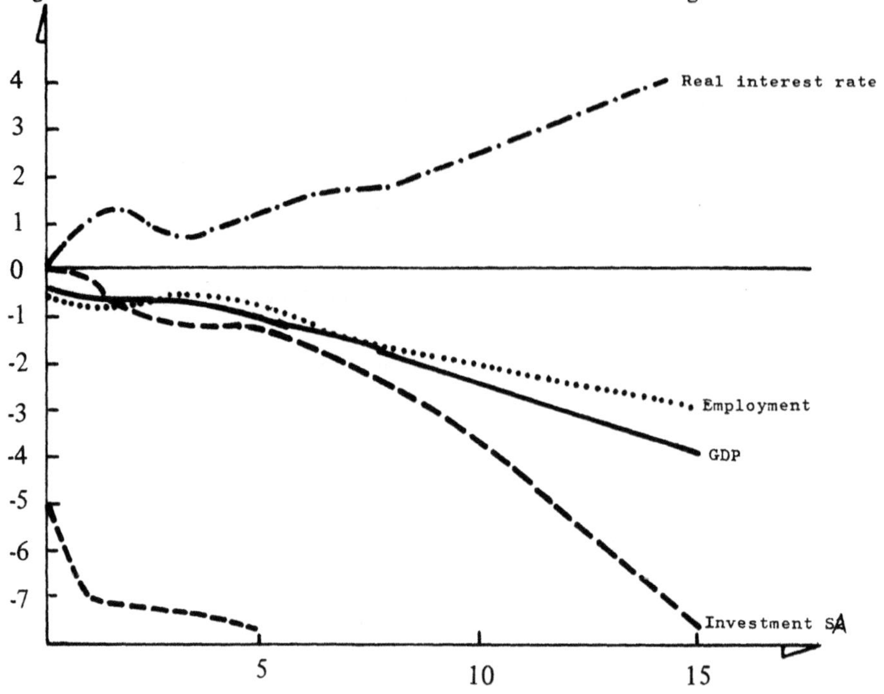

Figure 6: Credit limitation. Producers of non-rationed investment goods.

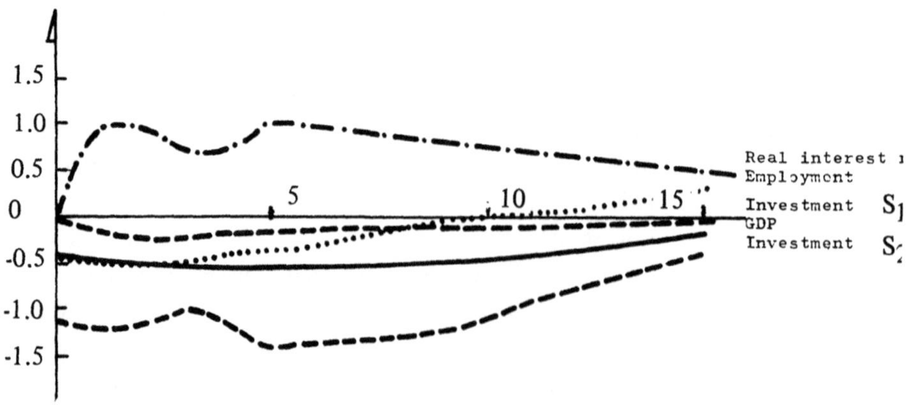

the competitiveness and explains why at the end of the period the cover rate has worsened with production lower than what it is on the reference path.

5. CONCLUSION

The development of a small-scale model, based mainly on the principles of the theory of disequilibrium and the assumption of monopolistic competition between firms in the productive sector, has enabled us to both show the links between this theory and empirical models, and catch a glimpse of the interest there is in expanding the usual static analyses by investigations into the dynamics of these models:

- by means of a few simplifying assumptions concerning the choice of the agents' objective functions, it has been possible to build a small-scale model integrating most of the elements present in the specifications of econometric models and supplying comparable simulations despite a few differences due to the over-restrictive periodisation of time. Moreover, it has been seen that the same micro-economic framework makes it possible to study other growth regimes than that of Keynesian unemployment;

  the desirability of basing dynamics on behavioural patterns consistent with those of the short term adjustment has led us to extend the existence of several types of adjustment, by means of appropriate price and investment equations; it can even be stated that the dynamic mechanisms essentially define the regime at work whilst the static equilibrium of Keynesian unemployment must be privileged.

NOTES

1) We ignore complementary intermediate consumptions for clarity. The modifications to be introduced to include them are straightforward.
2) The effective demand for credits is derived from an identical formula. The constraint on the supply of credits is then relaxed but a new constraint arises concerning the supply of good 1; whence:

$$\bar{Cr}_1 = \text{Min}\,[P_1^1 I_1, P_1^1 \bar{\bar{I}}_1] - \Pi_1$$

3) Indices are omitted, since the periodisation is defined in 3.2.

REFERENCES

Artus, P., P. Morin, J. Bournay, A. Pacaud, C. Peyroux, M. Sterdyniak and R. Teyssier (1981), 'Metric. Une modélisation de l'économie français', INSEE, Paris (mimeographed).

Artus, P. and P.A. Muet (1980), 'Une étude comparative des propriétés dynamiques de dix modèles français', *Revue économique,* Vol. 31, No 1, pp. 88-120.

Benassy, J.P. (1974), 'Théorie néokeynésienne du déséquilibre dans une économie monétaire', *Cahiers du séminaire d'économétrie,* INSEE, No 17, pp. 81-113.

Benassy, J.P. (1976), 'Théorie du déséquilibre et fondements microéconomiques de la macro-économie', *Revue économique,* Vol. 27, No 5, pp. 755-804.

Bertrand, H. (1978), 'La croissance française analysée en sections productives (1950-1974)', *Statistiques et Etudes Financières,* No 35.

Bureau, D. (1982), 'Anticipations des agents dans les modèles néokeynésiens: le cas de la courbe de demande perçue', Working Paper, Ministère de l'Economie et des Finances, Direction de la Prévision, Paris (mimeographed).

Deleau, M., J.P. Lafargue, P. Malgrange, G. de Ménil and P.A. Muet (1980), 'Recherches sur les fondements de la modélisation macroéconomique quantitative', CEPREMAP, Paris, mimeographed).

Deleau, M., P. Malgrange and P.A. Muet (1983), 'A Study of Short Run and Long Run Properties of Macroeconometric Dynamic Models by Means of an Aggregative Core Model', in: P. Malgrange and P.A. Muet (eds.), *Contemporary Macroeconomic Modelling,* Basil Blackwell, Oxford.

Drazen, A. (1980), 'Recent devlopments in macroeconomic disequilibrium theory', *Econometrica,* Vol. 48, No 2, pp. 283-306.

Grandmont, J.M. (1976), 'Théorie de l'équilibre temporaire général', *Revue économique,* Vol. 27, No 5, pp. 805-843.

Grandmont, J.M. and G. Laroque (1976), 'On temporary keynesian equilibria', *Review of Economic Studies,* No. 133, pp. 53-67.

Lévy Garboua, V. (1978), 'Le taux de change et la polititque monétaire dans une économie d'endettement', *Annales de l'INSEE,* No 32, pp. 3-33.

Malinvaud, E. (1977), *The theory of unemployment reconsidered',* Basil Blackwell, Oxford.

Muet, P.A. (1979), 'La modélisation macroéconomique: une étude de la structure et de la dynamique des modèles macroéconométriques', *Statistiques et Etudes Financières (*special issue).

CHAPTER 10

THE MONETARY SECTOR OF THE NETHERLANDS IN 50 EQUATIONS. A quarterly model for the Netherlands (1970–1979)

M.M.G. Fase
The Netherlands Bank and Erasmus University, Rotterdam, The Netherlands

1. INTRODUCTION

These are trying days for econometric modelling and the profession of model oriented policy analysis. Thus the present situation resembles 1936, when Tinbergen presented his first econometric model to the Dutch economics establishment (see Tinbergen (1936)). Tinbergen's econometric description of the Dutch economy of the interwar period, though containing an exchange rate variable, did not yet include a monetary sector. The model which he designed a short time later for the U.S. economy did have a fairly comprehensive monetary block. However, until quite recently official econometric modelling at the Dutch Central Planning Bureau did not expand on these lines, with the result that in the Dutch models the monetary sector hardly existed.

Since 1970 the Netherlands, too, has witnessed a revival of monetary econometric practice and hence of interest in empirically oriented monetary models. Van Loo (1974), Knoester (1974), Fase and Van Nieuwkerk (1975), Korteweg and Van Loo (1977), Schouten (1978), Bakhoven (1979), Knoester (1980) and De Ridder (1981) have published empirical structural models of the monetary sector. Fase and van Nieuwkerk, Schouten and Knoester have in addition, albeit with widely differing degrees of specification, incorporated the interaction between the monetary and the real sector. Of these authors, Knoester provided the most detailed specification. It might also be noted that Schouten, and to a much lesser extent, Fase and Van Nieuwkerk based their analyses on what might be termed global empiricism. In 1981 both the Netherlands Bank and the Planning Bureau published the first results of modelling the monetary sector (see Fase (1981) and Den Haan, Hasselman, Okker (1981)).

This chapter describes a quarterly model for the Netherlands. The model has been built in conformity with an old and now widely accepted tradition of describing the financial sector as a coherent system of the balance sheets of all sectors of the economy which together provide a cross-section of the holdership of the financial assets and liabilities. It is noted in passing that rudiments of this approach have always played a role in the Bank's monetary analysis. The balance sheets of money-creating institutions and institutional investors which are regularly published by the banks provide both a statistical illustration and a practical starting point for further analysis.

In the sections below, first a summary is given of the system of balance sheets which provides the theoretical framework of the model. Section 2 contains an overall description of the system of monetary equations. In the subsequent two sections a close look is taken at the *ex post* forecasting ability of the empirical model, and a number of impulse simulations is presented. In the epilogue the model is considered in the perspective of Dutch model building tradition and the present-day views about econometric models in monetary literature.

2. OUTLINE OF THE MONETARY RELATIONSHIPS

2.1. Introductory remarks

Formulated in a very general and abstract fashion, the monetary process in an economy is basically determined by either the supply of and demand for financial claims or interest rate and demand (supply) behaviour. As a matter of fact, the precise modelling depends on the type of market, the assumed market behaviour of the economic agents, the institutional setting and other actual market circumstances.

Supply of and demand for financial claims originate from the private sector, the financial institutions, the government and foreign countries. Equilibrium is achieved by quantity adjustments, changes in interest rates and wealth and by the interaction between the real and the monetary sector of the economy. Because foreign assets and liabilities are included, the exchange rate may also act as an adjustment mechanism. Due to inertia and institutional arrangements any adjustment towards a new equilibrium situation takes time. An additional factor is the lag with which economic agents adjust their actual asset holdings to the desired portfolio. Where this optimum portfolio conflicts with the situation sought by policy makers, policy measures will ensue. Here monetary policy comes into view. Its formulation requires a knowledge, or at any rate a notion, of the behavioural patterns of the agents involved. A monetary model is one of the sources from which to derive such knowledge, besides subjective judgement and insight into the actual economic situation and the institutional limitations.

As noted before, the above is most general. It does no more than outline a framework to embody any monetary model of an economy with financial intermediaries.

The principal specific characteristic of the monetary model presented below is the fact that it is based on a coherent system of balance sheets for the five sectors considered. The necessary equality of the assets' and the liabilities' side has been ensured for each sector by the introduction of a residual item. The balance sheets are interconnected. Table 1 shows a stylised representation of the financial relationships, considered here.

This representation shows first of all a breakdown of financial assets in the Netherlands and the distribution of their holdership among the private sector, the banking sector and the central bank. Table 1 also shows where the accumulated surpluses or deficits of the government's budget and the current account have their counterparts. Thirdly, the table illustrates the quantitative significance of the various financial assets and liabilities as at the end of 1979. Finally, it shows the equalities to be satisfied by a model based on a system of balance sheets.

In the chosen model design the banking sector is seen as a largely intermediary sector, whose role with regard to the size of the various balance sheet items is a relatively passive one. Banks' behaviour is apparent mainly in their pricing, as reflected notably in their interest rates on demand and savings deposits and in their lending rates. This would seem to be justified by the oligopolistic market situation in the Dutch banking system.

In this model design the behaviour of the central bank is mainly directed towards short term interest rates in order to achieve equilibrium in the foreign exchange market. The long term interest rate seeks to achieve equilibrium in the capital market.

No specific concept of money has been chosen. On the basis of demand for liquid assets, the allocation over the five components is described. Thus, the selection of an appropriate money concept is completely left to the user of the model.

The complete model contains 22 behavioural equations[1]. The equations have mostly been estimated using seasonally unadjusted quarterly figures for the period 1970–1979. Consequently, seasonal dummy variables are included in each of the equations. The scope of this chapter does not permit a detailed discussion of the individual equations and their economic theoretical justification. Such justification is, however, available and most of it is to be found in the relevant references to earlier research. Below, only some brief comments are given on the most important relationships. These concern the supply and demand equations, the interest rate equations and a few exchange rate relationships. In addition, the model embodies a large number of identities (or definitional equations). Their inclusion is partly due to the fact that the behavioural equations often relate to the individual sectors or variables, whereas the quantities which are relevant from a monetary point of view are frequently aggregated over sectors. The balance sheet equations for the separate sectors, with the exception of the central bank, follow directly from table 1 (see equations (1), (13), (43) and (45)). Summing the rows 'miscellaneous' and 'net assets' in the table produces equation (49), which shows private sector net assets as a residual item. Consequently, the balance sheet identity for the central bank

Table 1.1. Intersectoral liabilities and assets

assets / liabilities	private sector	banking sector	public sector	central bank	foreign sector	SUM of liabilities (SUMℓ)
private sector	$LK_{fi,gb}$ 110.6 S_{fi} 37.4	BL 71.9 $LK_{b,ps}$ 104.7	LB_{10} 2.8			327.4
banking sector	D 41.9 T 52.9 S_b 63.3 $LK_{ps,b}$ 33.7		KT_{ro} 0.8	VBL 5.6		198.2
public sector	CH_{ro} 1.0 KOS_{ps} 1.9 $LK_{ps,o}$ 100.4	KOS_b 20.4 $LK_{b,o}$ 13.8		KOS_{cb} 0.5 $LK_{cb,o}$ 0.5	ΣKBu_o −2.4	136.1
central bank	CH_{cb} 19.0	VR 0	SSCH 2.3			21.3
foreign sector	NFA_{ps} 14.7	NFA_b −0.4	NFA_o 0.0	IR 23.6		37.9
miscellaneous		DA_b 20.4	ΣFT_o 130.1		ΣLR 19.0 Σ(RBO+NBARV) 21.3	190.8
SUM of assets (SUMA)	$LK_{fi,gb}$+S+D+T+ +$LK_{ps,b}$+CH+ +KOS_{ps}+$LK_{ps,o}$+ +NFA_{ps} 476.8	BTB 230.8	LK_{10}+KT_{ro}+SSCH+ +NFA_o+ΣFT_o 136.0	VBL+KOS_{cb}+ +$LK_{cb,v}$+IR 30.2	Σ(LR+KBu_o+ +RBO+NBARV) 37.9	911.7
net wealth	$V_{ps}=SUMa_{ps}-$ $-SUM\ell_{ps}$ 149.4	$V_b^*=BTB-SUM\ell_b$ 32.6		$V_{cb}=SUMa_{cb}-$ $-SUM\ell_{cb}$ 8.9		

Explanatory note: Amounts are given in billions of guilders at end-1979; $V_b = V_b^* - DA_b = 12.2$; the summation index of Σ runs over time. For the sake of brevity, the sum of liabilities per sector is not shown in symbols.

$$IR + VBL + KOS_{cb} + LK_{cb} = VR + CH_{cb} + SSCH + V_{cb}$$

is no longer an independent relationship and, hence, cannot stand by itself.

2.2. Demand for liquid assets

The demand for liquid assets, M3, stems from the personal and business sector. M3 represents the domestic money supply plus savings deposits held by the private sector, so that by definition:

$$M3 = CH + D + T + S + KOS_{ps}$$

where CH represents currency, D demand deposits, T time deposits including foreign currency deposits of residents, S savings deposits with banks (S_b) and financial institutions (S_{fi}), and KOS_{ps} short term public authority debt held by the private sector. This definition shows that the financial institutions are partly included in the private sector. However, for the sake of analysis, no complete consolidation has been applied so as to allow the personal and business sector's savings deposits with the financial institutions, as well as its portfolio investments, to be distinguished. It must be noted, though, that this is attained by the introduction of additional behavioural equations.

For M3 a usual demand equation is postulated as suggested by previous studies of the demand for money (cf. Fase and Kuné (1973): Den Butter and Fase (1981)). A special feature of these studies is the incorporation of a cyclical variable q_ℓ. This is intended to allow for an increase in liquidity preference or a shift in the demand for liquid assets as the result of a cyclical downturn. The cyclical variable can, incidentally, also be interpreted on the basis of price theory if it is taken as a proxy for the yield on assets other than M3. The demand for money is assumed to be linear homogeneous in prices (see equation (2)).

The components of M3 result from an allocation model for liquid assets, which includes, in addition to interest rate differentials, income and the growth rate of net financial assets as explanatory variables (see equations (3) to (7)). For a theoretical justification, reference is again made to earlier research (see Fase (1977), (1978), (1979)). By analogy with the procedure used in these earlier studies, switching to and from demand deposits, time deposits and savings deposits is described by the inclusion of interest rate differentials. Contrary to what theory would lead to expect, no interest rate effect has been found to exist for short term public authority debt and currency holdings. As a result, the estimated allocation model is simple and does not satisfy the theoretical ideal with respect to interest rates. The dynamics are modelled within a simple stock-flow model with a growth rate of liquid assets. Consequently, the assumption of identical speed of adjustment for all monetary assets is less stringent than it would appear to be at first sight. For the interest rate on time deposits, the rate for three-month loans to local authorities is used. Taken together, this illustrates the problems which are encountered when attempting an empirical description of the monetary sector on the lines suggested by theory. Nevertheless, the estimated allocation model provides a useful starting point for the description of the balance sheet structure of the private sector.

2.3. Demand for credit

The private sector's demand for bank credit is described bt two equations. Equation (8) explains the demand for short term credit, BL, from expected sales, the lending rate, the long term interest rate as an indicator of an alternative source of finance, and industrial investment (see Fase (1977)). The demand for credit is assumed to be linear homogeneous in prices while allowance is made for lagged adjustment. The private sector's demand for long term credit, LOG_{ps}, is specified in a slightly different fashion (see equation (9)). Thus, BL is measured as a stock and LOG_{ps} as a flow. Demand for long term credit originates from two entirely different categories of borrowers: credit raised from banks by the private sector, $LK_{b,ps}$, and credit raised from financial institutions by the personal and business sector, $LK_{fi,gb}$. Consequently, equation (11):

$$LOG_{ps} = LK_{b,ps} + LK_{fi,gb}$$

results, with the last term on the right-hand side being the outcome of incomplete consolidation of the financial institutions with the private sector. It is obvious that the reasons underlying the demand differ between the two categories of borrowers. This conjecture is supported by the empirical explorations which preceded the final specification.

The long term funds raised by the private sector, LOG_{ps}, are granted by the banking system and the financial institutions. This distribution is described by equation (10) and an equation implied by equation (11). Apart from seasonal effects, this implicit equation reads as follows:

$$\Delta(LK_{fi,gb}/LOG_{ps}) = -0.1852\,\Delta(BTB/BTOT) - 0.0005\,r_k + 0.0039\,r_s + 0.0010\,kr$$

This is a supply equation in the form of an allocation model. The explanatory variables are two rates of interest, a dummy variable kr for the presence or absence of credit restrictions, and the growth of the relative balance sheet total BTB/BTOT. The last quantity represents the growth of the operations of the banking sector (BTB) relative to those of all financial institutions (BTOT). The growth of this balance sheet total is in part determined by exogenous factors and is for the other part the result of the portfolio behaviour of the banking system. This is described by equation (12) and identities (13), (14) and (15). The portfolio behaviour concerns savings deposits received from households, represented by the share in the savings market, S_b/S. This behaviour is described by equations (16) and (17), with the differential between the interest rate on savings deposits and the short term interest rate, and the presence of credit restrictions as the principal determinants.

2.4. International capital movements

In the present model, external capital transactions have been modelled in four behavioural equations, some of which extend across the sectors distinguished. The first set of equations concerns components of total net foreign assets, NFA, described as:

$$NFA = NFA_{ps} + NFA_b + NFA_o$$

For the private sector, an equation is postulated to describe net capital transactions, $KV = NFA_{ps} - NFA_{ps_{-1}}$ (cf. (18)). The principal determinants are the change in the interest rate differential vis-a-vis other countries, the surplus or deficit on the current account on a transactions basis[2] and the amount of long term government borrowing. It might be noted here that exchange rate expectations have been measured with respect to the Deutsche Mark. Equation (18) follows from a stock model and is based in part on a study by Huijser (1983). Equation (20) models the net foreign assets held by the banks, NFA_b and differs slightly from equation (18). The dollar swaps between the central bank and the authorised banks have been added as an explanatory variable, while government lending and exchange rate expectations have been deleted. The third component of NFA, the public authorities' net foreign assets, NFA_o, is assumed to be exogenous.

The second set of reaction equations describes the international trade credit received (ΔHKO_{bu}) and granted (ΔHKV_{bu}). Apart from timing differences in recording, the balance of the two constitutes the difference between the current account on a transactions basis and that on a cash basis (see equations (23) and (24)). Equation (21) explains trade credit received from the change in the interest rate for short term bank credit and the growth of imports. As shown in equation (22), trade credit granted is explained from the change in the lending rate abroad and the growth rate of exports. Equations (23) and (24) reconcile the current transactions with the balance sheet changes.

2.5. Interest rates

Any economy is marked by a spectrum of interest rates. Therefore, a number of interest rates must be distinguished in a monetary model. An interest rate is the result either of supply of and demand for financial assets or, in the absence of a supply relationship, of price setting behaviour. Knoester (1980), for instance, distinguishes three endogenous interest rates, two of which are determined by demand and price setting behaviour. The present model incorporates six endogenous rates of interest.

In the model presented here, the short term interest rate, r_k, and the long term interest rate, r_ℓ, play a central role. The other rates are closely connected with the short term rate. The short term rate responds to the situation in the money and capital markets and is described by the relevant reaction function of the central bank, stylised in equation (25). Thus, r_k is mainly governed by the exogenous interest rate in the Euro-DM market, $\underline{r}_k^{du}$, and the spot exchange rate of the Deutsche Mark. It has been assumed to be endogenous. As will be shown later, this exchange rate of the Deutsche Mark constitutes the link with the Bank's intervention policy in the foreign exchange market.

The long term interest rate follows from the discrepancy between demand and supply on the capital market, the expected appreciations and foreign interest rates, as described by equation (26). A particularly important element in assessing the discrepancy is capital market borrowing by public authorities ΔVAS, which is included in DVL′, as may be seen from equation (50). Furthermore, there is a link with capital market rates in the United States and the Federal Republic of Germany, and with the domestic short term interest rate. Finally, a role is played by inflationary expectations and by exchange rate expectations for the dollar, $\hat{\dot{e}}_\$$. The inclusion of this variable provides another direct link with the foreign exchange market through the –incidentally very simple– manner in which the exchange rate expectations are described by means of a linearly distributed lag model (see equation (35)).

As noted above, the other rates of interest are bound up with the short term rate. As shown in equation (27), the interest rate on demand deposits, r_d, is explained from the share of these deposits in the balance sheet total, D/BTB, and the lagged short term interest rate, r_k. A similar relationship is postulated for the interest rate on savings deposits r_s (see equation (28)). Both these equations reflect the relevant supply behaviour of the banking system. On empirical grounds, the rate on three-month Treasury paper, r_{sc}, has been linked to the rate on three-month loans to local authorities (see equation (29)).

The equation for the lending rate, r_{bl}, which is described in equation (30), is also a price setting relationship, where the lending is traditionally tied to the discount rate on promissory notes. Additionally, allowance has been made for a variable interest surcharge in so far as these are prompted by interest rate movements in the money market. The other interest rate equations (31) and (32) are definitional relationships in terms of the short term interest rates referred to above.

2.6. Foreign exchange market

In the present model the exchange rate of the dollar, expectations as to the dollar rate and the exchange rate of the Deutsche Mark are assumed to be endogenous. The required foreign exchange market block consists of equations (33) to (38). It is based in part on earlier research by Fase and Huijser (1980) and Huijser (1980).

Equation (33) is the main relationship in the exchange rate block and describes the relative change in the dollar's exchange rate in terms of guilders, $\dot{e}_{\$}$. The principal determinant is the dollar rate of the Deutsche Mark, $\dot{e}_{DM.\$}$, on account of the obligations ensuing from EMS membership. Consequently, the volume of the Bank's interventions in the foreign exchange market, ΔNFA_{cb}, has also been included as a determinant. Besides, changes in money market rates at home and abroad, differences in rates of inflation and the surplus or deficit on the current account play a role as explanatory variables. The volume of the interventions in the foreign exchange market is defined in equation (34) by distinguishing not only the endogenous change in the holdings of gold and foreign exchange but also an autonomous change, $\Delta \underline{IR}_{aut}$. Thus, the model's internal consistency is ensured. Equation (36) defines the changes in the cross rates and is, like equation (37), an identity. Equation (38) describes the significance of the exchange rates of the dollar and the Deutsche Mark for total Dutch imports. The weights have been 'guesstimated' in view of the distribution by currency of Dutch imports. This relationship endogenises, as it were, the value of imports within the monetary block and, hence, the exchange rate in the equation for capital transactions (18), the banks' net foreign assets (20), trade credit received (21) and, in part, the surplus or deficit on the current account (24). Equation (38) is in fact merely a worked out version of the definition $M = m.p_m.e$, where m is the volume of imports, p_m the price of imports in foreign currency and e the exchange rate in terms of guilders.

2.7. The overall monetary model

The preceding sections presented a broad outline of the main individual equations without going into the interrelationships which are characteristic of an economy and hence of a macro-economic model. The complete model of the monetary sector is presented in Appendix A. In addition, figure 1 presents a flow diagram of the assumed relationships between the endogenous variables (shown in circles), the instruments (shown in diamonds) and the external or exogenous and predetermined variables (shown in rectangles).

The diagram merely gives an overall view of the monetary model, ignoring the identities and the numerous other details, which are irrelevant for the understanding of the model.

Figure 1: Flow diagram of the monetary block

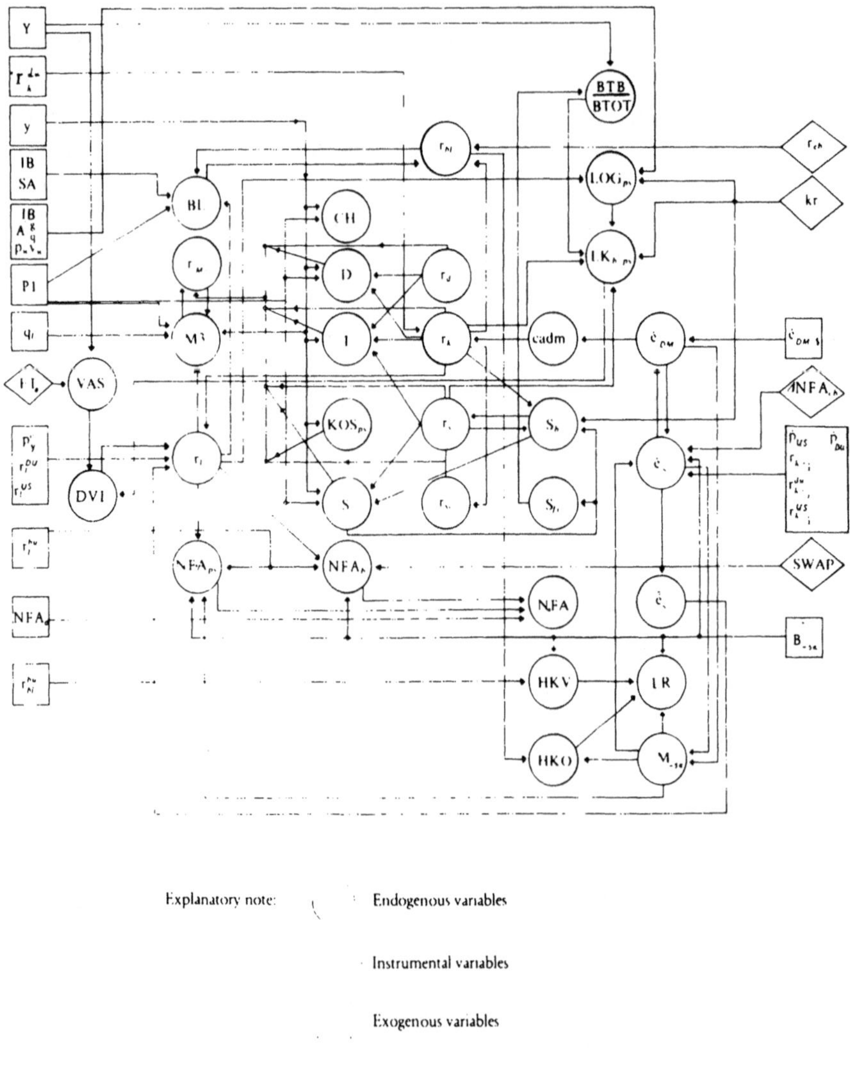

Essential to the model are the restrictions imposed on each sector which follow from the internal logic of a system of balance sheets. Consequently, the endogenous balance sheet items are split up into items which are explicitly described in behavioural equations, and exogenous or residual items. Despite the model's strict logic, the choice between explicitly explained and residual items is somewhat arbitrary. Thus, in our model, the private sector's net assets, V_{ps}, follow from the sector's balance sheet equality. Likewise, the borrowed reserves, VBL, result from the banking sector's balance sheet equality, while the private sector's long term loans to the government, $LK_{ps,o}$, ensue from the equality of the public sector's balance sheet. The change in the holdings of gold and foreign exchange, ΔIR, results from the balance of payments restriction.

Another feature to be noted is the role of interest rates. It is evident from figure 1 that, but for the exchange rate block, the short term rate is exogenously determined. The same would then be true of the long term interest rate. Furthermore, the balance sheet items exert only a minor influence on the other interest rates, so that an exogenous exchange rate would imply a virtual absence of causality between balance sheet items and interest rates. This reasoning illustrates the fundamental importance to the model of the inclusion of the exchange rate as an endogenous variable. As a result of this inclusion, the rates of interest become fully fledged endogenous variables.

The diagram shows five monetary instruments. Discount policy (r_{cb}), credit restriction policy (kr), intervention policy (ΔNFA_{cb}) and foreign exchange market transactions (SWAP) are instruments of the Bank. The financing of the budget deficit (FT_o) is currently an instrument of the central government. If it is assumed that the credit restriction policy is also aimed at controlling bank lending to the government, the financing of the budget deficit becomes part of the Bank's monetary policy. The other instruments of monetary policy are not included in the model. It might be noted here that the model allows various procedures to incorporate the effects of a system of direct credit restrictions. However, in the case of a system of credit restrictions by means of liquidity reserves, some adjustments are necessary. The discount rate acts primarily on the banks' short term lending rate. The latter rate influences both lending (BL) and the volume of trade credit received (HKO). The credit restrictions –which have so far been accounted for in the model in a very general fashion– directly affect the volume of long term lending to the private sector and the banking system's acquisition of long term funds. In the model the foreign exchange market transactions directly act upon the banking system's net foreign assets, but they ultimately affect the exchange rate and, hence, the interest rate and the monetary aggregates. The budget deficit exerts an influence on long term debt and thus on the long term interest rate.

The exogenous variables include the movements in income, the movements in prices an the balance of payments. Other important exogenous variables are the foreign rates of interest. Finally, the exogenous variables include the expected rate of inflation. Its assumed exogenous nature means that for its formation, unlike the exchange rate expectation, no link has been established with the model used. This is a restriction which would appear to be justified by practical reasons.

3. THE DESCRIPTIVE POWER OF THE MODEL

An economic model with numerical coefficients offers various interesting opportunities for experimentation. As a minimum requirement, the model must be capable of reproducing the past. We are concerned here with so-called dynamic simulations, in which, on the basis of historical initial values, the lagged endogenous variable is each time assigned the values produced by the model. It is evident that such a procedure makes heavy demands on the model. Moreover, such an experiment affords an insight into the simultaneity, the predictive ability and the dynamics of the empirical model.

Figures 2A and B show the time profile of predicted and historical values of eight variables, viz. the volume of short term bank lending to the private sector (BL), long term funds raised by the private sector (LOG_{ps}), the money supply (M2), time deposits with financial institutions (T), net foreign capital transactions (KV), borrowed reserves (VBL), the long term interest rate (r_{ℓ}) and the exchange rate of the dollar ($e_{\$}$). Of these quantities, the money supply, M2, is a quantity that does not follow directly from the model. It is obtained by aggregating the relevant components, which, with the exception of –the quantitatively negligible– liquid savings, result from the model ($M2 = CH + D + T + KOS_{ps}$ + liquid savings). For the assessment of the model this means that the performance of M2 also reflects the predictive ability of the underlying equations for currency, demand deposits, time deposits and short term public authority debt held by the private sector. The sample period was marked by substantial shifts between the components of M2 and savings deposits, not included in M2. This is reflected in the time profile of time deposits, which show sizeable discrepancies between the historical and the simulated values in 1974 and 1976. Thus, it is gratifying to note that the model describes this substitution satisfactorily. The model reproduces reasonably well the time profile of bank lending, long term borrowing and the \$ exchange rate. For the long term interest rate the level is considerably overpredicted in the early 1970's and underpredicted in the quarters of 1975–1977. The poor results of borrowed reserves reflect its residual character in our model. Of even greater significance, however, is the fact that turning points are adequately reproduced for the money supply, net capital transactions and interest rates.

The model's predictive ability for the principal variables during the sample period 1971:II–1979:IV is summarised in table 2.1. The table employs three usual statis-

Figure 2A: Dynamic simulation with the monetary model

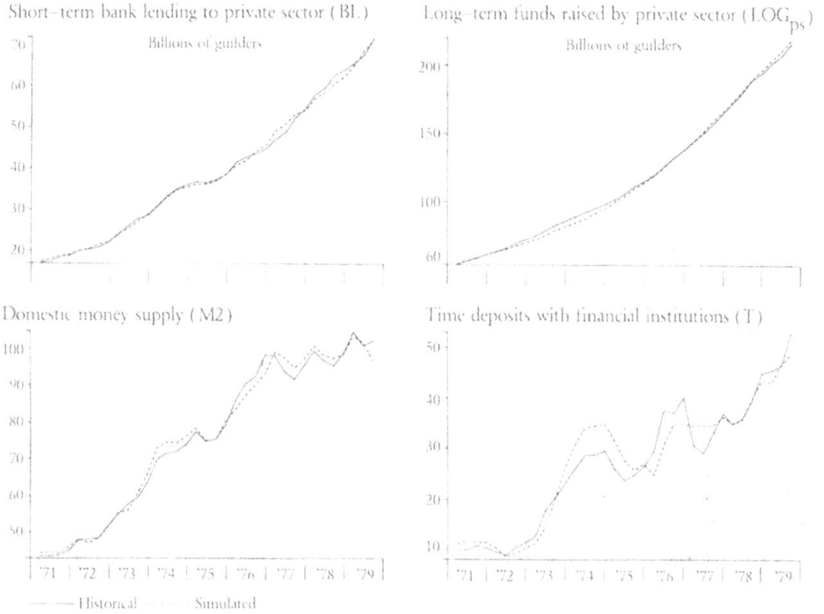

Figure 2B: Dynamic simulation with the monetary model

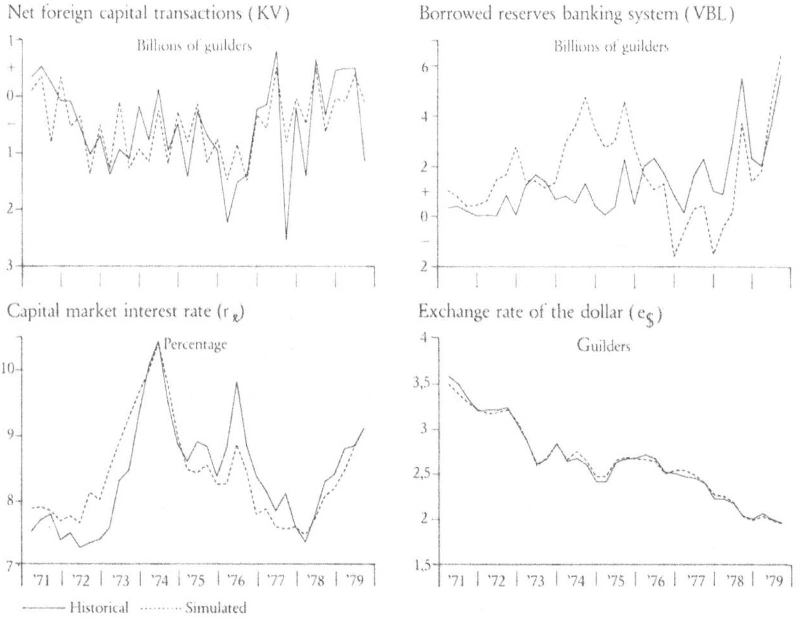

Table 2.1. Ex post forecasting errors in dynamic simulations, 1971:II – 1979:IV

Variable	Mean predictive error	Inequality coefficient	
		Theil	Verdoorn
M3	1.98	0.01	0.01
CH	0.32	0.01	0.02
D	2.05	0.03	0.06
T	3.23	0.05	0.11
S	1.39	0.01	0.02
KOS_{ps}	0.48	0.09	0.18
BL	0.83	0.01	0.02
LK_{gb}	3.06	0.02	0.04
LOG_{ps}	2.23	0.01	0.02
S_b	0.80	0.01	0.02
V_{ps}	0.72	0.00	0.01
KV	0.56	0.33	0.58
HKo_{bu}	0.40	0.32	0.58
HKV_{bu}	0.35	0.25	0.47
NFA_b	0.95	0.11	0.21
IR	1.69	0.05	0.09
VBL	1.75	0.39	0.90
r_k	1.24	0.09	0.17
r_ℓ	0.43	0.03	0.05
$\dot{e}_\$$	0.04	0.01	0.02

tics[3] for predictive ability, viz. the mean forecasting error and the inequality coefficients according to Theil and Verdoorn. By common standards, the quality of the predictions for the individual variables in the seventies seems very reasonable for most variables. The inequality coefficient is largest for borrowed bank reserves (VBL) and smallest for the exchange rate and the private sector's net assets. It must be pointed out here that both VBL and V_{ps} result from other behavioural equations, with V_{ps} moreover being a residual item, which is virtually exogenous (see equation (49)). As a result, the quantity actually concerned is merely the predictive error for net trade credit. Measured in absolute terms, the predictive error is fairly large for time deposits, T, and capital markets, LK_{gb}. A notable result is the small predictive error for the exchange rate of the dollar, bearing out the impression given in figure

2B.

Relatively high inequality coefficients are also found for the foreign capital transactions, KV, and the banking system's net foreign assets (NFA_b). Noteworthy, though not surprising, is the slight improvement in the quality of the predictions when the endogenous exchange rate block is omitted. For the sake of brevity, the relevant key figures are not reported here. We note that the inclusion of the exchange rate as an endogenous variable implies interaction between the money supply and the exchange rate and between interest rates and the exchange rate.

Table 3.1. Inequality coefficients of Theil

Period	coefficient
1971:IV	0.008
1973:IV	0.020
1975:IV	0.010
1977:IV	0.011
1979:IV	0.014

Dynamic simulation tends to produce cumulative predictive errors as one prediction is superimposed upon the other. To check this, the Theil inequality coefficients for the entire model have been computed for a number of years. The results are shown in table 3.1. It is evident that, with the progress of time, the model eminently stands the test of predictive ability. This provides a sound basis for policy simulations or impulse simulations.

4. POLICY SIMULATION

Apart from the assumed relationship, any prediction by a model is based on the values assigned to the exogenous and the predetermined variables. It is therefore important to see how a change in these values affects the prediction. This section seeks first of all to analyse this relationship. Additionally, on the basis of the assumed empirical relationships we attempt to establish how certain changes in the monetary or financial policy variables influence a number of major model variables.

4.1. External influences

First, the following cases were analysed:

– the effect of an additional balance of payments surplus of Fl. 5 billion brought

about by an increase in exports;
- the effect of an appreciation of the dollar by 20% against the Deutsche Mark;
- the consequences of an increase in interest rates abroad by 2 percentage points attended by an equally large increase in the domestic discount rate,
- the effect of an increase in inflationary expectations by 5 percentage points.

All these variants have been analysed on the basis of a certain initial situation, which in our experiments corresponds to the position in the first quarter of 1979. The results are presented in table 4.1.

It is once again pointed out that the results in table 4.1 are preliminary and tentative, owing to the absence of any link with the real economic sector. Nevertheless, within these limitations, the exercise does provide an impression of the relationships within the monetary model. Especially notable is the surprisingly strong impact of a long term appreciation of the dollar against the Deutsche Mark on the short term interest rate, differing markedly from the effect on the long term interest rate. As shown in table 4.1 the 20% appreciation of the dollar works out at about 18% appreciation vis-a-vis the guilder. As a result of the consequent depreciation of about 3% of the guilder against the Deutsche Mark, the short term interest rate decreases, followed, after an initial slight rise, by a much smaller fall in the long term interest rate. The resulting change in the structure of interest rates leads to a shift, at the expense of time deposits, in the composition of liquid assets. The supply of M2 decreases by about Fl. 8 billion after 8 quarters. The fact that, on balance, no capital inflows ensue from this change in interest rates is due to the exchange rate effect and the attendant deficit on the current account. The latter causes a decrease in net foreign exchange holdings. It must be noted that the adverse effects on the domestic price level have been ignored because of the absence of a link with the real economic sector. However, it can be shown that by linking this model to a real block the price level will increase with 0.2 percentage points.

The impact of foreign interest rate movements is evident from the third column of table 4.1. The increase in foreign interest rates has been combined with an increase in the domestic discount rate of equal size to simulate reality as closely as possible. This is justified by the experience that there is a close relationship between foreign interest rate movements and the Dutch discount rate. This does not mean, however, that it would be impossible for the Netherlands to conduct an independent discount policy. It does mean that such a policy responds to extraneous circumstances[4]. As a result of the discount rate impulse, after 8 quarters the short term interest rate goes up by 2.8 percentage points and the long term rate by slightly less than 2 percentage points. The dollar exchange rate of the guilder increases slightly. The change in the domestic interest rates leads to a sizeable increase in the money supply, notably because of the enhanced attraction of time deposits as a consequence of the disturbance of the interest rate structure.

Table 4.1. Effects of a long term change in four external variables

Effect on	after quarters	Fl. 5 billion increase in exports	20% appreciation of dollar against Deutsche Mark	2 percentage points increase of foreign interest rates and of the domestic discount rate	5 percentage points increase in inflationary expectations
Short term interest rate, r_k (percentage points)	1	−0.8	−2.0	2.6	0.0
	4	−0.2	−2.9	2.8	0.1
	8	1.1	−3.0	2.8	0.1
Long term interest rate, r_ℓ (percentage points)	1	0.2	0.1	1.7	0.4
	4	−0.3	−0.3	1.6	0.4
	8	−0.2	−0.3	1.6	0.4
Bank lending, BL (billions of guilders)	1	−0.0	0.1	0.3	0.1
	4	−0.2	0.0	0.9	0.3
	8	−0.3	0.0	1.2	0.5
Money supply, M2 (billions of guilders)	1	0.7	−2.0	1.7	−0.2
	4	0.9	−6.0	5.3	−0.2
	8	−1.8	−8.2	6.9	−0.2
Liquid assets, M3 (billions of guilders)	1	−0.1	0.6	−0.1	0.1
	4	−2.9	0.2	0.0	0.0
	8	−2.7	0.3	0.0	0.0
Dollar exchange rate $\dot{e}_\$$ (guilders)	1	−0.02	0.34	0.01	0.00
	4	−0.00	0.32	0.01	0.00
	8	0.02	0.27	0.01	0.00

The effects of the two other variants are modest. This particularly reflects the absence of feedback to the real sector, where increases in both exports and inflationary expectations have an immediate impact and would hence affect the monetary sector. This conjecture is supported by our first results with an integrated quarterly model for the monetary and real sector.

4.2. Monetary policy instruments

Successively, the quantitative effects of the following variants were analysed:

- an increase in the discount rate of 1 percentage point;
- a reduction in net money-creating operations of Fl. 2 billion;
- a reduction in external capital transactions of Fl. 2 billion.

To begin with, the 1 percentage point increase in the discount rate has been assumed to be attended by an initially equal rise in the short term endogenous interest rate. This results in a fall in bank lending, to an amount of Fl. 0.1 billion going up to Fl. 0.2 billion, and an ultimate increase in the money supply of almost Fl. 2.0 billion. This strange effect, at least at first sight, is due to the simultaneous rise in the short term interest rate which disturbs the term structure. The much weaker effect on the volume of liquid assets, M3, leads to an increase of Fl. 0.7 billion after 8 quarters. The assumed increase in the short term interest rate with the long term rate remaining unchanged causes a discrepancy between the short and the long term interest rate, which enhances the attraction of holding liquid assets, money in particular. The effect on the dollar's exchange rate is negligible.

Though barely topical at present, it would be obvious to compute the consequences of credit restrictions. As the instrument of credit restrictions has been included in the model in a rather crude way by means of a dummy variable, a credit restriction policy has been simulated by a reduction in net lending of Fl. 2 billion. This results in a slight increase in the long term interest rate and a decrease of the money supply.

A policy to curb capital inflows will be based mainly on the necessity to prevent domestic credit restrictions from being frustrated by unlimited lending by non-residents. Such a policy can be simulated in several ways. We have assumed that Fl. 2 billion is supplied in guilders by the private sector and that the central bank allows this supply to make itself felt fully in the exchange rate. The additional supply of guilders causes a decrease in the guilder's exchange rate and, consequently, the short term interest rate goes up by about 0.3 percentage points. This leads to increased demand for time deposits, mainly by switching funds from demand deposits and savings deposits. Ultimately, after 8 quarters, the money supply shows an expansion of almost Fl. 1 billion.

4.3. The public sector financial deficit

To conclude the simulations with policy variants, two, albeit very limited, experiments were conducted with respect to the public sector financial deficit. The effects of the following variants were analysed:

- a reduction in the financial deficit by Fl. 6 billion or 2% of net national income;
- an increase in monetary financing by Fl. 2 billion.

The assumptions underlying the model –especially equations (41) to (43)– cause the sustained reduction in the financial deficit (compared with the initial situation) to be immediately reflected in a Fl. 5 billion decrease in long term debt and a Fl. 1 billion decrease in short term debt. The decrease in long term debt results in a small decline in both the short and the long term interest rate. As a result, net capital export declines by Fl. 0.6 billion, but returns to its initial level after 8 quarters. Short term bank lending contracts slightly, while the exchange rate undergoes no significant change. However, if the real block is taken into account, the impact on bank lending is much stronger.

The impact of a Fl. 2 billion increase in monetary financing has been analysed subject to the assumptions that the financial deficit remains unchanged and that long term debt decreases by Fl. 2 billion. For the sake of argument it has been assumed that this decrease is effected by repayment to the banking system ($\Delta LK_{b,o}$ = – Fl. 2 billion).

The effects of the decrease in long term debt are similar, *mutatis mutandis*, to those in the earlier experiment, the impact on long term interest rate exceeds the impact on short term rate.

4.4. Concluding remarks

The question arises how our variants compare with those of other Dutch models. The opportunities for comparison are few because the policy variants studied sometimes differ from ours and because with one exception none of the previous studies are consistently based on a complete set of balance sheets or take the exchange rate to be an endogenous variable. Korteweg and Van Loo admittedly start from a complete set of balance sheets but, strictly speaking, they drop this starting point in their empirical elaboration. This, and the fact that they assume fixed rates of exchange, detracts greatly from the value which a comparison might have had for an assessment of the results produced by the present model. To a certain extent this is also true of the study by De Ridder. Though not basing himself on a coherent set of balance sheets, he does include the exchange rate as an endogenous variable. As his study is mainly concerned with policy variants, we have compared his results with those obtained by us. De Ridder calculates, for instance, that an increase of one percentage point in the interest rate abroad reduces the money supply after two years by about Fl. 400 million. This is considerably at variance with the increase of about Fl. 3 billion produced by our model. It must be noted, however, that in De Ridder's study it is not clear whether the discount rate remains unchanged. De Ridder's results for the effect on the long term domestic interest rate do not differ significantly from ours. The outcomes would also appear to correspond in the cases of a reduction in net money creating operations and a shift towards monetary financing at an unchanged financial deficit. Recently the Central Planning Bureau has published an annual monetary model (see Den Haan, Hasselman and Okker (1981)), which presents a few policy simulations along the same lines performed here. These show as far as the budget deficit is concerned, similar quantitative effects as ours. Different from us, however, they assume the exchange rate to be exogenous.

5. EPILOGUE

The preceding sections describe a quarterly model for the monetary sector, which is partly the result of the numerous studies of monetary sub-sectors conducted at the Bank in recent years. This model is consistently embedded in a system of balance sheets, and includes an endogenous exchange rate. The model has been estimated with quarterly data for the period following the Bretton Woods system.

The model does not contain an explicit formulation of base money. Although there is considerable doubt about the usefulness of this concept in an open economy (cf., for instance, Zijlstra (1979) and Fase (1980)), it is, in principle, possible to incorporate this monetary aggregate, say MO, into the model discussed here.

At present, the question is frequently raised whether macro-economic models are as useful for policy preparation as was believed not so long ago. After being cherished for many years in academic and also in policy-making circles, this branch of economics is now under fire from both scientists and politicians. A major objection which is often raised concerns the absence of an adequate incorporation of expectations regarding inflation, interest rates, exchange rates, etc. It is beyond doubt that this criticism deserves serious attention. On the other hand, it must also be recognised that the alternative of the rational expectations as advocated by the monetarist economists is not often much more than an empty shell, being filled up in practice with a reduced form equation which is far from satisfactory from the viewpoint of economic theory. However, this does not alter the fact that with regard to expectations further research is required for most models, including that presented in this paper.

Even though a monetary model has intrinsic merits, a link-up with a model of the real economic sector is essential for policy decisions. Such a model has been developed at the Bank. For many years the building of such a quarterly model was hampered by the absence of quarterly data[5] in the Netherlands. An alternative would have been to link the monetary model to the existing models in the Netherlands and to ignore differences in time spans or sample periods. However, this requires sufficient points of contact from a monetary point of view. Unfortunately, the possibilities are limited as a schematic survey of the existing Dutch models given in table 5.1 illustrates. In this survey VINTAF–II has been omitted as it lacks monetary

Table 5.1. Monetary factors in Dutch policy models

Equation	CS–model	Annual model (69c)	Quarterly model (CPB)	Knoester (1980)
Consumption	r_ℓ	r_ℓ, D+T	r_ℓ, LQ	r_{call}, MO
Investment				
Industrial fixed	LQ, r_ℓ	D+T	r_ℓ^a, LQ	r_{call}, MO
Dwellings	r_ℓ			
Local authorities				r_{call}, MO
Stockbuilding			r_ℓ	r_{call}, MO
Demand for labour		D+T	r_ℓ^a, LQ	MO^b
Consumer prices			r_{cb}	

Explanatory note: LQ is the national liquidity ratio M2/Y; r_{call} is the interest rate on call money; MO is the monetary disequilibrium indicator: $(\dot{MO} - \dot{Y})$. The other symbols have the same meaning as in MOKMON–1–82. The model FREIA has been ignored here because no published version is available.

a: Through the price of capital

b: In Knoester and Buitelaar (1975).

elements. The survey suggests that, apart from building a new model for the real economic sector, it might be possible to effect a link-up with the existing quarterly model of the Central Planning Bureau, provided that the concomitant data problems prove surmountable.

APPENDIX A. The equations of the monetary quarterly model for the Netherlands: MOKMON–1–82[6]

Unless indicated otherwise, the econometric equations of the model have been estimated with quarterly figures, not seasonally adjusted, for the period 1970:1 to 1979:IV. The coefficient for determination adjusted for degrees of freedom, $\bar{R}^2$, and the Durbin-Watson test statistic, DW, are given for each of the equations. The reporting of the DW statistics to each equation does not necessarily mean that this statistic has any real significance in each case. Often the addition is based on tradition only. Unless stated otherwise, the behavioural equations have been estimated with the ordinary least squares method. The t values are given in parentheses. The exogenous variables are underlined.

(1) Balance sheet equality of the private sector

$$M3 + LK_{gb} + LK_{fi,gb} + NFA_{ps} = BL + LOG_{ps} + S_{fi} + V_{ps} + \underline{LB}_{lo}$$

(2)
$$M3/\underline{p}_{y_{bnpm}} = \exp[\underset{(6.74)}{0.6074} \ln (M3/\underline{p}_{y_{bnpm}})_{-1} + \underset{(3.64)}{0.3187} \ln \underline{y}_{bnpm}$$
$$- \underset{(2.41)}{0.2975}\ \Delta^4 \ln \underline{p}_{y_{bnpm}} - \underset{(2.09)}{0.8381} \ln \underline{q}_{\ell} - \underset{(0.45)}{0.0230} \ln r_{\ell}$$
$$+ \underset{(1.07)}{0.0244} \ln r_{M3} + \underset{(5.92)}{0.044}\ \underline{d}_1 + \underset{(6.84)}{0.046}\ \underline{d}_2 + \underset{(2.08)}{0.013}\ \underline{d}_3 + \underset{(1.97)}{5.001}]$$

$\bar{R}^2 = 0.99$ DW = 2.09 sample period: 1970:II – 1979:IV

(3)
$$CH/M3 = \underset{(29.55)}{0.7761}\ CH_{-1}/M3 - \underset{(1.00)}{0.0306}\ \underline{Y}_{bnpm}/M3 - \underset{(6.54)}{0.0003}\ \underline{tr} - \underset{(3.47)}{0.0039}\ \underline{d}_1$$
$$+ \underset{(3.97)}{0.0037}\ \underline{d}_2 - \underset{(6.96)}{0.0046}\ \underline{d}_3 + \underset{(3.25)}{0.0446}$$

estimated with Zellner's (1962) seemingly unrelated regression method (SUR)

$\bar{R}^2 = 0.99$ DW = 2.02 sample period: 1970:II – 1979:IV

(4)
$$D/M3 = \underset{(7.28)}{0.0040}\,(r_d - r_k) + \underset{(29.55)}{0.7761}\,D_{-1}/M3 + \underset{(2.67)}{0.2458}\,\Delta M3/M3$$
$$+ \underset{(1.44)}{0.0649}\,\underline{Y}_{bnpm}/M3 + \underset{(0.06)}{0.0003}\,\underline{d}_1 + \underset{(2.59)}{0.0108}\,\underline{d}_2 - \underset{(2.43)}{0.0059}\,\underline{d}_3 + \underset{(2.34)}{0.0434}$$

estimated with Zellner's SUR

$\bar{R}^2 = 0.36$ DW = 1.63 sample period: 1970:II – 1979:IV

(5)
$$T/M3 = -\underset{(7.28)}{0.0040}\,(r_d - r_k) - \underset{(14.03)}{0.0030}\,(r_s - r_k) + \underset{(29.55)}{0.7761}\,T_{-1}/M3$$
$$+ \underset{(5.63)}{0.5303}\,\Delta M3/M3 + \underset{(6.59)}{0.0004}\,\underline{tr} - \underset{(1.07)}{0.0049}\,\underline{d}_1 - \underset{(3.89)}{0.0180}\,\underline{d}_2$$
$$+ \underset{(1.58)}{0.0054}\,\underline{d}_3 - \underset{(0.55)}{0.0026}$$

estimated with Zellner's SUR

$\bar{R}^2 = 0.92$ DW = 1.63 sample period: 1970:II – 1979:IV

(6)
$$S/M3 = \underset{(14.03)}{0.0030}\,(r_s - r_k) + \underset{(29.55)}{0.7761}\,S_{-1}/M3 - \underset{(0.92)}{0.0343}\,\underline{Y}_{bnpm}/M3$$
$$+ \underset{(2.99)}{0.0065}\,\underline{d}_1 + \underset{(0.90)}{0.0018}\,\underline{d}_2 + \underset{(0.04)}{0.0001}\,\underline{d}_3 + \underset{(6.69)}{0.1328}$$

estimated with Zellner's SUR

$\bar{R}^2 = 0.94$ DW = 1.38 sample period: 1970:II – 1979:IV

(7)
$$KOS_{ps}/M3 = \underset{(29.55)}{0.7761}\,(KOS_{ps})_{-1}/M3 - \underset{(3.73)}{0.0001}\,\underline{tr} + \underset{(1.73)}{0.0021}\,\underline{d}_1 + \underset{(1.48)}{0.0017}\,\underline{d}_2$$
$$+ \underset{(4.40)}{0.0051}\,\underline{d}_3 + \underset{(3.71)}{0.0056}$$

estimated with Zellner's SUR

$\bar{R}^2 = 0.91$ DW = 2.09 sample period: 1970:II – 1979:IV

(8)
$$BL/\underline{p}_{sa} = \exp[\underset{(12.42)}{0.7930}\,\ln\,(BL/\underline{p}_{sa})_{-1} + \underset{(3.38)}{0.5148}\,\ln\,(\underline{SA}_{-1}/\underline{p}_{sa}) - \underset{(0.35)}{0.0317}\,\ln r_{bl}$$

$$+ 0.0385 \ln r_{\ell} + 0.0034 \ln (\underline{IB}/\underline{p}_{sa})_{-1} - 0.033\ \underline{d}_1 + 0.015\ \underline{d}_2$$
$$\quad (0.49) \qquad\qquad (0.06) \qquad\qquad\qquad (2.00) \qquad (1.33)$$

$$- 0.018\ \underline{d}_3 - 3.651]$$
$$\quad (1.55) \qquad (5.14)$$

$\bar{R}^2 = 0.99$ DW = 1.78 sample period: 1970:II – 1979:IV

(9) $$\Delta LOG_{ps} = 0.7555\,\underline{IB} - 0.0880\ r_{\ell} \cdot \underline{IB} + 0.0176\, r_k \cdot \underline{IB} + 0.0056\ \underline{p}_w \cdot \underline{V}_w$$
$$\qquad (3.21) \qquad (3.47) \qquad (2.54) \qquad (3.89)$$

$$+ 15.642\ \underline{A}_q^g - 390\ \underline{kr} - 250\ \underline{d}_1 - 1.200\ \underline{d}_2 - 747\ \underline{d}_3 - 13.124$$
$$\quad (3.43) \qquad (1.48) \quad (0.67) \qquad (3.52) \qquad (1.84) \qquad (3.19)$$

$\bar{R}^2 = 0.93$ DW = 2.17 sample period: 1970:II – 1979:IV

(10) $$\Delta(LK_{b,ps}/LOG_{ps}) = 0.1852\ \Delta(BTB/BTOT) + 0.0005\ r_k - 0.0039\ r_s$$
$$\qquad (1.73) \qquad\qquad (3.43) \qquad (3.34)$$

$$- 0.0010\ \underline{kr} - 0.0010\ \underline{d}_1 + 0.0003\ \underline{d}_2 + 0.0023\ \underline{d}_3$$
$$\quad (1.46) \qquad (0.94) \qquad (2.43) \qquad (2.43)$$

$$+ 0.0170$$
$$(3.49)$$

$\bar{R}^2 = 0.44$ DW = 1.55 sample period: 1970:II – 1979:IV

(11) $$LK_{fi,gb} = LOG_{ps} - LK_{b,ps}$$

(12) $$\Delta(BTB/S_{fi}) = 0.0800\ \underline{Y}_{nnpmb}$$
$$(17.98)$$

$\bar{R}^2 = 0.89$ DW = 2.04 sample period: 1970:II – 1979:IV

(13) Balance sheet equality of the banking sector

$$\underline{VR} + NFA_b + BL + KOS_b + LK_b + \underline{DA}_b = D + T + S_b + LK_{ps,b} + VBL$$
$$+ \underline{KT}_{ro} + \underline{V}_b + \underline{DA}_b$$

(14) $$BTB = \underline{VR} + NFA_b + BL + KOS_b + LK_b + \underline{DA}_b$$

(15) $BTOT = BTB + S_{fi} + BTB|S_{fi}$

(16) $$S_b/S = \underset{(34.62)}{0.9413}\,(S_b/S)_{-1} + \underset{(5.24)}{0.0010}\,(r_s - r_k) + \underset{(1.26)}{0.0012}\,\underline{kr} + \underset{(2.44)}{0.003}\,\underline{d}_1$$

$$+ \underset{(3.78)}{0.005}\,\underline{d}_2 + \underset{(2.82)}{0.004}\,\underline{d}_3 + \underset{(2.14)}{0.036}$$

$\bar{R}^2 = 0.97$ DW = 1.40 sample period: 1970:II – 1979:IV

(17) $S_{fi} = S - S_b$

(18) $$KV = \underset{(1.42)}{628.2880}\,\Delta(r_\ell - \underline{r}_\ell^{bu})_{-½} - \underset{(1.40)}{0.2064}\,(\underline{B}_{-sa} - M_{-sa})$$

$$- \underset{(2.33)}{0.3439}\,(\underline{B}_{-sa} - M_{-sa})_{-1} + \underset{(0.71)}{0.1106}\,\Delta VAS$$

$$- \underset{(1.78)}{293.8325}\,\Delta\left[\frac{e_{DM} - \underline{\bar{e}}_{DM}}{\underline{\bar{e}}_{DM}} * 100\right]_{-½} - \underset{(1.43)}{561.5537}\,\underline{dumr}_k$$

$$+ \underset{(2.76)}{1047.8412}\,\underline{d}_1 + \underset{(1.02)}{370.0454}\,\underline{d}_2 + \underset{(2.39)}{993.4715}\,\underline{d}_3 - \underset{(2.15)}{855.4942}$$

$\bar{R}^2 = 0.39$ DW = 1.83 sample period: 1971:I – 1979:IV

(19) $NFA_{ps} = NFA_{ps_{-1}} - KV$

(20) $$NFA_b = \underset{(11.27)}{0.8029}\,NFA_{b_{-1}} - \underset{(0.36)}{103}\,(r_\ell - \underline{r}_\ell^{bu}) + \underset{(2.30)}{0.4034}\,(\underline{B}_{-sa} - M_{-sa})$$

$$- \underset{(2.12)}{0.6242}\,(\underline{SWAP} - 0.8029\,\underline{SWAP}_{-1}) + \underset{(2.93)}{1.864}\,\underline{dumkwart\ 2}$$

$$+ \underset{(1.13)}{534}\,\underline{d}_1 + \underset{(1.15)}{583}\,\underline{d}_2 + \underset{(0.88)}{409}\,\underline{d}_3 - \underset{(0.14)}{57}$$

$\bar{R}^2 = 0.86$ DW = 2.55 sample period: 1970:II – 1979:IV

(21) $$\Delta HKO_{bu}/M_{-sa_{-1}} = \underset{(1.56)}{0.0058}\,\Delta r_{bl} \cdot \underline{dum1975HKO} + \underset{(0.55)}{0.053}\,\Delta M_{-sa}/M_{-sa_{-1}}$$

$$+ \underset{(0.79)}{0.0759}\,(\Delta M_{-sa}/M_{-sa_{-1}})_{-1} + \underset{(2.44)}{0.034}\,\underline{d}_1 + \underset{(0.88)}{0.011}\,\underline{d}_2 - \underset{(1.99)}{0.024}\,\underline{d}_3$$

$$+ \underset{(1.46)}{0.023}\,\underline{d}_1\ 70/74 + \underset{(1.63)}{0.025}\,\underline{d}_2\ 70/74 + \underset{(1.91)}{0.028}\,\underline{d}_3\ 70/74 - \underset{(1.83)}{0.015}$$

$\bar{R}^2 = 0.48$ DW = 2.18 sample period: 1970:III – 1979:IV

$$(22)\quad \Delta HKV_{bu}/B_{-sa_{-1}} = \underset{(2.26)}{0.0114}\,\Delta \underline{r}_{bl}^{bu} + \underset{(2.80)}{0.1993}\,\Delta \underline{B}_{-sa}/\underline{B}_{-sa_{-1}}$$

$$+ \underset{(1.48)}{0.1071}\,(\Delta \underline{B}_{-sa}/\underline{B}_{-sa_{-1}})_{-1} - \underset{(0.56)}{0.008}\,\underline{d}_1 - \underset{(1.45)}{0.016}\,\underline{d}_2$$

$$- \underset{(2.97)}{0.036}\,\underline{d}_3 + \underset{(2.72)}{0.031}\,\underline{d}_1\ 70/74 + \underset{(2.42)}{0.029}\,\underline{d}_2\ 70/74$$

$$- \underset{(0.05)}{0.001}\,\underline{d}_3\ 70/74 \quad \underset{(1.87)}{0.020}\,\underline{d}_4\ 70/74 + \underset{(0.76)}{0.007}$$

$\bar{R}^2 = 0.69$ DW = 2.45 sample period: 1970:III – 1979:IV

$$(23)\quad \Delta HK_{bu} = \Delta HKO_{bu} - \Delta HKV_{bu}$$

$$(24)\quad LR = (\underline{B}_{-sa} - M_{-sa}) + \Delta HK_{bu} + \underline{LRRV}$$

$$(25)\quad r_k = \underset{(12.34)}{1.146}\,\underline{r}_k^{du} + \underset{(3.02)}{115.76}\,\text{cadm} + \underset{(7.30)}{4.356}\,\underline{\text{dumr}}_k - \underset{(0.40)}{0.255}$$

$\bar{R}^2 = 0.87$ DW = 2.05 sample period: 1973:III – 1979:IV

$$(26)\quad r_\ell = \underset{(0.70)}{2.192}\,\dot{\underline{p}}_{y_{bnpm}} + \underset{(4.21)}{0.102}\,r_k + \underset{(4.28)}{0.421}\,\underline{r}_\ell^{DU} + \underset{(3.36)}{0.281}\,\underline{r}_\ell^{US}$$

$$+ \underset{(2.05)}{4.352}\,\hat{e}_\$ + \underset{(1.55)}{11.039}\left(\sum_{j=0}^{3} DVL'_{-j} \Big/ \sum_{j=0}^{3} \underline{Y}_{nnpmb_{-j}}\right) + \underset{(0.94)}{1.163}$$

estimated with GLS

$\bar{R}^2 = 0.93$ DW = 1.61 $\rho = 0.82$ sample period: 1971:II – 1980:IV

(27) $r_d = \underset{(8.28)}{0.5483}\, r_{d_{-1}} + \underset{(8.18)}{0.0601}\, r_{k_{-1/2}} - \underset{(1.48)}{1.1837}\, \Delta D/BTB + \underset{(2.42)}{0.137}$

$\bar{R}^2 = 0.92$ DW = 1.69 sample period: 1970:II – 1979:IV

(28) $r_s = \underset{(11.61)}{0.7897}\, r_{s_{-1}} + \underset{(3.98)}{0.0429}\, r_{k_{-1/2}} - \underset{(1.03)}{2.9821}\, \Delta S_b/BTB + \underset{(2.61)}{0.684}$

$\bar{R}^2 = 0.88$ DW = 1.75 sample period: 1970:II – 1979:IV

(29) $r_{sc} = \underset{(17.46)}{0.7398}\, r_k + \underset{(1.16)}{0.709}$

estimated with GLS

$\bar{R}^2 = 0.94$ DW = 1.82 $\rho = 0.84$ sample period: 1970:II – 1979:IV

(30) $r_{bl} = \underline{r}_{cb} + \underset{(6.5)}{0.33}\, dumr_{bl}(r_k - \underline{r}_{cb}) + \underset{(5.5)}{0.23}\, dumr_{bl}(r_k - \underline{r}_{cb})_{-1}$

$+ \underset{(2.6)}{18.7}\, dumr_{bl}(\Delta BL/BTB)_{-1} - \underset{(4.8)}{1.1}\, \underline{dum1973r}_{bl} + \underset{(59.7)}{2.43}$

where $dumr_{bl} = 1$ if $r_k > \underline{r}_{cb}$

$= 0$ in other cases

$\bar{R}^2 = 0.88$ DW = 1.37 sample period: 1970:III – 1979:III

(31) $r_T = r_k$

(32) $r_{M3} = (D/M3)r_d + (KOS_{ps}/M3)r_{sc} + (T/M3)r_T + (S/M3)r_s$

(33) $\dot{e}_\$ = \underset{(-)}{20}\, \Delta NFA_{cb}/(\underline{B}_{-sa} + M_{-sa}) - \underset{(2.50)}{0.5448}\, \Delta r_{k_{-1/2}} + \underset{(2.63)}{0.9148}\, \Delta \underline{r}^{DU}_{k_{-1/2}}$

$+ \underset{(0.59)}{0.1534}\, \Delta \underline{r}^{US}_{k_{-1/2}} + \underset{(14.11)}{0.7844}\, \underline{\dot{e}}_{DM.\$} - \underset{(1.76)}{0.2454}\, \underline{dump}(\underline{\dot{p}}_{US} - \underline{\dot{p}}_{DU})$

$- \underset{(1.62)}{19.3757}\, \Delta(\underline{B}_{-sa} - M_{-sa})/(\underline{B}_{-sa} + M_{-sa}) + \underset{(0.31)}{0.102}$

$\bar{R}^2 = 0.87$ DW = 1.84 sample period: 1970:II – 1979:III

(34) $\Delta NFA_{cb} = \Delta IR - \Delta\underline{IR}_{aut}$

(35) $\hat{\dot{e}}_{\$} = 0.50\dot{e}_{\$} + 0.25\,\dot{e}_{\$_{-1}} + 0.15\,\dot{e}_{\$_{-2}} + 0.10\,\dot{e}_{\$_{-3}}$

(36) $\dot{e}_{DM} = \dot{e}_{\$} - \underline{\dot{e}}_{DM.\$}$

(37) $cadm = \dfrac{e_{DM} - \underline{\bar{e}}_{DM}}{\underline{\bar{e}}_{DM}}$

(38) $M_{-sa} = m_{-sa}\,\underline{p}m_{-sa}\; e_{DM}^{0.282}\; e_{\$}^{0.125}$

coefficients have been given a priori values and have not been estimated

(39) $CH_{cb} = CH - \underline{CH}_{ro}$

(40) $\Sigma FT^{*}_{o} = \Sigma\underline{FT}_{o} + \underline{NFA}_{o} - \underline{\Sigma KBu}_{o} + \underline{LB}_{1o}$

(41) $VAS = VAS_{-1} + \delta_1 FT^{*}_{o}$

(42) $VLS = VLS_{-1} + \delta_2 FT^{*}_{o}$

(43) Balance sheet equality of public authorities

$SSCH = SSCH_{-1} + (\delta_1 + \delta_2 - 1)FT^{*}_{o}$

(44) $KOS_{b} = VLS - KOS_{ps} - \underline{KOS}_{cb} - \underline{CH}_{ro} + \underline{KT}_{ro}$

(45) Balance of payments equality

$\Delta IR = LR + \underline{RBO} + \underline{NFARV} - \Delta NFA_{ps} - \Delta NFA_{b} - \Delta\underline{NFA}_{o} + \underline{KBu}_{o}$

(46) $LK_{ps,b} = LK_{gb} - LK_{ps,o}$

(47) $LK_{ps,o} = VAS - \underline{LK}_{b,o} - \underline{LK}_{cb,o}$

(48) $LK_{b} = LK_{b,ps} + \underline{LK}_{b,o}$

$$(49)\quad V_{ps} = \Sigma LR + \Sigma \underline{FT}_o + \Sigma \underline{NFARV} - \underline{V}_{cb} - \underline{V}_b + \Sigma \underline{RBO}$$

$$(50)\quad DVL' = \Delta VAS + \Delta LK_{b,ps} + \Delta LK_{fi,gb} + \Delta LK_{ps,b}$$

APPENDIX B. Symbols used

1. Endogenous variables

a. balance sheet items

BL	Short term bank lending to private sector
CH_{cb}	Currency issued by central bank, i.e. bank notes in circulation
D	Demand deposits
IR	Gold and foreign exchange holdings, i.e. stock of international reserves
KOS_b	Short term public authority debt placed with the banks
KOS_{ps}	Short term public authority debt placed with the private sector
$LK_{b,ps}$	Capital market investments of the banks with the private sector
$LK_{fi,gb}$	Long term funds raised from financial institutions by the personal and business sector = long term funds raised from the personal and business sector by financial institutions (= $LK_{gb,fi}$)
$LK_{ps,b}$	Long term funds raised from the private sector by the banks, i.e. long term lending by the private sector to the banks
$LK_{ps,o}$	Long term lending by the private sector to the public authorities
ΣLR	Acculated current account surplus on a cash basis
NFA_b	Net foreign assets of the banks
NFA_{ps}	Net foreign assets of the private sector
S_b	Savings deposits with the banks
S_{fi}	Savings deposits with financial institutions
SSCH	Treasury's balance
T	Time deposits with financial institutions
V_{ps}	Net assets of the private sector
VBL	Borrowed reserves of the banks

b. composite or derived balance sheet items

BTB	Balance sheet total of the banks
BTOT	Balance sheet total of the banks and financial institutions combined
BTB|S_{fi}	Balance sheet total of financial institutions less savings deposits with these institutions
CH	Currency
DVL'	Capital market disequilibrium

ΣFT_o^*	Accumulated financial surplus of the public authorities to the extent that it is distributed among long term debt, floating debt and the Treasury's balance
ΔHK_{bu}	Net external trade credit
ΔHKO_{bu}	External trade credit received
ΔHKV_{bu}	External trade credit granted
KV	Increase in the private sector's net foreign assets: net capital transactions
LK_b	Capital market investments of the banks
LK_{gb}	Capital market investments of the personal and business sector
LOG_{ps}	Long term funds raised by the private sector
M3	Domestic money supply plus savings deposits
ΔNFA_{cb}	Foreign exchange market intervention by the central bank
S	Savings deposits of the private sector
VAS	Long term public authority debt
VLS	Floating public authority debt

c. interest rate variables

r_{bl}	Interest rate on bank credit
r_d	Interest rate on ordinary current account balances
r_k	Short term interest rate (interest rate on three-month loans to local authorities)
r_ℓ	Capital market rate
r_{M3}	Interest rate on domestic money supply
r_s	Interest rate on savings deposits
r_{sc}	Interest rate on three-month Treasury paper
r_T	Interest rate on time deposits

d. exchange rate variables and other exogenous variables

cadm	Spot DM rate against parity ($= \bar{e}_{DM}$)
$\dot{e}_\$$	Relative change in the dollar rate ($= e_\$$)
$\dot{\hat{e}}_\$$	Relative change in the expected dollar rate ($= \hat{e}_\$$)
$\dot{e}_{DM}$	Relative change in the DM rate ($= e_{DM}$)
M_{-sa}	Imports of goods and services on a transactions basis; excluding ships and aircraft

2. Exogenous variables

a. balance sheet items

CH_{ro}	Currency issued by the central government
ΣFT_o	Accumulated public authorities' financial surplus
ΣKBu_o	Accumulated official external capital transactions
KOS_{cb}	Central bank's short term claims on the public authorities
KT_{ro}	Central government's cash and deposits
LB_{lo}	Local authorities' liquid assets holdings
$LK_{b,o}$	Long term funds raised by the public authorities from the banks
NFA_o	Public authorities' net foreign assets
NFARV	Timing differences in recording for the banks' net foreign assets
RBO	Items in transit plus exogenous items on the balance of payments on a cash basis
V_b	Banks' net assets
V_{cb}	Central banks' net assets
VR	Borrowed reserves

b. other exogenous variables

A_q^g	Labour income ratio
d_1,d_2,d_3	Seasonal dummy variables
d_1 70/74	Seasonal dummy variable for 1970:I – 1974:IV
d_2 70/74	Seasonal dummy variable for 1970:I – 1974:IV
d_3 70/74	Seasonal dummy variable for 1970:I – 1974:IV
d_4 70/74	Seasonal dummy variable for 1970:I – 1974:IV
DA_b	Miscellaneous bank assets
$dumr_k$	Dummy variable for periods marked by use of interest rate in support of the guilder (value 1 in 1976:III and 1978:IV; value 0 in other periods)
$dumr_{bl}$	Dummy variable for extra surcharge on banks' overdraft rates
dump	Dummy variable in exchange rate equation (value 0 in 1970:I – 1973:II; value 1 in other periods)
dum1975HKO	Dummy variable in equation for trade credit received (value 1 as from 1975:I)
$dum1973r_{bl}$	Dummy variable for extreme money market conditions in 1973:IV
dumkwart 2	Dummy variable in connection with banks' net foreign assets (value 1 in 1974:II, 1975:II and 1976:II; value 0 in other periods)
B_{-sa}	Export of goods and services on a transactions basis; excluding ships and aircraft

$\dot{e}_{DM \cdot \$}$	Relative change in the exchange rate of the Deutsche Mark in terms of dollars
IB	Industrial investment
kr	Credit restriction variable
LRRV	Timing differences in recording between current account on a cash basis and that on a transactions basis
m_{-sa}	Imports of goods and services on a transactions basis, excluding ships and aircraft in real terms
p_{sa}	Price index of sales
p_{DU}	Price index of the Federal Republic of Germany's export in D-mark
$p_{m_{-sa}}$	Price index of imports of goods and services
p_{US}	Price index of US export in dollars
p_w	Price index of dwellings
$p_{y_{bnpm}}$	Price index of the national product
r_{cb}	Discount rate on promissory notes
q_ℓ	Cyclical indicator: degree of utilisation of labour
r_{bl}^{bu}	Average discount rate in the Federal Republic of Germany, the United Kingdom and the United States
r_k^{US}	Short term interest rate in the United States
r_k^{DU}	Interest rate on Deutsche Marks in the Eurocurrency market
r_ℓ^{bu}	Capital market rate abroad
r_ℓ^{DU}	Capital market rate in the Federal Republic of Germany
r_ℓ^{US}	Capital market rate in the United States
SA	Industrial sales
SA^e	Expected industrial sales ($= SA_{-1}$)
SWAP	Dollar swaps between the central bank and the authorised banks
tr	Trend term
V_w	Housing stock
Y_{nnpmb}	Net disposable income
Y_{bnpm}	National product
y_{bnpm}	National product in real terms
δ_1	Ratio of public authority capital market borrowing to public authority financial deficit
δ_2	Ratio of increase in public authority floating debt and public authority financial deficit

NOTES

1) These are shown in Appendix A, together with the other equations. This appendix also shows the sample period and the estimation method. Appendix B lists the symbols used and their meanings.
2) The ideal theoretical basis for this specification is provided by the so-called stock-flow model from the portfolio theory, which covers both reallocations of the existing portfolio (stock) induced by changes in interest rates, and the distribution of new savings (flows) induced by the interest rate differential vis-a-vis other countries. In this reasoning, total wealth, the interest rate differential vis-a-vis other countries and the change in this differential are viewed as the primary determinants (cf. Branson and Hill (1971)).
3) Leaving aside the characteristics and merits of these statistics, it is merely noted that the first mainly indicates the absolute magnitude of the predictive errors in the unit used. The two inequality coefficients are between 0 and 1 (Theil) and above 0 (Verdoorn). With perfect prediction, all criteria assume the value 0.
4) See Fase and Den Butter (1977) for a technical elaboration.
5) A first draft of this quarterly model of the real sector is presented in M.M.G. Fase (1982).
6) This is a slightly revised version of MOKMON-1-81, published by Fase (1981).

REFERENCES

Bakhoven, A.F. (1979), 'Het herstel van evenwicht tussen de vraag naar en het aanbod van liquiditeiten', in: J.J. Klant, W. Driehuis, H.J. Bierens and A.J. Butter (eds.), *Samenleving en onderzoek*, Stenfert Kroese, Leyden, pp. 225-255.

Branson, W.H. and R.D. Hill jr. (1971), 'Capital Movements in the OECD Area', *OECD Economic Outlook, Occasional Studies.*

Butter, F.A.G. den and M.M.G. Fase (1981), 'The Demand for Money in EEC Countries', *Journal of Monetary Economics*, 8, pp.201-230.

Fase, M.M.G. (1977), 'The Demand for Bank Credit and the Commercial Bank Lending Rate', *De Nederlandsche Bank N.V., Onderzoekrapport*, No 7710 (revised in March 1979).

Fase, M.M.G. (1977), 'Savings Deposits, Time Deposits and Interest Rate Differentials: an econometric analysis', *De Nederlandsche Bank N.V., Quarterly Statistics*, No 2, pp. 78-88.

Fase, M.M.G. (1978), 'Een verdeelmodel voor liquide activa', *Economisch-Statistische Berichten*, 63, pp. 215-218.

Fase, M.M.G. (1979), 'The Demand for Financial Assets', *European Economic Review*, 12, pp. 381-394.

Fase, M.M.G. (1980), 'Monetary Base Control: a useful alternative for the Netherlands?', *De Economist*, 128, pp. 189-204.

Fase, M.M.G. (1981), 'Financiële activa, rentevorming en monetaire beheersbaarheid: proeve van een monetair kwartaalmodel voor Nederland', in: E. den Dunnen, M.M.G. Fase and A. Szász, Zoeklicht op Beleid, Leyden, 1981, pp. 43-81.

Fase, M.M.G. (1982), 'Een reël kwartaalmodel voor Nederland, REKMON-1-82', *De Nederlandsche Bank N.V., Onderzoekrapport*, No 8204 (August 1982).

Fase, M.M.G. and F.A.G. den Butter (1977), 'The Endogeneity of Monetary Policy in the Netherlands: two reaction functions of the central bank', *Cahiers économiques et monétaires*

(Banque de France, Paris), pp. 177-204.

Fase, M.M.G. and A.P. Huijser (1980), 'A Reaction Function for Foreign Exchange Intervention in the Netherlands', *Kredit und Kapital*, 6, pp. 290-319.

Fase, M.M.G. and J.B. Kuné (1974), 'De vraag naar liquiditeiten in Nederland, 1952-1971', *De Economist*, 122, pp. 326-356.

Fase, M.M.G. and M. van Nieuwkerk (1975), 'Anticipated Inflation and Interest Rates in an Open Economy: a study of the Gibson paradox for the Netherlands', in: F. Masera, A. Fazio and T. Padoa-Schioppa (eds.), *Econometric Research in European Central Banks* (Banca d'Italia, Rome), pp. 297-321.

Haan, R.J.A. den, B.H. Hasselman and V.R. Okker (1981), 'Een monetair submodel voor Nederland', *CPB Occasional Paper*, No 26, s'-Gravenhage.

Huijser, A.P. (1980), 'De samenhang tussen de geldmarkt en de valutamarkt: een eenvoudig structuurmodel', *Maandschrift Economie*, 44, pp. 291-307.

Huijser, A.P. (1983), 'Het kapitaalverkeer van de private sector', *De Nederlandsche Bank N.V., Onderzoekrapport*, No 8206 (revised version February 1983).

Knoester, A. (1974), 'Een stelsel monetaire vergelijkingen ten behoeve van een empirisch macromodel voor Nederland', *Maandschrift Economie*, 38, pp. 473-530.

Knoester, A. (1980), *Over geld en economische politiek*, Stenfert Kroese, Leyden.

Knoester A. and P. Buitelaar (1975), 'De interacties tussen monetaire en reële sector in een empirisch macromodel voor Nederland', *Maandschrift Economie*, 39, pp. 493-556.

Korteweg, P. and P.D. van Loo (1977), *The Demand for Money and the Market for Credit'*, Martinus Nijhoff, Leyden.

Loo, P.D. van (1974), 'A Monetary Submodel for the Dutch Economy', *De Economist*, 122, pp. 243-283.

Schouten, D.B.J. (1978), 'Internationale stagflatie bij vaste en flexibele wisselkoersen', in: *Preadviezen van de Vereeniging voor de Staathuishoudkunde*, Stenfert Kroese, Leyden, pp. 1-29.

Ridder, P.B. de, (1981), 'Enkele monetaire samenhangen rond een endogene wisselkoers', *Maandschrift Economie*, 45, pp. 14-33.

Tinbergen J. (1936), 'Kan hier te lande, al dan niet na overheidsingrijpen, een verbetering van de binnenlandse conjunctuur intreden, ook zonder verbetering van onze exportpositie? Welke lering kan ten aanzien van dit vraagstuk worden getrokken uit de ervaringen van andere landen?', in: *Preadviezen van de Vereeniging voor de Staathuishoudkunde en de Statistiek*, Martinus Nijhoff, The Hague, pp. 62-108.

Zellner, A. (1962), An Efficient Method of Estimating Seemingly Unrelated Regressions and Tests for Aggregation Bias', *Journal of the American Statistical Association*, 57, pp. 348-368.

Zijlstra, J (1979), 'Central Banking: a moderate monetarist's view', *Speech at Jerusalem*, Nov. 1979 (mimeographed).

CHAPTER 11

SPECIFICATION OF THE IMPORT FUNCTION AND THE DETERMI - NATION OF SHORT AND LONG TERM EQUILIBRIA IN A MACRO-ECONOMETRIC MODEL

C. Le Van

University of Paris X and Groupe d'Analyse Macroéconomique Appliquée – CNRS France

1. INTRODUCTION

Some macroeconometric model builders wish to generalise the theoretical foundation of their models. On one hand, they try, in the short term (keynesian situation), to describe both the situations of full employment and underemployment of production capacities, on the other hand, to reconciliate a short term situation where the demand plays an essential role, and a long term situation where this role is played by the supply side. For example, this theoretical approach holds for the model DMS (see Fouquet et al. (1978)) and especially for the model MOGLI (see Courbis et al. (1980)) which has a theoretical framework (see Courbis (1980)) explaining its economic foundation.

Our purpose in this paper is to verify whether this generalisation is always possible.

The principal tool of our analysis is the generally admitted formulation of the import function; it includes the effects of demand, relative prices and possibly the rate of capacity utilisation. For the short term, we have the following result: if the elasticity of demand in the import function is smaller than one, one can describe both the situations of underemployment and full employment of production capacities; if this elasticity is greater than one, then these models cannot describe the situation of full employment of capacities; moreover, there exists a 'perverse' effect if we simulate a demand policy with these models.

To study the long term behaviour we use a very small model which possesses a unique equilibriated growth path qualified as classical path. Out of this path one is in a neo-keynesian situation. But does every neo-keynesian path converge to the classical one? In other words, is the classical path asymptotically stable? We show, in a special model, that the growth path is unstable if the elasticity of demand in the import function is strictly smaller than a value $\alpha \leqslant 1$. So, to have a model which can reconciliate the short and the long term, it seems to us that the elasticity of demand of the traditional import function must belong to a 'narrow' interval bounded by unity; as this condition is quite unrealistic in practice (generally this elasticity is greater than one), we think that the models which adopt such an import function cannot describe, on the one hand, the classical situation for the long term, and on the other hand, *both* the full employment and underemployment situations in the short term.

The paper is organised as follows: in section 2 the theoretical scheme of determination of short term equilibrium is presented. In section 3 we examine the importance of the elasticity of demand of the import function in the determination of this equilibrium. In section 4 we study the stability of the classical growth path of a very small model.

2. SHORT TERM EQUILIBRIUM

Let us consider the following system giving the short term equilibrium:

$$\begin{cases} Q + M = D & (1a) \\ M = f(D, p/p^e, Q/\hat{Q}) & (1b) \end{cases}$$

where Q. M, D, $\hat{Q}$ are respectively production, imports, demand and production capacity, p/p^e is the relative price (national/foreign).

The general assumptions are the following:

$$f > 0; \quad \frac{\partial f}{\partial D} > 0; \quad \frac{\partial f}{\partial (p/p^e)} > 0; \quad \frac{\partial f}{\partial (Q/\hat{Q})} > 0,$$

$$f(D, p/p^e, Q/\hat{Q}) \rightarrow A \leqslant +\infty \quad \text{when } Q \rightarrow \hat{Q}.$$

In the short term we assume that D, p, p^e and $\hat{Q}$ are given. The system (1) is then equivalent to the following one:

$$\begin{cases} Q + M = D & (2a) \\ M = \varphi(Q+M, Q) & (2b) \end{cases}$$

where φ is obtained by replacing D by Q+M, and 'omitting' p, p^e, $\hat{Q}$ (these variables are fixed in the short term). We have always:

$$\varphi > 0; \quad \frac{\partial \varphi}{\partial (Q+M)} > 0; \quad \frac{\partial \varphi}{\partial Q} > 0;$$

$$\varphi(Q+M,Q) \rightarrow A \leqslant +\infty \quad \text{when } Q \rightarrow \hat{Q}.$$

Some macroeconomic model builders (see e.g. Fouquet et al. (1978), Courbis et al. (1980), Courbis (1980)) assume that the second relation of (2) implies:

$$M = \psi(Q) > 0$$

where $\psi'(Q) > 0$, and $\psi(Q) \rightarrow A \leqslant +\infty$ when $Q \rightarrow \hat{Q}$. Graphically, the short term equilibrium is the intersection point, in the (M,Q)-plane, of the line (Δ):

$$Q + M = D$$

and the curve (Γ):

$$M = \psi(Q).$$

In figures 1 and 2 the graphs of (Δ) and (Γ) are plotted.

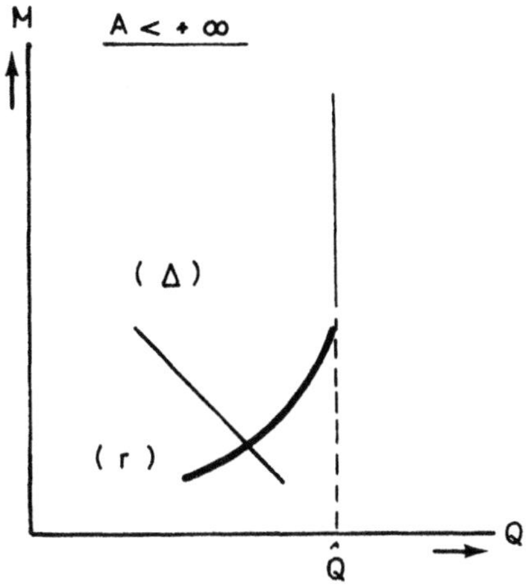

Figure 1.

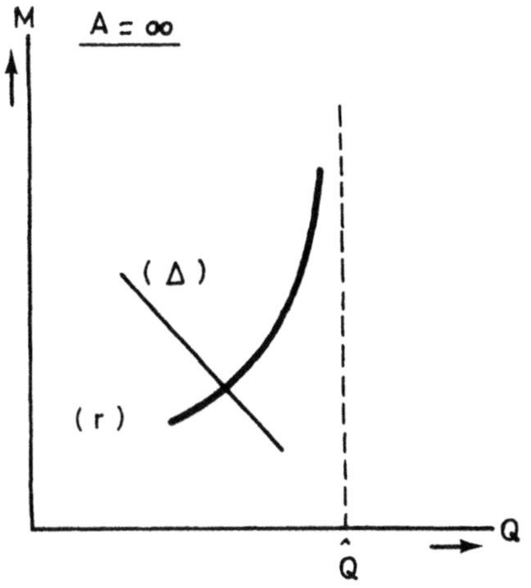

Figure 2.

When the demand D increases, the line (Δ) moves up to the right. Also in the neighbourhood of the full employment level $\hat{Q}$, an increase of D is almost absorbed by the imports.

3. THE ELASTICITY OF DEMAND OF IMPORT FUNCTIONS AND THE DETERMINATION OF THE SHORT TERM EQUILIBRIUM

In this section we examine whether the theoretical scheme described in the previous section is always obtained by a traditional import function.

We assume that the import function has the following form:

$$M = A\,D^{\alpha}\,\varphi(Q/\hat{Q})$$

where $Q+M = D$

$\hat{Q}$ is capacity of production

A depends on p/p^e, fixed in the short term.

As $\hat{Q}$ is given in the short term, one can write:

$$M = A\,D^{\alpha}\,f(Q).$$

We shall find the appropriate values of α to provide a graph of M versus Q similar to those of the previous section. Writing

$$M = \psi_Q(M)$$

with

$$\psi_Q(M) = A(Q+M)^{\alpha}\,f(Q)$$

$$f(Q) > 0;\quad f'(Q) > 0 \quad \forall\, Q \in [0, \hat{Q}[\,.$$

We have successively:

$$\frac{\partial \psi_Q(M)}{\partial Q} = A\,\alpha(Q+M)^{\alpha-1}\,f(Q) + A(Q+M)^{\alpha}\,f'(Q) > 0$$

$$\frac{\partial \psi_Q(M)}{\partial Q} = A\,\alpha(Q+M)^{\alpha-1}\,f(Q) > 0$$

$$\frac{\partial_2 \psi_Q(M)}{\partial M^2} = A\,\alpha(\alpha-1)(M+Q)^{\alpha-2} f(Q)$$

It is readily verified that the graphs of $\psi_Q(M)$ versus M, indexed by Q, move up when Q increases, $\psi_Q(M)$ being increasing functions of M, convex if $\alpha > 1$, concave if $\alpha < 1$. These curves go through the origin if and only if Q=0. The graph of M versus Q will be obtained by solving the following equation graphically:

$$M = \psi_Q(M) . \tag{3}$$

For each value of Q, this relation gives one (or many) value(s) of M; thus by varying Q we obtain the graph of M versus Q.

Case 1: $\alpha < 1$

We obtain figure 3 showing the shape of the family of graphs of $\psi_Q(M)$:

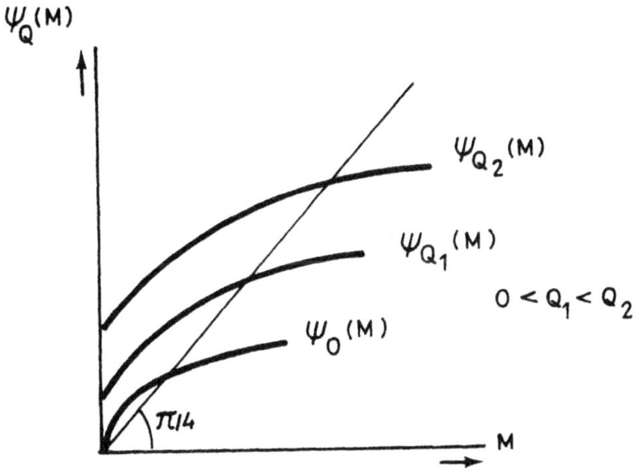

Figure 3.

From this figure we deduce the graphs of M versus Q:

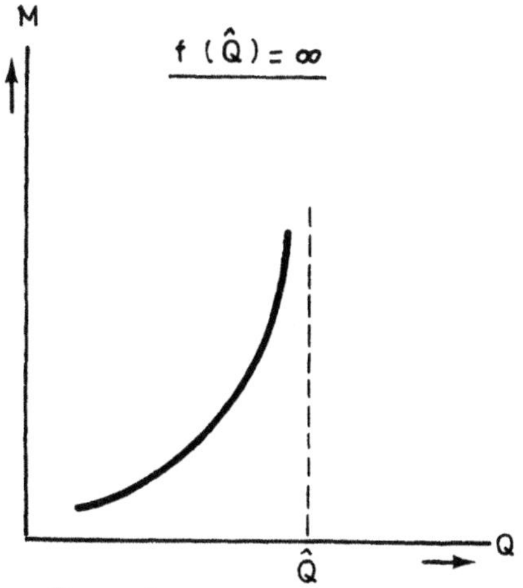

Figure 4.

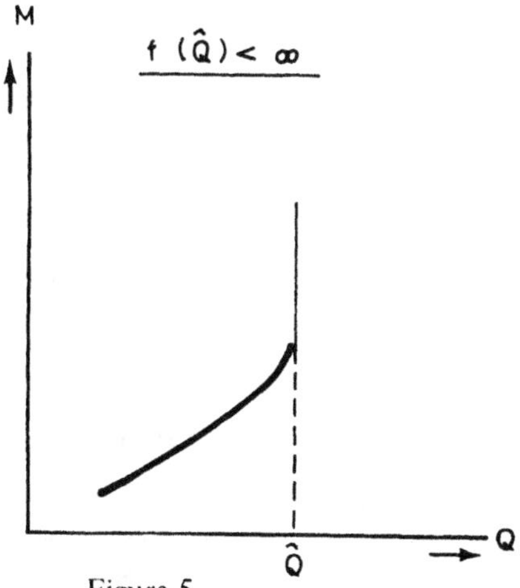

Figure 5.

When the demand D increases beyond some value, there is perfect substitution between imports and production. These graphs correspond then to the theoretical scheme of the previous section.

Case 2: $\alpha > 1$

The solutions of (3) are illustrated in figure 6:

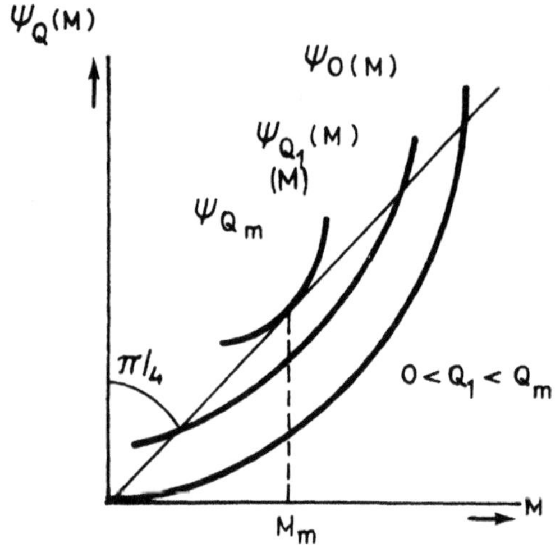

Figure 6.

One can see that there exists a critical value Q_m where the graph of $\psi_{Q_m}(M)$ is tangent to the first bisector. If $Q > Q_m$, equation (3) has not solution; for $Q < Q_m$ there are two solutions. The graphs of M versus Q can be easily deduced:

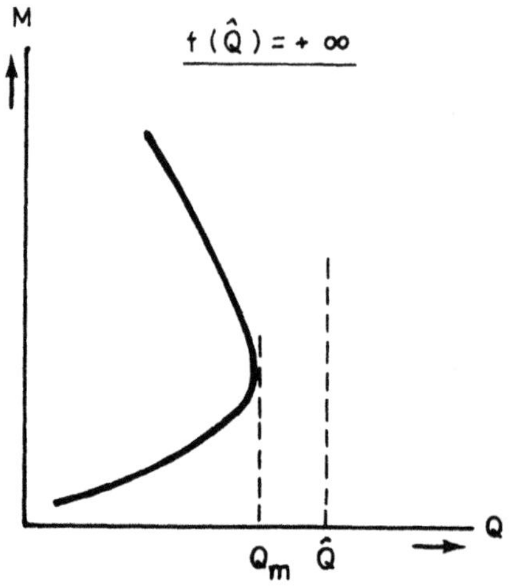

Figure 7.

According to the values of Q_m we obtain two graphs (figures 8 and 9).

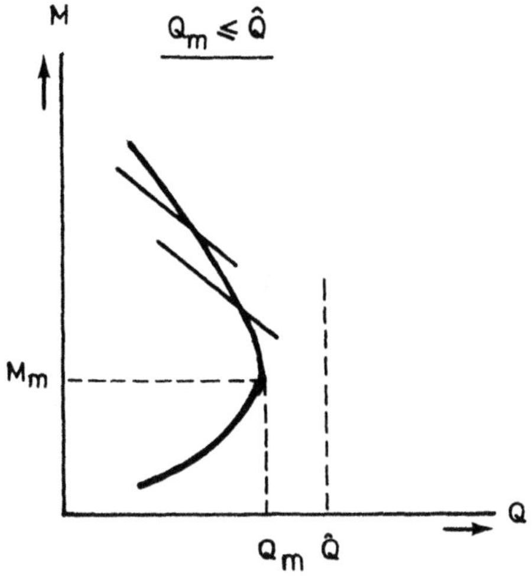

Figure 8.

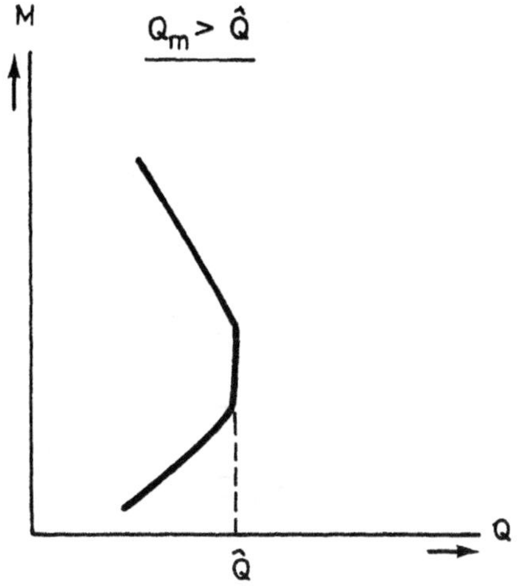

Figure 9.

It is readily proved that for $M > M_m$, one has $\alpha M/(Q+M) > 1$, and

$$\left|\frac{dM}{dQ}\right| = \frac{\alpha/(Q+M) + f'(Q)/f(Q)}{\alpha/(Q+M) - 1/M} > 1.$$

Thus, when the demand D increases beyond a critical value, we have an *increase of imports* and a *decrease of production*. We call this situation 'perverse' effect of the demand policy. *It is due only to the specification of the import functions.*

Case 3: $\alpha = 1$

It is easily checked that the function $\psi_Q(M)$ is then represented by a family of lines, the envelop of which is $Af(Q)$, increasing with respect to Q. Let Q_A denote the value of Q such that

$$Af(Q_A) = 1.$$

The solutions of (3) are given in figure 10:

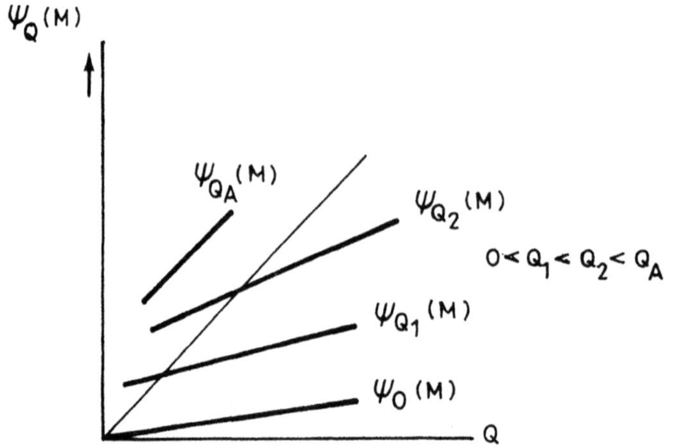

Figure 10.

Hence, one deduces the graphs of M versus Q (figures 11, 12 and 13):

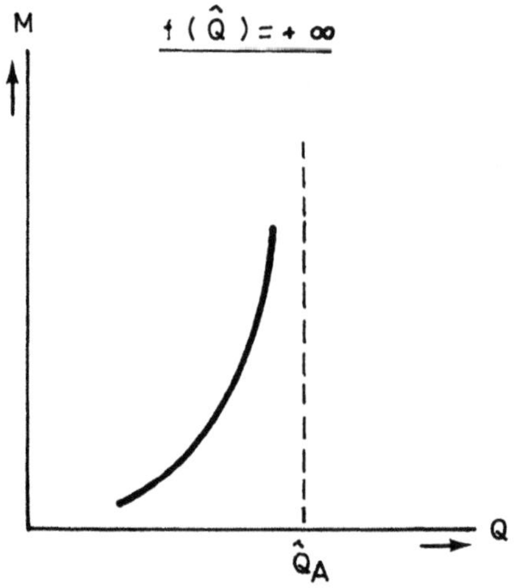

Figure 11.

When $f(\hat{Q}) < +\infty$, we have two possible configurations according to the sign of $Q_A - \hat{Q}$ (see figures 12 and 13).

One can conclude that, in the short term, with a traditional import function like the one we use in this section, one can describe both the underemployment and the full employment production capacities if the elasticity of demand in the import function is less than one.

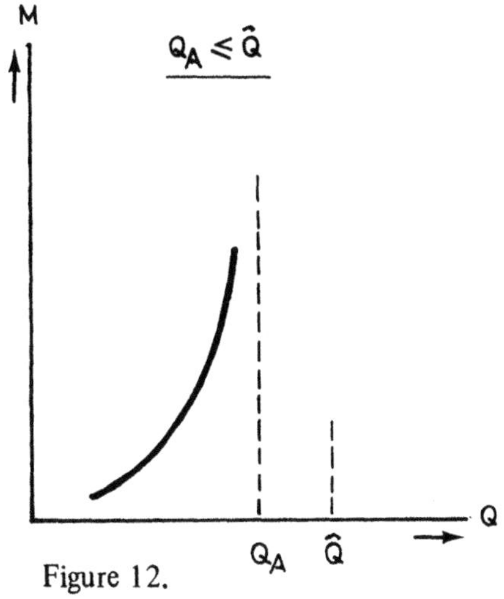

Figure 12.

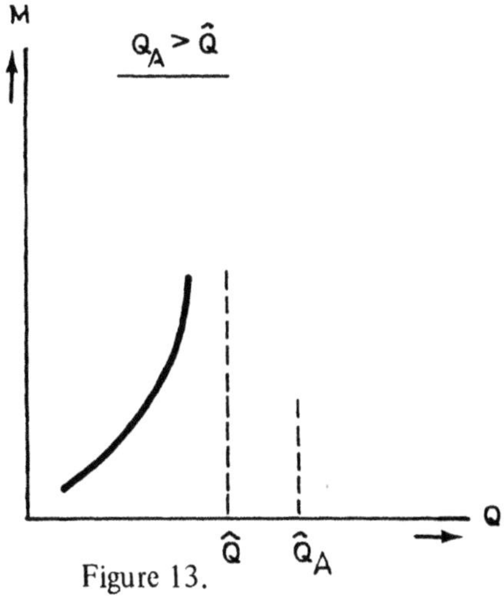

Figure 13.

4. THE LONG TERM GROWTH PATH OF A SMALL DYNAMIC MODEL: STABILITY CONDITIONS

In order to study the stability of the long term growth path we shall use a small dynamic model with a keynesian short term structure. Production is determined by effective demand; we have excess supplies on both goods and labour markets. We assume, in this model, that investment depends only on self-financing. (The long run stability of a model with an investment function depending on both the accelerator and self-financing is studied in Le Van (1983)). We assume also that the productivity is exogenous with a constant growth rate. The wage relation is the standard Phillips curve. Inflation depends on the rate of growth of production costs. In the import function we have included a trend, as in Deleau et al. (1981): this specification allows for the existence of an equilibrated growth path characterised by constant growth rates. In this paper, as we focus the attention on the role of the import function, we assume that exports and government expenditures are exogenous. The equations of the model are given in table 1. The long run solution variables are given in table 2. We shall briefly study the long term path. One can refer to Le Van (1983) or Deleau et al. (1981) for a complete study of such growth paths. First, this long term solution is characterised by four growth rates:

- γ : rate of growth of quantities
- ϵ : rate of growth of prices
- ℓ : rate of growth of population
- π : rate of growth of technical progress

Table 1. The equations

Goods market equilibrium	
$Q = cQ + I + \bar{A} - M$	(4)
Imports	
$M = \tilde{M}_0 (Q+M)^{e_1} (P/\bar{P}^e)^{e_2} (1-U_c)^{-e_3} e^{-\gamma e_1 t}$	(5)
Employment	
$N = \bar{\omega}_0 e^{-\pi t}$	(6)
Unemployment rate	
$U_n = 1 - N/\bar{N}$	(7)
Investment	
$I = \theta Q(1 - \frac{WN}{PQ})$	(8)
Capital	
$\frac{dK}{dt} = I$	(9)
Production capacity	
$\hat{Q} = K/v$	(10)
Capacity utilisation rate	
$U_c = Q/\hat{Q}$	(11)
Nominal wage rate	
$\overset{o}{W} = g_1 \overset{o}{P} + g_2 U_n + g_3;\ g_2 < 0$	(12)
Inflation	
$\overset{o}{P} = f_1 U_c + f_2(\overset{o}{W} + \overset{o}{N} - \overset{o}{Q}) + f_3$	(13)
Exogenous variables	
Autonomous expenditures	
$\bar{A} = \bar{A}_0 e^{\gamma t}$	
Labour supply	
$\bar{N} = \bar{N}_0 e^{\ell t}$	
Foreign price	
$\bar{P}^e = \bar{P}^e_0 e^{\epsilon t}$	
$(\gamma = \ell + \pi)$	
Notation	
$\overset{o}{X} = \frac{1}{X} \frac{dX}{dt}$	

Table 2. The long run solution

Growth rates

rate of growth of production, investment, capital, imports: $\gamma = \ell + \Pi$
rate of growth of employment: ℓ
rate of growth of price: ϵ
rate of growth of nominal wage: $\epsilon + \pi$

Initial values

Unemployment rate	$U_{n_o} = \dfrac{\epsilon(1-g_1)+\pi-g_3}{g_2}$
Capacity utilisation rate	$U_{c_o} = \dfrac{\epsilon(1-f_2)-f_3}{f_1}$
Employment	$N_o = (1-U_{n_o})\bar{N}_o$
Production	$Q_o = N_o/\bar{\omega}_o$
Capital stock	$K_o = vQ_o/U_{c_o}$
Investment	$I_o = \gamma K_o$
Imports	$M_o = (c-1)Q_o + I_o + \bar{A}_o$
Price	$P_o = \bar{P}_o^{e}\left(\dfrac{M_o}{\tilde{M}_o}(Q_o+M_o)^{-e_1}(1-U_{c_o})^{e_3}\right)^{1/e_2}$
Nominal wage	$W_o = P_o\,\dfrac{(1-I_o/(\theta Q_o))}{\bar{\omega}_o}$

(In our model ℓ and π are exogenous; given the form of the production function we have: $\gamma = \ell + \pi$).

Then the Phillips curve yields a relation between the rate of growth of prices ϵ and the unemployment rate U_{n_o} : therefore U_{n_o} is constant in the long term, since the rate of growth of domestic prices equals the rate of growth of foreign prices given the form of the import function. In other words, employment is determined by the labour supply and yields the level of production (given the form of the production function). The price equation implies, in the long term, a constant capacity utilisation rate; thus we obtain the level of capital stock necessary to attain the production level. One deduces investment; imports and price level are obtained through the goods market equilibrium relation and the import function. The long term system is a pure supply model in which government expenditures have no effect on output and increase imports.

To study the long run stability we express the variables in *reduced form* (see Malgrange (1981)), i.e. we divide each variable by its long run value. Doing this, we obtain a reduced system which possesses a steady state in terms of the initial values of the long term solution. The equations of this reduced system are given in table 3.

Table 3. The equations of the reduced system

$$q = cq + i + \bar{A}_0 - m \tag{14}$$

$$m = \tilde{M}_0 (q+m)^{e_1} (P/\bar{P}^{e}_{0})^{e_2} (1-vk/q)^{-e_3} \tag{15}$$

$$n = \bar{\omega}_0 q \tag{16}$$

$$i = \theta q(1 - \bar{\omega}_0 w/p) \tag{17}$$

$$\overset{o}{k} = i/k - \gamma \tag{18}$$

$$\overset{o}{w} = g_1 \overset{o}{p} + g_2(1 - n/\bar{N}_0) + g_3' \tag{19}$$

$$\overset{o}{p} = f_1 vq/k + f_2 \overset{o}{w} + f_3' \tag{20}$$

$$g_3' = g_3 + g_1 \epsilon - \epsilon - \pi$$

$$f_3' = f3 - \epsilon\,(1 - f_2)$$

Combining different equations we have the following differential system in (w, p, k):

$$\begin{cases} \overset{o}{w} = \dfrac{1}{1-g_1 f_2}(f_1 g_1 vq/k - g_2 \bar{\omega}_o q/\bar{N}_o + g_3'') & \text{(21a)} \\ \overset{o}{p} = \dfrac{1}{1-g_1 f_2}(f_1 vq/k - f_2 g_2 \bar{\omega}_o q/\bar{N}_o + f_3'') & \text{(21b)} \\ \overset{o}{k} = \theta q/k(1-\bar{\omega}_o w/p) - \gamma & \text{(21c)} \end{cases}$$

where q is related to the variables w, p, k through the following relation:

$$cq + \theta q(1-\bar{\omega}_o w/p) + \bar{A}_o - q = \tilde{M}_o(cq+\theta q(1-\bar{\omega}_o w/p)+\bar{A}_o)^{e_1}(p/\bar{P}_o)^{-e\,e_2}(1-vq/k)^{-e_3}$$

obtained by replacing imports and investment by their expressions in the goods market equilibrium relation.

In its reduced form, $\overset{o}{w}$ depends only on q; its expression has an economic meaning if $1-g_1f_2>0$.

Let us denote: $x = (x_1, x_2, x_3) = (\text{Log } w, \text{Log } p, \text{Log } k)$; then we obtain the non-linear differential system:

$$\frac{dx_i}{dt} = h_i(x), \qquad i=1, 2, 3$$

which has a steady state x*,

$$h_i(x^*) = 0.$$

We shall compute the product of the eigenvalues of the Jacobian matrix $h'(x^*)$. If it is strictly positive, one of the eigenvalues is also strictly positive: the steady state of the system (21) is locally unstable (see Hirsch and Smale (1974)). The computation is tedious: the reader can refer to the appendix for details. The sign of the product of the eigenvalues is that of the expression:

$$1 - \frac{\bar{A}_o}{m^*} - e_1\left(1 - \frac{\bar{A}_o}{m^*+q^*}\right) - e_3\frac{U_{c_o}}{1-U_{c_o}}$$

If $\quad e_1 < \dfrac{1-\bar{A}_o/m^* - e_3U_{c_o}/(1-U_{c_o})}{1-\bar{A}_o/(m^*+q^*)}$

the steady state is locally unstable. In our model, since exports and government expenditures are assumed exogenous, $\overline{A}_0$ is greater than m*: this sufficient condition is not satisfied. But if we assume that $\overline{A} = gQ$ then the steady state is locally unstable if

$$e_1 < 1 - e_3 \frac{U_{c_0}}{1 - U_{c_0}}$$

If the import function does not take (explicitly) the effect of capacity utilisation rate into account (see Courbis et al. (1980), Courbis (1980)), then the sufficient condition of unstability is

$$e_1 < 1.$$

5. CONCLUSION

In this paper we have shown that a macroeconometric model which adopts a traditional import function can describe, in the short term, both the situations of full employment and underemployment of production capacities, if and only if the elasticity of demand in the import function is less than unity. Moreover, if the same model wants to reconciliate a neo-keynesian structure for the short term with a classical one for the long term, then the elasticity of demand of the import function must belong to an interval (which could be 'narrow' or empty) bounded by unity. But it is obvious that this condition is practically never satisfied: generally this elasticity is greater than one (unfortunately, this condition is not sufficient to warrant a stable long run path; see Le Van (1983)). The main conclusion of this paper is that generally the macroeconometric model, with a traditional import function, cannot describe, in the short term, *both* the situations of underemployment and full employment of capacitites.

APPENDIX

Let us consider the system:

$$\left\{\begin{aligned} \overset{o}{w} &= \frac{1}{1-g_1 f_2}(f_1 g_1 vq/k - g_2\bar{\omega}_0 q/\bar{N}_0 + g_3'') \\ \overset{o}{p} &= \frac{1}{1-g_1 f_2}(f_1 vq/k - g_2 f_2 \bar{\omega}_0 q/\bar{N}_0 + f_3'') \\ \overset{o}{k} &= \theta q/k(1-\bar{\omega}_0 w/p) - \gamma \end{aligned}\right. \tag{I}$$

where q is related to w, p, k by the following relation:

$$cq + \theta q(1-\bar{\omega}_0 w/p) + \bar{A}_0 - q = \tilde{M}_0(cq+\theta q(1-\bar{\omega}_0 w/p)+\bar{A}_0)^{e_1}(p/\bar{P}_0^{e})^{e_2}(1-vq/k)^{-e_3}$$

The differentiation of this last relation gives:

$$((1-\bar{A}_0/m)-e_1(1-\frac{\bar{A}_0}{m+q}) - e_3\frac{U_{c_0}}{1-U_{c_0}})\frac{dq}{q} = \theta\bar{\omega}_0 w/p(\frac{q}{m}-e_1\frac{q}{m+q})\frac{dw}{w}$$
$$+(e_2-\bar{\omega}_0\theta w/p(\frac{q}{m}-\frac{e_1 q}{m+q}))\frac{dp}{p} - e_3\frac{U_{c_0}}{1-U_{c_0}}\frac{dk}{k}$$

Let us denote $x = (x_1, x_2, x_3) = (\log w, \log p, \log k)$. The system (I) can be written as:

$$\frac{dx_i}{dt} = h_i(x), i=1, 2, 3.$$

We shall compute the Jacobian matrix $h'(x^*)$, x^* being the steady state of (I). We have successively:

$$\frac{\partial h_1}{\partial x_1} = \lambda_1\alpha\,; \quad \frac{\partial h_1}{\partial x_2} = \lambda_1\beta\,; \quad \frac{\partial h_1}{\partial x_3} = \lambda_1\epsilon - \zeta_1\,;$$

$$\frac{\partial h_2}{\partial x_1} = \lambda_2\alpha \, ; \quad \frac{\partial h_2}{\partial x_2} = \lambda_2\beta \, ; \quad \frac{\partial h_2}{\partial x_3} = \lambda_2\epsilon - \zeta_2 \, ;$$

$$\frac{\partial h_3}{\partial x_1} = \lambda_3\alpha - \mu \, ; \quad \frac{\partial h_3}{\partial x_2} = \lambda_3\beta + \mu \, ; \quad \frac{\partial h_3}{\partial x_3} = \lambda_3(\epsilon - 1) \, ;$$

where:

$$\lambda_1 = \frac{f_1 g_1 vq/k - g_2 \bar{\omega}_o q/\bar{N}_o}{1 - g_1 f_2}$$

$$\lambda_2 = \frac{f_1 vq/k - f_2 g_2 \bar{\omega}_o q/\bar{N}_o}{1 - g_1 f_2}$$

$$\lambda_3 = \gamma$$

$$\zeta_1 = -\frac{f_1 g_1 vq/k}{1 - g_1 f_2}$$

$$\zeta_2 = -\frac{f_1 vq/k}{1 - g_1 f_2}$$

$$\mu = \theta q/k\bar{\omega}_o \, w/p$$

$$\alpha = \frac{\partial \log q}{\partial \log w} \, ; \quad \beta = \frac{\partial \log q}{\partial \log p} \, ; \quad \epsilon = \frac{\partial \log q}{\partial \log k}$$

The product of the eigenvalues of $h'(x^*)$ equals its determinant. It is easily proved that the latter equals:

$$(\alpha + \beta)\, \mu(\lambda_1\zeta_2 - \lambda_2\zeta_1)$$

with:

$$\lambda_1\zeta_2 - \lambda_2\zeta_1 = -\frac{f_1 g_2 \bar{\omega}_o q/\bar{N}_o vq/k}{1 - g_1 f_2} > 0$$

$\mu > 0$

$$\alpha + \beta = \frac{e_2}{1 - \frac{\bar{A}_0}{m} - e_1\left(1 - \frac{\bar{A}_0}{m+q}\right) - e_3 \frac{U_{c_0}}{1-U_{c_0}}}$$

REFERENCES

Courbis, R. (1980), 'Une relormulation dynamique de la théorie des économies concurrencées', *Economie Appliquée,* Tome XXXIII, No 1, pp. 5-43, Paris.

Courbis, R., A. Fonteneau, C. Le Van and P. Voisin (1980), 'Le modèle MOGLI', *Prévision et Analyse Economique,* Cahiers du GAMA, Vol. 1, No 2-3, Economica, Paris.

Deleau, M., P. Malgrange and P.A. Muet (1981), 'Une maquette représentative des modèles macro-économiques', *Annales de l'INSEE,* No 42, pp. 53-91, Paris.

Fouquet, D., J.M. Charpin, H. Guillaume, P.A. Muet and D. Vallet (1978), 'DMS, Modèle dynamique multi-sectoriel', *Les Collections de l'INSEE,* Série C, No 64-65.

Hirsch, M.W. and S. Smale (1974), 'Differential Equations, Dynamic Systems and Linear Algebra', *Academic Press,* New York, San Francisco, London.

Le Van, C. (1983), 'Etude de la stabilité du sentier d'équilibre d'une maquette d'économie ouverte', *Annales des l'INSEE,* No 50, pp. 93-111, Paris.

Malgrange, P. (1981), 'Note sur le calcul des valeurs propres d'un modèle macroéconométrique', *Annales de l'INSEE,* No 41, pp. 67-77, Paris.

CHAPTER 12

AN ALTERNATIVE TO DEBREU'S DATED AND LOCATED COMMODITIES (OR THE ECONOMY AS AN ONION)

Thijs ten Raa
Erasmus University, Rotterdam, The Netherlands

1. DATED AND LOCATED COMMODITIES

The usual framework of general equilibrium analysis, since the inception of Debreu (1959), is an ℓ–dimensional Euclidean space with one dimension for each commodity. Thus there are ℓ commodities and with each one a single real number is associated: its quantity.

Now let the real world contain n physically different goods and services. Debreu's example is wheat. What is the quantity of wheat? To avoid infinity, we must consider a quantity of wheat per unit of time. But then we have a variety of wheat quantities, one for each date. To meet the condition that a single real number is associated with a commodity, we must define wheat at a certain date as a distinct commodity. That is, commodities are dated. Let the number of dates be T. Then there are nT commodities, so far.

Another complication is that wheat in one location, say Kansas, cannot be the same commodity as wheat in another, say New York. For if it were, transportation would be nonsense, on the assumption that one can always produce a commodity out of itself by doing nothing. Therefore, commodities are also located. Let the number of locations be S. Then the total number of commodities equals the number of goods multiplied with the numbers of dates and locations: $\ell = nTS$.

Note that since the commodity space is ℓ–dimensional Euclidean, ℓ is finite, and, therefore, T and S too. Time and space must be discrete and have finite horizons. We end up with one very long list of commodities, $1, 2, 3, \ldots, \ell$. These commodities are independent actors in the general equilibrium performance. Whether they are differentiated by physical, temporal or spatial pecularities is inessential.

2. DISCUSSION

The economy is much like an onion. It has a kaleidoscopic structure as that of spheres, rings and segments. Adopting alternative points of view one can form a mosaic of beautiful patterns. The general equilibrium analysist, however, peels the onion apart to separate layers of different vintages which, on their turn, are cut into pieces of different locations. To make sure that no parts remain connected, the remainders are thoroughly chopped up. The smahed substance is served and swallowed down. Since mashed onions are not exactly a delicacy, a strong wine must finish off digestion. A Chateau Brouwer of 1910 serves the purpose quite well.

The draw-back of dating and locating goods is, paradoxally, the destruction of time and space. Time and space are reduced to an index set of date and location labels for commodities. The index set has no structure. The order of the dates and locations is arbitrary. Once the onion is chopped, its structure is lost. Temporal and spatial subtleties such as accumulation or diffusion are treated in the same way as differences between forks and knives.

Our comprehension is lessened too. Initially we recognised a whole nest of spheres in the onion, but now there is just a mess of tiny bits. The original economy consisted of n goods plus time and space. But the resulting model comprises numerous commodities, namely $\ell = nTS$. And, if equilibrium between supply and demand is analysed for all commodities, the number of equations is equally sizeable.

These considerations motivate our search for an alternative framework for economic analysis. The new space should facilitate whole goods, including their temporal and spatial extensions. It must be richer than Euclidean space to avoid dating and locating. We should be able to associate a whole temporal and/or spatial distribution of quantities with a good, rather than just a single real number. Therefore, it is natural to propose as an alternative framework the space of n-vector valued distributions over time and/or space. The introduction of the new framework is simplified by confining ourselves, for the time being, to time, and considering a Leontief technology.

3. TIME

Consider a dynamic economy with n goods. Let $y(t)$ be the n-vector of quantities supplied at time t. Then $\dot{y}(t)$ is the vector of accumulation rates at time t, dot denoting differentiation with respect to time. This requires investment of $B\dot{y}(t)$ at time t, assuming fixed capital coefficients which are arranged in the nxn-matrix B. Let $x(t)$ be the n-vector of quantities demanded at time t, other than for investment. Then the condition of equilibrium is

$$y(t) = B\dot{y}(t) + x(t).$$

Since this must hold for all t, we obtain

$$y = B\dot{y} + x.$$

This is an n-vector valued equation of equilibrium of simple form. The dating device consists of restricting t to the index set $\{1, \ldots, T\}$ and to define the T y(t)'s as distinct commodity vectors. $\dot{y}(t)$ is replaced by $y(t+1) - y(t)$. Then the equation becomes

$$\begin{pmatrix} y(1) \\ \cdot \\ \cdot \\ \cdot \\ y(T) \end{pmatrix} = A \begin{pmatrix} y(1) \\ \cdot \\ \cdot \\ \cdot \\ y(T) \end{pmatrix} + \begin{pmatrix} x(1) \\ \cdot \\ \cdot \\ \cdot \\ x(T) \end{pmatrix}$$

where the nTxnT-matrix

$$A = \begin{pmatrix} -B & B & & 0 \\ & \ddots & \ddots & \\ & & \ddots & B \\ 0 & & & -B \end{pmatrix}$$

This system can be solved for $(y(1) \ldots y(T))$ given $(x(1) \ldots x(T))$. Note that the analysis is essentially the same as that of a static economy with nT commodities arranged in one long vector which is subjected to an input–output matrix. Formally, the commodity space is R^{nT} and technology is in R^{nTxnT}, applying through the ordinary matrix product.

Alternatively, we consider y itself as an element of a commodity space. This space, then, is, heuristically, the space of functions from R (time) to R^n (quantities of goods). We preserve n, the number of goods. There is, however, a problem in placing the equation of equilibrium. The first term is clear: it is an element of the commodity space. But the second term, $B\dot{y}$, is opaque. Is B a technology and $\dot{y}$ a commodity? Our approach to clarification of the meaning of the terms is to generalise the notion of a function in the sense of Schwartz (1957). Formally, we take $D'(R,R^n)$ as commodity space, i.e. the space of n-vector generalised functions, also called distributions, over time. The generalisation of technology is similar: we position it in $D'(R,R^{nxn})$, the space of nxn-matrix distributions over time.

Now let us check the equation of equilibrium. The first term remains, albeit reinterpreted as a distribution. The second term reflects an application of technology on the commodity vector distribution. The application is immediate, no lags are involved. That is, technology is concentrated in time, like $B\delta$, where B is an ordinary nxn-matrix and δ is the unit point mass on the time axis, i.e. Dirac distribution. Introducing the convolution product, $*$, extended in component by component fashion to matrix distributions, our second term becomes $B\delta*\dot{y}$. (δ is the unit element of the convolution product; heuristically $(B\delta*\dot{y})(t) = \int B\delta(s)\dot{y}(t-s)ds$ $= B\delta(0)\dot{y}(t-0) = B\dot{y}(t)$. For sound mathematical detail see Schwartz (1957).) The differentiation dot may be transferred to the first factor. (This elementary fact is established by partial integration). The whole term, $B\dot{\delta}*y$, now consists of a technical nxn-matrix distribution applying through the convolution product on the original commodity space element. In sum, we have commodities x and y in $D'(R,R^n)$, a technology $B\dot{\delta}$ in $D'(R,R^{nxn})$, and an equation for their equilibrium interrelationship:

$$y = B\dot{\delta}*y + x.$$

This equation can be solved for y given x, even when B is singular (as is true for real capital structures), along the lines established in ten Raa (1983). The present choice of spaces also facilitates treatment of investment lead times. This is done by simple extension of $B\delta$ beyond the origin of time. The equation and the calculus remain essentially unaltered. For details see ten Raa (1983).

4. SPACE

Spatial economics can be cast in the same mould. The appropriate commodity space is $D'(R^2,R^n)$, consisting of n-vector distributions over the plane. Similarly, the technology space is now $D'(R^2,R^{nxn})$. A simple example is constituted by a spatialisation of the Keynesian consumption equation. Then n=1 (the national pie), $y \in D'(R^2,R))$ is the national product, $c \in D'(R^2,R)$ a spatial propensity to consume (describing the expenditure distribution of one dollar income), and $x \in D'(R^2,R)$ represents non-consumption demand. The equation equilibrium is

$$y = c*y + x.$$

For details see ten Raa (1984).

5. SPACE–TIME

This section addresses the delicate issue of mathematical space selection for a dynamic spatial economy. Such an economy combines dynamic and spatial elements such as the described investment and consumption terms. Perhaps the most natural commodity space to embed those elements in is $D'(RxR^2,R^n)$ which consists of n-vector distributions over time and space jointly. However, often one traces a spatial economy, considered as a whole, through time. This view is especially useful when studying initial value problems for spatial economies, e.g. the ones formulated in Puu (1982). Then such problems can be solved as if they were textbook initial value problems; the only modification is that values do not lie in the reals but in the space of spatial distributions. In this case one takes the alternative commodity space of distributions over time with values in the space of spatial distributions.

A n-vector (spatial) distribution valued distribution (over time) A is a linear continuous functional from the test functions on time, $\phi \in D(R)$, to the n-vector distributions over space, $A(\phi) \in D'(R^2,R^n)$. (Test functions are defined to be infinitely differentiable and to have compact support.) The linearity and continuity conditions are captured elegantly by the following formal definition: $A: D(R) \rightarrow D'(R^2,R^n)$ is a *distribution valued distribution* if $\phi \mapsto \langle A(\phi), \psi \rangle$ is a distribution for all $\psi \in D(R^2)$.

Summing up, we take as the commodity space either $D'(RxR^2,R^n)$, consisting of n-vector distributions over time-space or $L[D(R),D'(R^2,R^n)]$, consisting of n-vector spatial distribution valued distribution over time. The choice is a matter of convenience.

Is the choise of mathematical commodity space a pure matter of convenience, i.e. otherwise immaterial? Yes, the choice can be made on purely opportunistic grounds. The justification of this proposition lies in a deep theorem which states that the space of distributions over time-space and the space of spatial distribution valued distributions over time are essentially the same. More precisely, by the Schwartz (1953–54) kernel theorem there is a bijection between $A \in L[D(R),D'(R^2,R^n)]$ and (its kernel) $a \in D'(RxR^2,R^n)$. a is obviously defined for separable test functions on time-space, say $\phi \times \psi$ where x is the direct tensor product: $\langle a, \phi \times \psi \rangle = \langle A(\phi), \psi \rangle$. The deepness of the theorem lies in the extension of a to all test functions on time-space).

As before, the casting of technology is much the same. For technologies we take either $A \in L[D(R),D'(R^2,R^{nxn})]$ or $A \in D'(RxR^2,R^{nxn})$.

6. APPLICATION

To illustrate the use of our commodity framework for specific models we shall now briefly discuss the application to the trade cycle model of Puu (1982). Detailed analysis would go beyond the scope of the present paper.

Puu studies local income Y and local net export X as functions of time t and location in space, denoted by Euclidean coordinates x and y. He regards X and Y as deviations from equilibrium. Puu assumes that income adjusts in proportion to the degree savings fall short of net export:

$$\dot{Y} = \lambda(X - \sigma Y),$$

where σ is the savings quote, λ denotes adjustment speed and dot time differentiation. He notes that it is usual to relate net exports to income 'abroad' relative to local income. Relative income 'abroad' is measured by the 'curvature' of Y, that is $\partial^2 Y/\partial x^2 + \partial^2 Y/\partial y^2$ or the Laplacean ΔY. Assuming an import propensity μ and an adjustment process with the same delay as above, Puu obtains

$$\dot{X} = \lambda(\mu\Delta Y - X).$$

The model is reduced by elimination of X:

$$\ddot{Y} + \lambda(1+\sigma)\dot{Y} + \lambda^2\sigma Y = \lambda^2\mu\Delta Y.$$

This is Puu's equation of a dynamic spatial economy. The initial value conditions are

$$Y(x,y,0) = Y_0(x,y) \quad \text{and} \quad \dot{Y}(x,y,0) = Y_1(x,y).$$

Now we consider the unknown Y as a distribution over time (with spatial distribution values) and incorporate the initial value conditions in the equation by going to HY where H is the Heaviside function (zero on the negatives and one on the positives). Then HY can be shown to fulfill

$$(HY)^{\cdot\cdot} + \lambda(1+\sigma)(HY)^{\cdot} + \lambda^2\sigma HY = \lambda^2\mu\Delta(HY) + [\lambda(1+\sigma)Y_0 + Y_1]\,\delta + Y_0\dot{\delta}.$$

This is a second order differential equation in HY.

Reconsidering HY as a distribution over time-space by the Schwartz kernel theorem and letting E be the fundamental solution of the differential operator we obtain by convolution through E,

$$HY = [\lambda(1+\sigma)Y_0 + Y_1]*E + Y_0*\dot{E},$$

where * denotes the convolution product with respect to space.

This is the formal solution of the initial value problem. For the concepts involved we refer the Schwartz (1957). The main task which remains to be done is substantiation of E, but that will not be undertaken here.

7. SUMMARY AND CONCLUSION

The economy is much like an onion (figure 1).

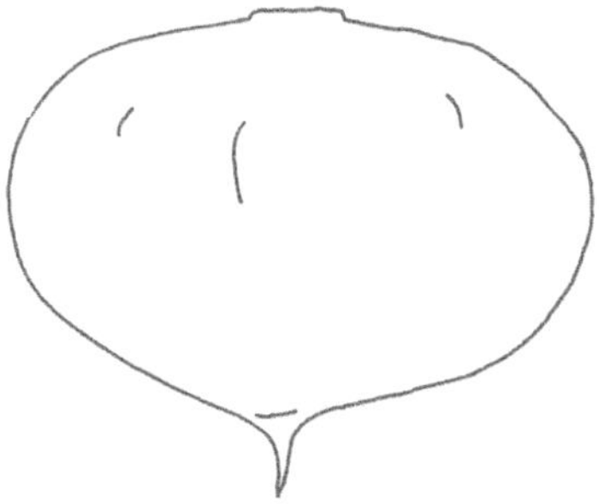

Figure 1

Time and space are treated by dating and locating the commodities. The onion is peeled and the layers are cut. The result is a mashed onion (figure 2).

Figure 2

This paper has developed alternative means of analysis. The onion is respected as a full distribution over time and/or space. For dynamic analysis we make a spatial cut and recognise a distribution over time (figure 3).

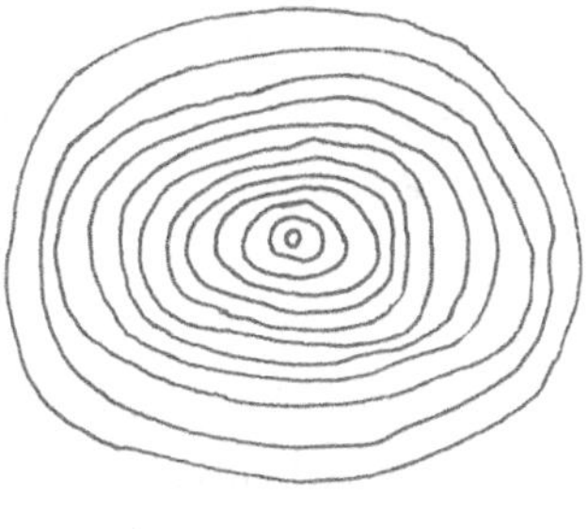

Figure 3

For spatial analysis we separate one layer from the other and obtain a nice spatial distribution (figure 4).

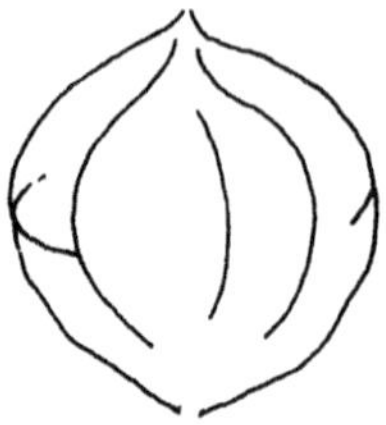

Figure 4

Analysing the dynamics of a spatial system we may adopt alternative points of view. One is to integrate figures 3 and 4 into an onion distribution over time and space jointly (figure 5).

Figure 5

The other point of view is closer to the dynamics at hand. It facilitates analysis of the distribution over time of the spatial onion layers (figure 6).

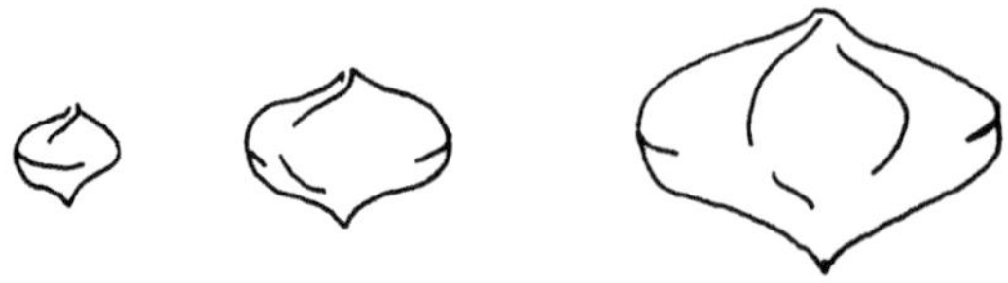

Figure 6

The two points of view on the onion (figures 5 and 6) are equivalent by the Schwartz kernel theorem. This allows opportunistic use of the alternative commodity spaces. For example, the space of time-space distributions (figure 5) is useful for the determination of so-called elementary solutions of particular nonhomogeneous equations, while the space of spatial distribution valued distributions over time (figure 6) is appropriate for handling initial value conditions. I plan to solve the initial value problem for Puu's trade cycle in full detail in a subsequent paper. The proof of the onion is in the eating.

REFERENCES

Debreu, G. (1959), *Theory of Value*, Wiley and Sons, New York.

Puu, T. (1982), 'Outline of a Trade Cycle Model in Continuous Space and Time', *Geographical Analysis*, 14, pp. 1-9.

ten Raa, Th. (1983), 'Dynamic Input–Output Analysis with Distributed Activities', IFAC/IFORS Conference on the Modelling and Control of National Economies, Washington.

ten Raa, Th. (1984), 'The Distribution Approach to Spatial Economics', *Journal of Regional Science*.

Schwartz, L. (1953-54), 'Produits Tensoriels Topologiques', *Séminaire Schwartz* 1, Exposition No 11.

Schwartz, L. (1957), *Théorie des Distributions*, Hermann, Paris.

GPSR Compliance

The European Union's (EU) General Product Safety Regulation (GPSR) is a set of rules that requires consumer products to be safe and our obligations to ensure this.

If you have any concerns about our products, you can contact us on ProductSafety@springernature.com

In case Publisher is established outside the EU, the EU authorized representative is:

Springer Nature Customer Service Center GmbH
Europaplatz 3
69115 Heidelberg, Germany

Batch number: 10824484

Printed by Printforce, the Netherlands